D0887859

Gift of the Holy Spirit

What Every Christian Should Know About the Holy Spirit

By Paul S. Ragan

St. Luke's Publications, Atlanta GA, USA

Dedication

To my nieces and nephews.

To Katie, Christie, and Allie McElyea,

and to John-Paul and Conor Fenn.

May the Holy Spirit greatly enrich your life;
may He strengthen you with an abounding faith in Jesus;
and may He bring forth in you an abundance of his sanctifying
and charismatic graces, all to God's glory. Amen.

.

Table of Contents

See Appendix 4 for explanation of abbreviations used in the footnotes.

Table of Contents - continued

Appendices

Introduction

Every Sunday, millions of Christians around the world (*Catholics, Orthodox, and Protestants, alike*) recite the Nicene Creed. In that Creed, we profess our belief in "the Holy Spirit, the Lord, the giver of life." Yet how many of us understand these words? How many of us believe what we say?

Unfortunately, for many Christians, the Holy Spirit is the great unknown. In our faith journeys, we rightly focus on Jesus, his teachings, his death and resurrection, and on the Father who sent him. Yet few Christians focus on the Holy Spirit, whom the Father also sent. The Father sent the Holy Spirit as a gift to Creation, to the Church, and to every believer. Pope Francis describes the Holy Spirit as "the supreme gift of the risen Christ."[1]

The Holy Spirit is truly a wonderful gift, who comes to us at an exceptionally high price. Saint Paul tells us that Jesus endured the suffering of the Cross "so that we might receive . . . the Spirit."[2] Jesus' body nailed to the Cross was the price,[3] and this gift is nothing less than friendship with God. Our openness to this gift is life's key to peace, joy, and fulfillment, now and forever.

Who, then, is the Holy Spirit? Who is this forgotten Person of God? Why is the Holy Spirit important to our lives? What did Jesus and his Apostles teach about the Holy Spirit? Throughout history, what did the great Christian saints teach about the Holy Spirit? Today, what does the Catholic Church teach about the Holy Spirit? This book explores these questions primarily as a Bible study. As Pope Benedict XVI suggested, study of the Bible's revelations concerning the Holy Spirit "opens us up to great and inspiring insights"[4] – not only about the Holy Spirit, but also about ourselves.

While reading this volume, be aware that Christians understand God as One, yet within the Oneness of God are three Persons: the Father, the Son, and the Holy Spirit. They are co-eternal and co-equal.

---

[1] Pope Francis, homily, May 19, 2013. Cf. Pope Benedict XVI, Letter to Youth, July 20, 2007, section 4; St. Augustine, *On the Trinity*, book 15, chapters 18 and 19.
[2] Galatians 3:14 (NAB).
[3] Cf. 1 Corinthians 6:20, Galatians 3:13-14, 1 Peter 1:18-19.
[4] Pope Benedict XVI, Letter to Youth, July 20, 2007, section 2.

They share one nature and act together in all matters. Nevertheless, each has a unique role in salvation history. As for Jesus and the Holy Spirit, their roles include a divine mission here on earth.

Jesus' mission is that of Redeemer. *He is the visible face of the invisible God.*[5] He came to proclaim the kingdom of God to a wayward people and to lay down his life as a ransom for all.[6] He came to show us the way to eternal reconciliation with God the Father. Jesus, himself, is the way. He is "the way and the truth and the life."[7]

God the Holy Spirit continues the mission of Jesus. The Holy Spirit works in our hearts, drawing us to Jesus and through Jesus to the Father.[8] If we already know Jesus in a personal sense, then, whether we realize it or not, we already know the Holy Spirit to some extent.[9] However, if our minds are unaware of the Holy Spirit, his purposes, and his graces, our lack of awareness limits his work within us.

This study begins by considering various titles for the Holy Spirit, titles that speak to the Holy Spirit's personal involvement in our respective lives. The study then considers aspects of the Spirit-filled life, including the Spirit's sacramental and charismatic graces. Throughout this book, we will consider practical applications of what we study. In addition, prayers follow at the end of each chapter to aid our study and strengthen our faith. You may want to read each prayer first to acquaint yourself with its contents and then read it again as a prayer to God. Modify each prayer as seems appropriate to you. Let each prayer be your own.

This volume follows the Christian practice of referring to the Holy Spirit using masculine pronouns ("he," "him," "his"). This may seem odd when we consider that the Holy Spirit is pure spirit, neither male nor female. Christians use these pronouns for the Holy Spirit because Jesus did so.[10] Perhaps Jesus used these pronouns to emphasize that the Holy Spirit is a Person, someone we can encounter and come to know.

---

[5] Cf. John 14:9, Colossians 1:15; CCC section 689.
[6] Cf. Mathew 20:28.
[7] John 14:6 (NAB).
[8] Cf. Ephesians 2:18; Pope John Paul II, RM, section 5.
[9] Cf. 1 Corinthians 12:3, Galatians 4:6; CCC section 683.
[10] Cf. John 14:16-17, 16:7-15; Pope John Paul II, GA, April 26, 1989, section 5; Sheed, Frank, *The Holy Spirit in Action,* Servant Books, 1981, page 27.

A proper understanding of any aspect of the Holy Spirit – or of God the Father, or of Jesus, or of any divine mystery – comes only through revelation from God. Our personal philosophies, opinions, and theories do not matter because the mysteries of God are so much greater than anything our human minds can ever imagine or reason on their own. What matters is our openness to what God reveals. God's revelations come to us most surely through the Bible and the teachings of the Church. God's revelations also come to us through the experiences of fellow Christians, including the great saints of the Church, and our own personal experiences.

This volume presents quotes from Sacred Scripture using several different Bible translations. Why? For three reasons: First, some translations of a particular text are easier to read and understand. Second, various nuances of Biblical thought often shine more brilliantly in one translation, and other nuances more brilliantly in other translations. Third, some scriptures can become so familiar to us that we skim past them, and by hearing another translation or a paraphrase of the text, we hear the text with a new freshness.

As you engage in this study, I hope you seek not merely to know about the Holy Spirit, but more importantly to know the Holy Spirit and to experience his presence and action in your life. This book's main objective is to enable each reader to receive the gift of the Holy Spirit in an ever more meaningful way. God created each of us with a definite purpose and plan for our lives. Only with the help of the Holy Spirit will any of us experience the fulfillment of those plans.

Yes, God has a plan for your life. By virtue of your existence, you are his creature. Yet he desires more for you and everyone. He desires that we become his beloved children. No matter our age, our health, our past sins, or our present struggles – *today* – we can connect to God's plan for our lives. That is good news for us all. So then, let us get started. Let us pray.

Heavenly Father, You are holy. You are wonderful. With Jesus and the Holy Spirit, you are God. Father, please bless me as I begin this study of the Holy Spirit. Please breathe new life into my heart and mind, awakening me to your purposes for my life. Please breathe the Holy Spirit upon me and strengthen me to live those purposes. In the name of Jesus, I pray. Amen.

The Holy Spirit and You

I have said these things to you while I am still with you. But the Advocate, the Holy Spirit, whom the Father will send in my name, will teach you everything, and remind you of all that I have said to you.

John 14:25-26 (NRSV)

Helper

1

Where does one begin a study of the Holy Spirit, a study that in many respects is abstract and theological, and in other respects deeply personal, cutting to the core of who we are and who God calls us to be. A good start may be with the Greek word "*parakletos*" which Jesus used as a title for the Holy Spirit. Our English Bibles commonly translate this word as "Paraclete" or "Advocate" or "Counselor" or "Helper." It means "the One who comes alongside to help." Jesus was a Helper or Advocate himself and the Holy Spirit, Jesus said, was another.[11]

Both Jesus and the Holy Spirit help us in various ways. One way they help us is by speaking to us. While Jesus came to speak to us from without, that is, from Jesus' mouth to our ears, the Holy Spirit comes to speak to us from within. He speaks to us quietly from deep within our hearts. The Holy Spirit is the love of God poured into our hearts calling us out of our sins, out of the worldly distractions and worldly ambitions that fill our lives, and into a loving relationship with God. The Holy Spirit is not our conscience. Instead, he is the one who rightly informs and inspires our conscience, if only we let him.

The more we engage our Christian faith, the more we awaken not only to Jesus as our Savior, but also to the Holy Spirit as our unseen Helper. As St. Cyril taught, "[T]he Spirit comes with the tenderness of a true friend and protector to save, to heal, to teach, to counsel, to strengthen, to console."[12]

When we speak of the Holy Spirit as Helper, it is important to understand that he is not some heavenly valet who comes to aid us with our various wants and whims. Instead, he comes to help us understand, accept, and live the Father's plan for our lives. He comes to train us from within concerning the ways of God. In the process, we must unlearn the ways of the world.

Most importantly, the Holy Spirit comes to reveal Jesus to us. He comes to guide us into a personal relationship with Jesus and with the Father and into healthy relationships with our fellow human beings. If

---

[11] Cf. John 14:16, 1 John 2:1.
[12] Saint Cyril of Jerusalem, *Catechetical Lecture #16*. Cf. CCC section 1697.

we earnestly pursue our faith in Jesus, the Holy Spirit brings the love of Jesus to perfection within us.

Many Christians may think that spiritual growth is something we accomplish on our own, but this is never the case. The Holy Spirit inspires us, and we achieve spiritual growth only with his help. The Spirit helps our religious experience move from our heads to our hearts, from an intellectual exercise centered on what we think or have been taught about God, to a faith exercise centered on a relationship we actually have with God.

The Holy Spirit accomplishes his work within us by "grace." Grace is God's *"free and undeserved help."*[13] By grace, God extends to us forgiveness, healing, guidance, and strength. In the present age, the Holy Spirit is the primary agent through whom God's many graces touch our lives. These graces provide believers the desire and ability to be fully united to God. As the theologian Karl Barth put it, grace is the means by which we are "made fit for God by God."[14]

How important is God's grace? Well, without it, there is no relationship with God, no forgiveness of sins, no inner healing, no holiness, and no eternal life with God in heaven. Without God's grace, it is literally impossible for us to attain the ultimate end for which God created us.[15]

We cannot earn or merit any of God's grace, it is all a gift. Some aspects of his grace, such as life itself, God unconditionally gives to us and all peoples. However, other aspects of his grace God gives on a conditional basis. With respect to God's conditional grace, we can only receive it pursuant to the Giver's terms. These terms require that we first seek God's kingdom. The primary way we seek God's kingdom is by following Jesus and worshipping him above all else.

Special aspects of the Holy Spirit's grace are often categorized as prevenient, sanctifying, sacramental, and charismatic. *Prevenient grace* prepares us to receive the Gospel message, draws us closer to Jesus, and encourages us to faith and prayer.[16] *Sanctifying grace* works to restore the image and likeness of God within repentant sinners, which

---

[13] CCC section 1996.

[14] Barth, Karl, *The Holy Spirit and the Christian Life,* Fredrick Mueller LTD, 1938, page 29. Karl Barth was a prominent Protestant theologian of the 20th century.

[15] Cf. CCC section 308.

[16] Cf. CCC sections 2001, 2670.

has been otherwise damaged by sin.[17] *Sacramental grace* is sanctifying grace conveyed through the sacraments of the Church. *Charismatic grace* empowers us to serve more effectively in God's kingdom, in ways such as teaching, healing, extending mercy, and prophesying.[18]

The Holy Spirit's grace is at the center of all true spirituality. However, in our day, "spirituality" is a much abused word. Some use it to philosophize about life or to espouse a false religion. For example, New Age, Transcendental Meditation, astrology, fortune telling, Voodoo, and the use of psychics or so-called "spirit guides" are false and dangerous spiritualities. A spirituality is authentic only if it originates from the Spirit of God.

In life, all instances of true goodness and true greatness involve the Holy Spirit's grace. Mary, the mother of Jesus, for example, is great among God's creatures not because of anything she has done or is doing of her own intelligence or strength or beauty. She is great because of the Holy Spirit who is at work within her and with whom she cooperates. Thus, we say, she is "full of grace."

Pope John Paul II taught, "[N]othing of what is good, true, and holy in the world can be explained without reference to the Spirit of God."[19] Nothing! Similarly, the Church sings in an ancient hymn to the Holy Spirit: "Nothing thrives apart from you [the Holy Spirit]!"[20] Nothing! For all the good we may attribute to such things as philosophy, education, art, science, commerce, and civil government, absent the Spirit of God, these fields of human endeavor only have the appearance of goodness. Their value to society is fleeting and temporal at best.

Only that which is in agreement with God, inspired by the very Spirit of God, truly deserves being called good or great. In our own lives, we are capable of no true or lasting goodness on our own. Without grace, we are incapable of anything that, by heaven's standard, is truly praiseworthy. There is no greater attainment in life than to be an instrument of God's grace through whom the Spirit works. We need his grace! *Do we understand that? Do we desire that?*

---

[17] Cf. CCC sections 734, 1999.
[18] Cf. CCC section 2003; 1 Corinthians 12:4-11, Ephesians 4:11-13, 1 Peter 4:10.
[19] Pope John Paul II, GA, May 13, 1998, section 2. Cf. CCC section 291.
[20] Cf. *Veni Sancte Spiritus*, a 13th century hymn that is commonly sung each year on the eve of Pentecost.

In the struggles of life, if we feel we may be missing something that would make life or religion more meaningful, joyful, or peaceful – the answer may be "the Holy Spirit's grace." We should all ask ourselves, am I open to the Spirit's grace as much as I could be? And if not, why not?

Grace is not only the various helps or kindnesses by which the Holy Spirit touches our lives. Grace is also the very presence of the Holy Spirit in our lives. Understandably, one of the Biblical titles we have for the Holy Spirit is "Spirit of Grace."[21] Moreover, the hymn "Amazing Grace" is actually an anthem to the Holy Spirit.

Dear Holy Spirit, Thank you for all the ways your grace touches my life. I need more of you in my life. I want more of you in my life. Please come ever more deeply into my heart with "the tenderness of a true friend and protector to save, to heal, to teach, to counsel, to strengthen, to console."

Please awaken me to the eternal truths of God's kingdom and to the truths of my own life. Please help me to live a life of true holiness and love. I ask this in Jesus' name. Amen.

---

[21] Cf. Hebrews 10:29.

2   Lord & Giver of Life

The Nicene Creed describes the Holy Spirit as "the Lord, the giver of life." This title originates from Saint Paul. In his second letter to the Corinthians, St. Paul tells us "the Lord is the Spirit" and "the Spirit gives life."[22]

When we refer to the Holy Spirit as "the Lord," we are saying he is God. He is not a created being. He is not an angel. He is not a force of nature. Instead, he is a Person of God. The Holy Spirit is a Person who loves, speaks, listens, creates, guides, protects, comforts, rejoices, and even grieves. In short, he is a Person we can encounter and know.

Our understanding of the Holy Spirit as "giver of life" includes his role in the creation of the world, the creation of each living being in the course of history, and the re-creation and ongoing renewal of every believer's spiritual life. Let us consider each of these ways by which the Spirit gives life.

Creation of the World. The Book of Genesis reveals that in Creation, the Holy Spirit was the mighty wind who blew over the ancient waters bringing forth beauty and life.[23] He was the source of life for all angelic beings, all plants, and all animals. At the pinnacle of the Creation event, he was the Breath of the Father who blew into the bodies of Adam and Eve giving them life.[24] The Book of Genesis tells us that God made these first humans in his image and likeness.[25] To be in God's *image* means that each was a unique person, not just something, but someone – someone capable of self-knowledge, self-control, and freely giving themselves to others.[26] God's *likeness* was his holiness that filled their hearts.[27]

Creation of Each Human Life Throughout History. Since Creation, human beings have been allowed to participate in the procreation of new human lives through the sexual act. However, the creation of each human life ultimately depends on God. Why? Because God authored human sexuality and he alone creates each person's

---

[22] Cf. 2 Corinthians 3:6, 17.
[23] Cf. Genesis 1:2.
[24] Cf. Genesis 2:7.
[25] Cf. Genesis 1:26-27.
[26] Cf. CCC section 357.
[27] Cf. Ephesians 4:23-24.

immortal spirit.[28] The ongoing creative work of God is a ministry of the Holy Spirit.

The Holy Spirit's giving of life includes not only our coming into existence, but also our continued existence. Pope John Paul II emphasized this point stating, "God's vital and life giving breath . . . keeps all creation in existence and gives it life by continuously renewing it."[29] Every person may say with Job, "[T]he Spirit of God has made me, the breath of the Almighty keeps me alive."[30] Without the Spirit's life-sustaining grace, the angelic choir, human beings, and all other creatures, the good and the bad, would cease to exist.[31]

In the Creation event and throughout time, God creates persons for himself. He creates each of us to live in "a personal relationship"[32] with himself. God created us to know him, to love him, and to serve him.[33] The Holy Spirit facilitates our relationship with God. However, this relationship requires our cooperation. For in his wisdom, God gives each of us free will. He gives us the freedom to choose him or to reject him, freedom to cooperate with his grace or to go our own way.

In his first letter to the Thessalonians, St. Paul provides a helpful framework to consider the totality of the human person. In that letter, he describes us as a combination of spirit, soul, and body.[34]

Term	Greek Derivative	Meaning
Spirit	*Pneuma*	Spiritual Nature
Soul	*Psyche*	Psychological Nature
Body	*Soma*	Physical Nature

---

[28] Cf. Zechariah 12:1, Isaiah 42:5, 57:15-16, 2 Maccabees 7:22-23; CCC section 366.

[29] Pope John Paul II, GA, May 13, 1998, section 3. Cf. Genesis 7:15, Wisdom 11:25-12:1, Psalm 104:27-30, Hebrews 1:3; CCC sections 301, 302.

[30] Job 33:4 (NAB). Cf. Job 34:15, Judith 16:14, Psalm 104:29-30, 139:7, 13-16, Acts 17:28.

[31] Cf. St. Ambrose, *On the Holy Spirit*, book 1, chapter 5, section 62; CCC section 308.

[32] CCC section 299.

[33] Cf. Baltimore Catechism.

[34] Cf. 1 Thessalonians 5:23. See also Psalm 16:9, Luke 1:46, Hebrews 4:12; CCC section 367; Chrism Mass, prayer of blessing over the oils to anoint the sick.

The *spirit* is the inner most part of our being, often associated with the heart. It is that part of us most capable of experiencing God. The *soul* is the psychological part of our being, often associated with the mind. It is the repository of our intellect, will, and emotions. The conscious and unconscious regions of our soul include our memories and imagination. The *body* is the physical part of our being. As persons, we are spiritual, psychological, and physical beings. Each of these dimensions of our humanity is important and a gift from God; the spiritual dimension is the most important. Throughout this volume, we will periodically refer to and build upon this framework.

The previous chapter points out that the Holy Spirit helps move our religious experience from our heads to our hearts. To fully appreciate this transformation, we must note that in this framework of understanding, emotions are associated with our *soul/mind*, not our *spirit/heart*. Thus, to move from our heads to our hearts is not to move from our intellect to our emotions. Instead, it is to move our religious experience from our *soul* to our *spirit* – from what we know and feel about God, to a trusting relationship we actually have with God. It is proper for our religious experiences to engage our intellect and our emotions, but the deeper experience of God occurs in our spirit.

Re-Creation of Human Life. While the Bible's first mention of the Holy Spirit concerns the *creation* of life, Jesus' first mention of the Holy Spirit concerns the *re-creation* of human life. This happened when Jesus had a famous encounter with a respected teacher of the Jewish faith named Nicodemus. During their discussion, Jesus told Nicodemus that "[N]o one can enter the kingdom of God without being born through water and the Spirit; what is born of human nature is human; what is born of the Spirit is spirit. Do not be surprised when I say: You must be born from above."[35] With this new birth, the Holy Spirit comes to dwell within our spirits, and thereby begins a process to restore God's likeness within us.[36] This new birth involves a washing and renewal of our hearts and minds by the Holy Spirit.[37] What sin destroys, the Holy Spirit restores. Where sin brings death, the Holy Spirit brings life.

In this new life, it is through the Holy Spirit's indwelling that we become Christians, or, as some say, that we become "born-again."

---

[35] John 3:5-7 (NJB). Cf. John 3:3.
[36] Cf. Romans 5:5, 8:10-11; CCC section 734.
[37] Cf. Acts 22:16, Titus 3:5.

Within us, the Spirit sows the seeds of faith, hope, and love, and he thereby enables us to enter into a personal relationship with God. Peter spoke of this experience as a "new birth into a living hope"[38] whereby we come to "share in the divine nature."[39] Concerning the new birth, St. Paul tells us, "All of this is from God."[40] However, for this new birth to bring about the fullness of God's purposes, we must accept it and do our part to develop it.[41]

The Bible presents two ways by which the Holy Spirit comes to dwell within us. The first way is the Sacrament of Baptism. When Jesus told Nicodemus that to enter God's kingdom we must be born "through water and the Spirit,"[42] the water of which he spoke is the water of baptism.[43] As if to punctuate this teaching, Jesus and his disciples then engaged in a ministry of baptism.[44] After his resurrection, Jesus again emphasized baptism as part of the Great Commission. Jesus told his Apostles, "Go therefore and make disciples of all the nations, baptizing them in the name of the Father and of the Son and of the Holy Spirit, and teaching them to obey everything that I have commanded you."[45] He also told them, "Whoever believes and is baptized will be saved."[46] At Pentecost, Peter also emphasized baptism saying "Repent and be baptized, every one of you . . . And you will receive the gift of the Holy Spirit."[47] Pope John Paul II reminds us that in baptism, even infants receive "the presence of the Holy Spirit" and a "capacity to believe."[48]

St. Paul's conversion illustrates the importance of baptism for receiving the indwelling of the Holy Spirit. Around the year 35 AD, while traveling from Jerusalem to Damascus to arrest Christians, an intensely bright light blinded him and knocked him to the ground. From the light, Paul (whose Jewish name was Saul) heard a voice say, "Saul, Saul, why are you persecuting me?"[49] It was Jesus, speaking to

---

[38] 1 Peter 1:3 (NIV).
[39] 2 Peter 1:4 (NAB).
[40] 2 Corinthians 5:18 (NRSV).
[41] Cf. Pope John Paul II, RM, section 7.
[42] Cf. John 3:5.
[43] Cf. CCC section 1215.
[44] Cf. John 3:22, 26, 4:1-2.
[45] Matthew 28:19-20 (NRSV).
[46] Mark 16:16 (NAB).
[47] Acts 2:38 (NIV).
[48] Pope John Paul II, CT, section 19. Cf. CCC section 1266.
[49] Acts 9:4 (NJB).

Saul, holding him accountable for his persecution of the early Church. This experience greatly shook Saul's emotional and spiritual foundations, yet this was not his conversion, nor his spiritual rebirth as many commentators incorrectly suggest. It was an event leading to his conversion, three days later. While Saul was still on the ground, Jesus commanded him, "Now get up and go into the city and you will be told what you must do."[50] Still blind, Saul's companions led him by the hand into Damascus. For three days, he sat in darkness.

On the third day, Jesus spoke to a Christian named Ananias, instructing him to find Saul. When Ananias reached Saul, he said, "Brother Saul, I have been sent by the Lord Jesus, who appeared to you on your way here, so that you may recover your sight and be filled with the Holy Spirit."[51] "Get up, be baptized, and have your sins washed away, calling on [Jesus'] name."[52] As Ananias laid hands on Saul, something like scales fell from Saul's eyes. Then Ananias baptized him. Through baptism, Saul experienced spiritual rebirth. His sins were washed away. He was the proverbial *new wineskin* and the Holy Spirit filling him in that moment was the *new wine*.[53]

The Sacrament of Baptism is the principal means by which we receive the indwelling of the Holy Spirit. This indwelling can also happen when a non-Christian, after hearing the Gospel message, accepts it by faith.[54] Thus, Paul asked the Galatians, did you not receive the Spirit "because you believed what you heard?"[55] We can also look at Peter's encounter with Cornelius and his household. They received the Holy Spirit while listening to the proclamation of the Gospel. The Bible tells us, "[T]he Holy Spirit came on all who heard

---

[50] Acts 9:6 (NAB).

[51] Acts 9:17 (NJB).

[52] Acts 22:16 (NRSV). Similarly, in Paul's encounter with believers from Ephesus and Philip's encounter with the Ethiopian eunuch, we clearly see the link between baptism and a believer's initial receiving of the Holy Spirit (Acts 8:26-39, 19:1-7).

[53] Cf. Matthew 9:15-18, Mark 2:21-22, Luke 5:36-39.

[54] Some refer to the experience of the Holy Spirit coming to dwell within a person solely by faith as "baptism by desire." The Catholic Church uses this term almost exclusively in two situations: One, for persons who have come to faith in Jesus and are preparing for the Sacrament of Baptism in a worthy manner, but who die before receiving the sacrament. Two, for persons of goodwill who seek truth, strive to live it with integrity, and would have desired baptism had they known of the need for it. See CCC sections 1258-1260.

[55] Galatians 3:2 (NIV). Cf. John 1:12-13, 7:37-39, Galatians 3:5,14, Ephesians 1:13; St. John of Avila, *The Holy Spirit Within*, Scepter Publishers, 2012, page 75.

the message."[56] As they listened to Peter, the Holy Spirit "purified their hearts by faith"[57] and manifested in them various spiritual gifts. Even so, moments later Cornelius and his household received the Sacrament of Baptism. For persons who profess faith in Jesus, but have not been baptized, the Catholic Church considers it a necessity that they be baptized, as Jesus instructed.[58]

Developing Our Capacity to Believe. Having received the indwelling of the Holy Spirit, we must continually develop our "capacity to believe."[59] This is essential because the Spirit's indwelling in our lives is no guarantee that the Spirit's grace will bear fruit within us, most importantly the fruit of salvation. Pope John Paul II taught that without an "explicit personal attachment to Jesus Christ,"[60] our capacity to believe remains just a capacity.

Even a child can form an explicit personal attachment to Jesus by hearing the good news of Jesus, experiencing the kindness and holiness of Jesus' disciples, seeking Jesus in prayer, learning his commands, and striving to obey those commands. The more any of us encounters Jesus by these and other means, the more we then come to know him and form an attachment to him through the power of the Holy Spirit.

For those of us who have reached the *age of reason*, to either acquire or maintain an explicit personal attachment to Jesus requires us to purposefully turn to Jesus in prayer, sincerely repent of our sins, and invite him into our hearts as Lord. If we have been properly prepared for and have worthily received the Sacraments of Reconciliation and Confirmation, then this explicit attachment has been established. What follows these acts of faith is a flow of grace that launches us, as adults, into the spiritual life. By repenting of our sins and committing of our lives to Jesus, no matter how imperfectly, our relationship with Jesus becomes increasingly personal, through the power of the Holy Spirit. As we cooperate with the Holy Spirit, Jesus is no longer a stranger, an historical figure, or an abstract concept. Instead, he is increasingly real to us and alive. We feel his presence. We begin to hear his voice.

In our faith journeys, it is not enough for us to have a lofty opinion about who Jesus is and to agree with Jesus' spiritual, moral, or

---

[56] Acts 10:44 (NIV).
[57] Acts 15:9 (NJB).
[58] Cf. CCC section 1257.
[59] Pope John Paul II, CT, section 19.
[60] Pope John Paul II, CT, section 19.

social teachings. Nor is it enough to be a good person by society's standard or our own self-assessment. We must repent of our sins and invite Jesus into our hearts as Lord. If we do not, we will never enter into true belief in Jesus. We will be filled with information and opinions about Jesus, but not faith in him. We will, in effect, languish outside the borders of God's kingdom failing to enter into it.

Spirit and the Flesh. St. Paul contrasts the new life of a Christian and their old or worldly life as a battle between the Spirit and the flesh.[61] For Paul, "the flesh" is a metaphor for our sinful desires, our fears, our anxieties, and our addictions. We are living "in the flesh" if our daily lives are driven by urges originating in our soul, our body, or the world around us. Conversely, we are living "in the Spirit" if our lives are guided by the Holy Spirit dwelling within our spirit. Paul warns us, "[T]hose who are in the flesh cannot please God."[62]

Conversion is the transformation from the old self to the new self. This experience brings changes in attitudes, understandings, desires, and priorities. Gradually, the temptations of the world lose their grip on us, and the Spirit of God becomes a major influence within us. For all believers, this is a life-long process of continuous development. Yet, sometimes conversion involves dramatic changes in a short period of time. Conversion is always a work of grace.

Repentance is our participation in the Spirit's work of conversion. It is not a mere will-power approach to fighting sin, whereby we fix ourselves. True repentance is all about turning to God and seeking his mercy and asking him to fix us. We must acknowledge to God that we have sinned, that we are sorry for our sins, and that we want to stop sinning. We must ask for his forgiveness and the grace to sin no more.

The Holy Spirit helps us in the conversion process by first making us aware of our sins. In this process, awareness of sin is critical. If we are in denial about the existence of sin in our lives or the harmful nature of sin, then we are not properly open to the forgiveness and renewal that the Spirit provides. Awareness of our own sins requires self-reflection. It requires an inward look at our own brokenness.

Human pride resists the work of repentance and obstructs a sincere self-reflection. Most of us just don't like admitting we are

---

[61] Cf. Romans 8:1-13, Galatians 5:16-17.
[62] Romans 8:8 (NAB).

sinners. We don't like admitting that some of our attitudes about right and wrong *are just plain wrong.* Yet, amazingly, sincere repentance before God is the quickest way to the deeper peace and joy in life that we all desire. Such repentance is a form of sacrifice to God. It is the sacrifice of our pride and the idolatry embedded in the sins from which we repent. Having repented of our sins and having received God's forgiveness, we will still have to deal with certain earthly consequences relating to our past mistakes and with temptations to sin in the future. However, by the action of the Spirit's grace, we can know a new freedom and our interior wounds can begin to heal.

For the new birth to take root and flourish in our lives, we must cooperate with the Holy Spirit who fuels and shapes it. If we have not been baptized, we should seek that sacrament with a repentant heart. If we have been baptized, yet we have fallen away from the Christian faith or never allowed it to develop, we should repent of our sins and allow the grace of the new birth to flourish within us. If Catholic, we should also seek healing in the Sacrament of Reconciliation.

Honest self-reflection and repentance are choices. Committing our lives to Jesus is a choice. Working to keep our commitment is a daily choice. Conversely, ignoring Jesus is a choice. Living life on our own terms is a choice. Each sin is a choice. Our lives unfold based, in large part, on our choices. The sooner we make a choice for Jesus and work to follow through on that choice, the sooner we begin growing in ways meaningful to the kingdom of God and our own best interests.

Consider your own life. Is the new birth flourishing within you? Or is something missing? Consider taking a few moments to offer aloud the following prayer. Pray it from your heart.

Come Holy Spirit. Please assist me in my prayer. Please help me honestly acknowledge my sins and the harm they cause. Please help me appreciate that I am a sinner in need of a Savior. Please help me turn away from sin and turn to Jesus.

Take a few minutes to think about the sins in your life, past and present. Be specific. Consider the harm your sins have caused to you, to others, and to God's kingdom. Remember the sins of omission – your failure to love God above all else, to pray regularly, to live a morally upright life, to show kindness and respect to others, etc. Those sins cause harm too. Then, with a contrite heart, continue the prayer.

Dear Jesus, I acknowledge my sins, those that I recall and those that I do not recall, the things I have done wrong and the things that I have failed to do right. I am sorry that each sin has caused harm to others, to me, and to your kingdom. Please forgive me.

I now turn away from everything I know to be wrong and I turn to you, Jesus. I invite you into my heart as Lord and Savior. I desire your dominion over every facet of my life. Please send the Holy Spirit to fill me afresh with heavenly light and love. May the Holy Spirit cleanse my heart, renew my mind, and lead me in the ways of eternal salvation.

Thank you, Jesus, for your death on the Cross – your suffering for the sins of all humanity, and your suffering for my sins. Thank you as well for the forgiveness of my sins. I (re)dedicate my life to you.

Jesus, in your holy name I pray, Amen.

Rest for a few moments in silence. Softly push away distracting thoughts with the words "Thank you Jesus."

---

3 Spirit of Truth

Jesus delivered his most important teachings on the Holy Spirit when he celebrated the Jewish Passover feast, on the night before he died. At that gathering, what Christians remember as the Last Supper, Jesus prepared his disciples for the next chapter in salvation history. In these teachings, Jesus referred to the Holy Spirit as the "Spirit of Truth" and "the Advocate."

To put Jesus' teachings into perspective, it may help to remember the moment. The days leading up to the Last Supper were some of the most jubilant of Jesus' public ministry. The week began with much fanfare as he approached Jerusalem. A vast crowd of pilgrims were there for the feast, and they lined the road as Jesus approached the city. They waved palms in the air and sang songs of praise. The moment was filled with great expectation. The Messiah might finally be coming into his glory! The tyranny of Roman rule might finally be coming to an end! The House of David might finally be restored!

During the days following his arrival into Jerusalem, Jesus preached in the Temple. He taught God's Law and explained it with authority. He rebuked the religious establishment, which too often misinterpreted God's Law. He performed miracles and excited the crowds of ordinary people. On the fifth night, Jesus sat down with his friends to celebrate the feast. As was the custom, they remembered Israel's Exodus from Egypt and the first Passover night, 1500 years earlier. In the solemnity of that moment, Jesus began preparing them for the events of Good Friday and thereafter. He spoke of his impending death, of someone who would betray him, and of the hardships that they would soon experience.

Jesus shared many things with his disciples that night. However, it was probably his impending death that most disturbed them. In a matter of minutes, their emotions swung from the joyous high of that week's opening toward the sorrowful low of that week's close. They asked themselves: Why must Jesus die? Is our work together all over? What will happen to us?

At this gathering, Jesus taught about the Holy Spirit. He told them, "If you love me, you will keep my commandments. And I will ask the Father, and he will give you another Advocate, to be with you forever. This is the Spirit of truth, whom the world cannot receive, because it neither sees him nor knows him. You know him, because he abides with you, and he will be in you. I will not leave you orphans."[63]

Jesus continued, "[T]he Advocate, the Holy Spirit, whom the Father will send in my name, will teach you everything, and remind you of all that I have said to you."[64] "When the Advocate comes whom I will send you from the Father . . . he will testify to me."[65]

Then, Jesus explained to his disciples the reason, in part, for his impending death: "I tell you the truth, it is better for you that I go. For if I do not go, the Advocate will not come to you. But if I go, I will send him to you. And when he comes he will convict the world in regard to sin and righteousness and condemnation: sin, because they do not believe in me; righteousness, because I am going to the Father and you will no longer see me; condemnation, because the ruler of this world has been condemned. I have much more to tell you, but you cannot bear it now. But when he comes, the Spirit of truth, he will guide you to all truth. He will not speak on his own, but he will speak what he hears, and will declare to you the things that are coming. He will glorify me, because he will take from what is mine and declare it to you."[66]

In these teachings, Jesus makes five important promises concerning the Holy Spirit:

- The Holy Spirit will come.
- The Holy Spirit will testify about Jesus.
- The Holy Spirit will remind the disciples of all Jesus said.
- The Holy Spirit will convict the world in regard to sin and righteousness and condemnation.
- The Holy Spirit will glorify Jesus.

The Holy Spirit Will Come. Jesus promised that he would not leave his disciples orphaned. He promised to send the Holy Spirit to be with them always, yet he conditioned the Spirit's coming on his own departure, on his own death. "[I]f I do not go, the Advocate will not come to you."[67]

---

[63] John 14:15-18 (NRSV).
[64] John 14:25-26 (NRSV).
[65] John 15:26 (NAB).
[66] John 16:7-14 (NAB).
[67] John 16:7 (NAB).

15

Although Jesus promised to send the Holy Spirit to his disciples, this would not be humanity's or their first experience of the Holy Spirit. As we have already noted, the Spirit of God had been present to humanity since the beginning of time. Moreover, the Old Testament describes how the Holy Spirit journeyed with ancient Israel and spoke through her prophets. The Spirit was also with the Apostles in their ministries prior to Jesus' death, as they healed the sick and cast out demons. Speaking to his disciples, Jesus even said of the Spirit, "You know him, because he abides with you,"[68] which no doubt puzzled them. However, something different was about to happen. The Holy Spirit would soon enter their lives with a deeper presence. This promise was not just for Jesus' disciples. It was for all of humanity. It relates to the indwelling of the Holy Spirit through baptism, to the fullness of the Spirit's sacramental and charismatic graces, and to the fullness of the Christian experience.

Jesus also told them, "[I]t is better for you that I go."[69] How were his disciples to understand this statement? Jesus, their beloved Master, Teacher, and Friend, must die and that is the *better* course of events? What they would come to learn is that the Holy Spirit more abundantly present in their own lives would take their friendship with Jesus to new places and would allow them to participate in Jesus' work of salvation with greater boldness and power. The Spirit would not only replace Jesus as "another Advocate,"[70] the Spirit would unite the disciples more closely to Jesus. Further, while Jesus in his humanity was only in one place at one time, the Spirit is everywhere at all times.

The Holy Spirit Will Testify About Jesus. The Holy Spirit testifies (or witnesses) to Jesus in several ways. One way is that the Spirit inspires faithful transmission of the truths Jesus taught – first through the Apostles, and later through bishops, councils, priests, evangelists, and teachers throughout the generations. Though false teachers and false teachings abound in every generation, the Holy Spirit keeps the truth about Jesus alive.

The Spirit of Truth testifies about Jesus through Sacred Scripture by inspiring both its writers and readers. He testifies through signs and wonders that often accompany the work of evangelization. The Spirit also testifies in our hearts as we listen to powerful preaching. This

---

[68] John 14:17 (NRSV).
[69] John 16:7 (NAB).
[70] Cf. John 14:16, 1 John 2:1.

16

revelation gives us an inner awareness of truth and inspires us to know and trust Jesus. As St. Gregory Nazianzen taught, "[B]y the Spirit alone is Jesus known."[71]

The Holy Spirit Will Remind the Disciples of All Jesus Said. One of the blessings that the Holy Spirit bestows on believers is memory of Jesus and of all that he did and taught. The Spirit, if we let him, quietly continues the teaching mission of Jesus in our hearts, helping us to recall Jesus' teachings when that knowledge is needed. The Spirit helps us understand the proper application of those teachings to various situations of life. Pope Francis emphasizes this point: "[The Spirit of Truth] reminds us of Christ's words and convinces us of their saving truth. As the source of our new life in Christ, he awakens in our hearts that supernatural 'sense of the faith' by which we hold fast to God's word, come to a deeper understanding of its meaning, and apply it in our daily lives."[72]

The Spirit of Truth invites us ever deeper into the mystery of God. Jesus by his death became our gateway for truth. The Holy Spirit, as Pope John Paul II taught, is our "supreme guide."[73] God the Father is our destination. On our own, we cannot make this journey. With the Spirit's help, we can.

The Holy Spirit Will Convict the World. Jesus promised that the Holy Spirit would *convict* or *prove wrong* or *convince* the world regarding sin, righteousness, and condemnation. The Holy Spirit's work to convict us of our sins relates, in part, to the Final Judgment – a time when the Spirit will bring to light the fullness of each person's thoughts and actions.[74] He will be an Advocate for truth. He will convince God's saints into eternity on the harm of each and every sin. As Pope John Paul II taught, "The fundamental sin which the Paraclete will make known is not to have believed in Christ."[75]

More importantly, the Spirit, if we let him, convinces our hearts in the present life to turn away from sin and turn to Jesus. This turning requires an act of faith. For behind every sin is unbelief. We often don't believe God can or will save us or guide us in the present moment or we don't believe his way is the best way. Instead, we often

---

[71] St. Gregory Nazianzen, *Orations 41*, section 9.
[72] Pope Francis, GA, May 15, 2013.
[73] Pope John Paul II, DeV, section 6.
[74] Cf. John 12:48, Romans 2:16, 1 Corinthians 3:13, 4:5; CCC section 1039.
[75] Pope John Paul II, GA, May 20, 1998, section 4. Cf. John 16:9.

rely on ourselves or others or the ways of the world. In these moments, we need the Holy Spirit convicting our hearts away from sin.

The Holy Spirit's work convicting us of our sins facilitates the conversion process. This process is essential to our attaining the fruit of salvation. All too often we resist this work of the Spirit. For example, St. Augustine, in his *Confessions*, wrote about his own struggle with the sin of sexual impurity that lasted several years. But eventually, by grace, the Holy Spirit awakened him, convinced him, and empowered him toward greater conversion and holiness. While the pursuit of sexual purity seemed a torment for him at first, the more he accepted and cooperated with the Spirit's work in him, his sexual and spiritual purity became a source of joy.

When we resist the convicting power of the Spirit, we open the door for sin, mistakes in judgment, weaknesses of character, and fears to enter our lives and make a home within us. As a consequence of these negative developments, we can feel sorrow and shame. Relating to our sins, the Bible identifies two types of sorrow or shame that we may feel: (1) Godly sorrow and (2) worldly sorrow. Saint Paul identifies enormous differences between these two types of sorrow: "Godly sorrow brings repentance that leads to salvation and leaves no regret, but worldly sorrow brings death."[76]

Godly sorrow aids us in our conversion by helping us to see our sins for what they are, repent of them before God, experience interior healing, and attain freedom. Even though it may hurt at first, it is for our good. *Worldly sorrow* stems from Satan. It works to condemn us for our sins and, at the same time, to perpetuate those and other sins within us. For some, worldly sorrow leads to despair and low self-esteem; for others, it leads to a prideful arrogance that feels no regret for one's sins; for others, it leads to denial, anger, and blame. Both Godly sorrow and worldly sorrow are often at work within us at the same time. We should be mindful of these very different forms of sorrow or shame – cooperating with that which comes from God, and rejecting that which comes from Satan.

The Holy Spirit will also convince us regarding righteousness: the supreme righteousness of Jesus and the way of righteousness, which comes through faith in Jesus. Concerning the way of righteousness, the

---

[76] 2 Corinthians 7:10 (NIV).

Spirit's inspirations will always conform to the Word of God, which the Holy Spirit gives us to aid our ongoing conversion.

The Spirit will also convict our hearts regarding condemnation: the reality of the Final Judgment and of the punishment we are due, absent God's mercy. Jesus tells us that the ruler of this world (a reference to Satan), has already been condemned. We avoid the same fate by cooperating with the Spirit's work of conversion.

The Holy Spirit Will Glorify Jesus. The Holy Spirit glorifies Jesus in many ways. One way is through personal revelation, when the Spirit in a particular moment lets us sense how awesome Jesus is and how unbelievably valuable was (and is) Jesus' sacrifice on the Cross. Most importantly, the Spirit's work of conversion within us glorifies Jesus. As we become authentic disciples of Jesus, the glory of God shines through us and brings honor to Jesus' name.

Holy Spirit, you are the Spirit of Truth. With the Father and Son, you are God. Thank you for your presence in my life. Thank you for not giving up on me in times past, even as I have turned from you and sinned. Please awaken me ever more fully to the Truth of Jesus and the truth of my own life. Please convict my heart concerning sin, righteousness, and condemnation. Please free my mind from all misunderstandings of spiritual matters, and help me to rightly understand all Biblical truths. Please inflame my heart with love for Jesus. Please help me to know and trust Jesus as I ought. Amen.

4   Spirit of Love

Two special names for the Holy Spirit that come to us from St. Paul's writings are "the Spirit of Love" and "the Spirit of Adoption."[77] Both of these names provide insight into the Personality of the Holy Spirit and his mission in our lives.

Theologians have long described the Holy Spirit as the love of God the Father for the Son and the love of God the Son for the Father, a mutual love so strong that he is a separate Person.[78] This love "proceeds from the Father and the Son"[79] forming creation from chaos into beauty. In our lives as well, if we let him, the Spirit transforms human brokenness from chaos into beauty. He is the love of God poured into the hearts of all who believe.[80]

The Holy Spirit comes into our respective lives in an intense way at baptism because he loves us. He knows each of us by name. He knows our joys and pains, our triumphs and struggles, our virtues and our vices. He knows us and wants us to know him.

The title "Spirit of Adoption" flows from the title "Spirit of Love," for adoption into a family is a wonderful act of love. As a human parent might travel a great distance to an impoverished country where children are suffering to find one to whom they will give a new life, the Holy Spirit similarly comes to us. He comes to invite us to a new life in Christ. Despite our sins, despite our impoverished spiritual and moral state, the Spirit comes to us and chooses us to be his own. Without him, we are diseased and dying. With him, we are on the road to recovery and everlasting joy.

Saint Basil taught, "Through the Holy Spirit we are restored to paradise, led back to the Kingdom of heaven, and adopted as children, given confidence to call God 'Father' and to share in Christ's grace, called children of light and given a share of eternal glory."[81]

---

[77] Cf. Galatians 5:22 (Spirit of Love); Romans 8:5, Galatians 4:4-7 (Spirit of Adoption).

[78] Cf. St. Augustine, *On the Trinity*, n.7,3, 6; Pope John Paul II, GA, July 8, 1998.

[79] Nicene Creed.

[80] Cf. 1 John 4:8, 16, Romans 5:5.

[81] Saint Basil, *De Spiritu Sancto (On the Holy Spirit)*, chapter 15, sect. 36 (PG 32, 132), as quoted in CCC section 736.

Since the fall of Adam and Eve, God has extended an offer of adoption to every man, woman, and child. This offer is an invitation to joy, to peace of mind, and to friendship. In our sins, we are children of darkness, but God invites us to be children of light, children of love. This is not an invitation to know about God's existence, but instead it is an invitation to know God, to experience his presence in our lives, to feel his love, and to live in his love.

God offers us lives of spiritual abundance, lives filled with inner peace. His abundance is not about money or power or fame or worldly success. It is about the Holy Spirit who peacefully comes into our lives to heal, transform, and restore. Understanding God's offer of abundance, St. Augustine rightly prayed, "You made us for yourself, O Lord, and our souls are restless until they rest in you."[82]

Says God to each human being, "I know well the plans I have in mind for you . . . plans for your welfare, not for woe! plans to give you a future full of hope."[83] This is God's invitation to each of us today. The Cross is our invitation, for "While we were still sinners, Christ died for us."[84] Jesus suffered the agony of the Cross "so that we might receive the promise of the Spirit."[85]

The Importance of Encountering Jesus. Pope Benedict XVI taught that the Christian faith "is not born from the acceptance of a doctrine but from an encounter with a person, with Christ."[86] Our encounters with Jesus give "life a new horizon and a decisive direction."[87]

When several of Jesus' disciples first encountered him, it is interesting to note that Jesus did not inundate them with rules. Jesus merely invited them – Peter, Andrew, James, John, and others – to "Come, follow me."[88] Jesus did not even reprimand Matthew, who was a tax collector collaborating with the Romans. Instead, Jesus invited him into a relationship. Jesus said to Matthew, "Come, follow me."[89]

---

[82] Saint Augustine, *Confessions*, book I, chapter 1.
[83] Jeremiah 29:11 (NAB).
[84] Romans 5:8 (NIV). Cf. John 3:16.
[85] Galatians 3:14 (NAB).
[86] Pope Benedict XVI, RC, April 9, 2007.
[87] Pope Benedict XVI, DCE, section 1.
[88] Cf. Matthew 4:19, Mark 1:17, 19-20, Luke 5:10-11, John 1:39, 43.
[89] Cf. Matthew 9:9, Mark 2:14, Luke 5:27.

With similar words, Phillip invited his friend Nathanael to meet Jesus: "Come and see."[90]

The Holy Spirit helps us to hear and accept this same invitation directed to each of us. Rules come later. Rules help us grow in faith and find freedom from sin. But first we must encounter Jesus, appreciate his deep love for us, and then exercise our capacity to believe by committing our lives to him. Christianity is fundamentally about relationship with God, and allowing that relationship to orient the rest of our lives. An authentic Christian life is filled with daily encounters with Jesus, whereby his gift of the Spirit changes us, bit by bit. We can encounter Jesus in the proclamation of the Gospel, in Bible study, in prayer, in service to others, in the kindness of others to us, in the beauty of nature, and in all of the sacraments, most uniquely in the Sacrament of Holy Eucharist. It is a beautiful thing when we appreciate these encounters, realize how deeply Jesus loves us, and respond with faith and love, with reverence and awe.

Gift of an Identity. With adoption into God's family, we receive an identity in Jesus given by the Holy Spirit. Our challenge is to appreciate, accept, and live this identity. For our truest identity is not in ourselves; not in our families or friends; not in our race or national affiliation; not in our work or hobbies or accomplishments; not in our sexuality or looks or personality; not in money or things, but in Jesus. All these other things are passing away. One of the great tragedies of our day is all the many ways people seek identities for themselves that have nothing to do with eternal life in Christ.

The gift of Christian identity tells us "whose we are" and "who we are." We belong to Jesus. We are his. For the Christian, Jesus must be the core of our identity. From that core, everything else finds its place or is discarded.

Gift of a Calling. With adoption comes not only an identity but also a calling, many callings. First and foremost, we are called to life. This is implicit in our creation.[91] We are called "according to his purpose"[92] not to just any life, but life in God, in his Spirit, in his Love. This is our first calling which is all about relationship with God – faith, holiness, and love. This is eternal life now, to be perfected in the life to

---

[90] Cf. John 1:46.

[91] Cf. Philippe, Jacques, *Called to Life*, Scepter Publishers, 2008, page 20.

[92] Romans 8:28 (NRSV).

come. It is all about *knowing God* and letting our *knowledge of God* form our character, personality, and direction in life.

Second, God calls us to have an exterior focus for our lives that he determines. This calling will relate to a particular state in life: to holy matrimony, chaste singlehood, the priesthood, or religious life. Along with our state in life comes our work, our daily responsibilities to earn a living and manage a home, as well as areas of service in the Church community. The Spirit bestows on us spiritual gifts (charisms) that empower us to serve in the roles to which God call us. We will discuss these gifts in later chapters.

While St. Paul gives us a hierarchy of roles in the Church, which facilitates order in the community,[93] the highest calling for any individual is precisely that calling the Lord has for us. As for our roles of service in the Church, these will arise for a season (be it days, weeks, months, or many years).

Third, the *present moment* is a calling. Twenty-four hours a day, seven days a week, as Christians we are Christ's ambassadors to others. Thus, Paul tells us, "[W]hatever you say or do, let it be [done] in the name of the Lord Jesus."[94] We are always on-call for the Lord. Do we realize that? Many calls of service will unexpectedly come to us. They will be divine appointments from God, inspirations of the Spirit to act in a certain way in the moment. We must learn to be attentive to these inspirations.

Discerning a call is always an act of prayer seeking clarity from the Holy Spirit. It will require an exercise of faith. Depending on its nature, discernment of a call may last a split-second, or it may take a few minutes, many days, or sometimes much longer.

I love you Holy Spirit, you who are Love. Please fill me with your presence. Please fill me with love. Help me, I pray, find in Jesus the core of my identity. I am called to relationship with Jesus, the Father, and yourself, please help me to hear and faithfully respond to this call. Breath in me Holy Spirit, breathe your love into my heart and drive out all fear. Please help me to live your love each day. In the name of Jesus, I pray. Amen.

---

[93] Cf. 1 Corinthians 12:23, Ephesians 4:11.
[94] Colossians 3:17 (NJB).

23

5

Artisan of Prayer

The Catholic Church teaches, "Whether we realize it or not, prayer is the encounter of God's thirst with ours. God thirsts that we may thirst for him."[95] God desires that we know him intimately, and that we know him through prayer. The Catholic Church also teaches, "The Holy Spirit is the *living water* 'welling up to eternal life' in the heart that prays."[96] Through prayer, the Spirit helps us encounter Jesus not only as Lord and Savior, but also as Teacher and Friend.

The Apostle Paul taught, "No one can say 'Jesus is Lord' except by the Holy Spirit."[97] Of course, anyone can speak these words. However, only with the help of the Holy Spirit can we mean them, or enter into the mystery they signify. Mother Teresa taught that we should "Start and end the day with prayer. Come to God as a child. If you find it hard to pray you can say, 'Come Holy Spirit guide me, protect me, clear out my mind so that I can pray.'"[98]

Prayer is a wonderful gift from God whereby he allows us the privilege of communicating with him: to speak to him and to listen. Through prayer, we come to know the One who loves us most. It is through the mystery of prayer that a believer enters into "a vital and personal relationship with the living and true God."[99] Humble prayer is the primary way we draw closer to God and submit ourselves to the Spirit's influences. *For the devout Christian, times of prayer are literally the high points of each day.*

In the beginning, prayer was a gift enjoyed by Adam and Eve in a particularly beautiful way. The Bible tells how they walked in the coolness of each day alongside God, conversing with him.[100] God offers us the same gift today, through the Holy Spirit, who is the Artisan of Prayer.[101]

---

[95] CCC section 2560. Cf. St. Augustine, *De diversis quaestionibus octoginta tribus* 64, 4: PL 40, 56.

[96] CCC section 2652. Cf. John 4:14.

[97] 1 Corinthians 12:3 (NIV).

[98] Mother Teresa, *A Simple Path*, Ballentine Books, 1995, page 13.

[99] CCC section 2558.

[100] Cf. Genesis 3:8.

[101] Cf. CCC section 2672.

Prayer usually involves words. Those words can be spoken aloud, or sung, or mediated upon. They can follow a set pattern or be spontaneous. Different types of prayer include the following:

- Praise (Jesus you are awesome!)
- Thanksgiving (Thank you Jesus.)
- Repentance (Forgive me Lord.)
- Supplication (Please help.)
- Sharing (Lord, this was my day.)
- Lamentation (I feel horrible.)
- Lectio Divina (praying Scripture)
- Meditation (prayerful pondering)
- Contemplation (quiet resting)
- Blessing
- Tongues
- Formulated prayers
- Holy Mass
- Rosary / Divine Mercy Chaplet

The Bible tells us that Jesus' prayers to the Father were heard because of "his reverence."[102] The same is true for us. We express reverence for God in our efforts to live faithful and obedient lives, and to go to God in prayer deeply aware of his greatness and his presence. If we approach God with reverence, we can be assured that no matter how imperfect our prayers are, they please him. Moreover, the Holy Spirit within us "helps us in our weakness; for we do not know how to pray as we ought."[103] However, if our hearts are far from God and we speak to him from our selfishness or pride, our words will be in vain.[104] Yet, if despite our sins, we turn to God and pray from a place of humility, sorry for our sins, we can be assured he hears us.

Often, our prayers follow a set pattern, which can be from the Bible, the Church, a saint, a favorite hymn, or from our own personal pattern of prayer. The Bible contains hundreds of formulated prayers, including each of the psalms. Jesus himself gave us the most important formulated prayer, the Our Father. While with most other forms of prayer our thoughts precede our words, with formulated prayer the words go out first, and, if we are sincere, we adapt our thoughts to those words. There is a benefit here, because often our personal prayers can be self-centered and lacking a proper understanding of what prayer really is.[105] The formulated prayers of the Bible, the Church, and the saints teach us how to form our spontaneous prayers.

---

[102] Hebrews 5:7 (NJB).
[103] Romans 8:26 (NRSV).
[104] Cf. Psalm 66:18, Proverbs 15:8, 28:9, Isaiah 1:13, 66:2-3, Luke 18:9-14, James 4:3; CCC section 2562.
[105] Cf. Pope Benedict XVI, *Jesus of Nazareth*, Part I, Doubleday, 2007, pages 130-131.

During Jesus' public ministry, his Apostles made this request: "Lord, teach us to pray."[106] These men, raised in Judaism, who were probably familiar with the scriptures of the Old Testament and the prayers recited in their synagogues, were nevertheless confused about the practice of prayer. In his response, Jesus gave them the Our Father.

Regarding the Our Father prayer, St. Thomas Aquinas observed, "The Lord's Prayer is the most perfect of prayers. . . . In it we ask, not only for all the things we can rightly desire, but also in the sequence that they should be desired."[107] That sequence begins with praise of God. Pope Benedict XVI commented on this sequence: "If man is to petition God in the right way, he must stand in truth. And the truth is: first God, first his kingdom. The first thing we must do is step outside ourselves and open ourselves to God."[108] We do that with praise. St. Edmund taught, "It is better to pray one Our Father fervently and devoutly than a thousand with no devotion and full of distraction." This advice holds true for all our prayers.

A good way to order our prayers is ACTS: Adoration, Confession, Thanksgiving, and Supplication. Too often, supplication – our asking of God for things – dominate our prayers. If we are to pray with the right spirit, we should first give God the adoration he deserves, we should honestly confess our sins, and we should thank God for our lives and his blessings. These should precede our requests.

Throughout the Bible, we observe that devout believers pray together. The practice of prayer is not just about God and me; it is about God and us. Jesus, in the shortness of the Our Father prayer, emphasized this point using plural pronouns ("our," "we," and "us") nine times. On the night before he died, Jesus spent the entire evening in prayer with his Apostles, first at the Last Supper and then in the Garden of Gethsemane. The Apostles and Mary spent several days together in prayer waiting for the events of Pentecost. As with personal prayer, communal prayer is a call to intimacy, humility, and reverence.

Mother Teresa offered this advice concerning prayer. "I always begin my prayer in silence, for it is in the silence of the heart that God speaks. God is the friend of silence – we need to listen to God because

---

[106] Luke 11:1 (NAB).

[107] Thomas Aquinas, *Summa Theologiae*, II-II, 83, 9 as quoted in the CCC section 2763.

[108] Pope Benedict XVI, *Jesus of Nazareth*, Part I, Doubleday, 2007, page 134.

it's not what we say [to Him] but what He says to us and through us that matters. Prayer feeds the soul – as blood is to the body, prayer is to the soul – and it brings us closer to God. It gives you a clean and pure heart. A clean heart can see God, can speak to God, and can see the love of God in others."[109]

Importance of Prayer. Not only by his teachings, but also by his example, Jesus showed us the importance of prayer. It was his custom to arise early in the mornings to pray. Luke tells us that he "often withdrew to lonely places and prayed."[110] His public ministry began with forty-days of prayer. He prayed at each decisive moment in his ministry. His last hours were filled with prayer: not only at the Last Supper and in the Garden of Gethsemane, but also throughout the next day, even as he hung upon the Cross. Prayer filled him with purpose, power, and peace. He was "filled up" with the Holy Spirit through prayer. If Jesus needed to set aside so much time to pray, how much more do we as his followers need to do the same.

To enjoy a healthy prayer life, we must set aside time each day to pray. We must be disciplined about it. We must make it a priority. We should include time for silence to soak in the Spirit's power and time for Bible study to soak in his Word. To help prayer be most effective, St. Francis de Sales encourages us to first place ourselves quietly in God's presence and realize He is there.[111] When asked how to pray, St. Philip Neri responded, "be humble and obedient and the Holy Spirit will teach you."

Pray Constantly. Jesus taught his disciples to "pray continually and never lose heart."[112] Paul, likewise, taught fellow Christians to "pray without ceasing."[113] Beyond our set times for prayer, they are instructing us to be in a prayerful state of mind throughout each day – at work, school, shopping, socializing, as we engage in our hobbies, in times of hardship, etc. – letting God influence our thoughts and attitudes at all times. Toward that goal, we can spontaneously sing songs and offer up praises to God in our mind, as we go about our day. "*Thy will be done*" should be frequently on our minds.

---

[109] Mother Teresa, *A Simple Path*, Ballentine Books, 1995, pages 7-8.
[110] Luke 5:16 (NIV).
[111] Cf. St. Francis De Sales, *Introduction to the Devout Life*, Part II, Section 1.
[112] Luke 18:1 (NJB). Cf. Luke 21:36.
[113] 1 Thessalonians 5:17 (NRSV). Cf. Romans 12:12, Colossians 4:2.

Praying constantly is the choice to live life in the presence of God, in all that we do. It includes not merely our words, but also our attitudes and actions. Pope Benedict XVI taught, "the more prayer is the foundation that upholds our entire existence, the more we will become men of peace."[114] One of the ways we can pray without ceasing is to frequently proclaim Jesus' name or one of his titles with love. *Jesus, Jesus, Jesus. You are the Son of God, the Son of Man, the Lord of lords and the King of kings, my Savior, my Teacher, my Friend.* The Catholic Church teaches, "The invocation of the holy name of Jesus is the simplest way of praying always."[115]

We should not only pray to the Father and Jesus, but also to the Holy Spirit. Perhaps the simplest prayer to the Holy Spirit is the invitation to come. *"Holy Spirit, come. Help me focus on what is good and holy. Please help me be about the Father's perfect will."* The Catholic Church encourages all Christians "to call upon the Holy Spirit every day, especially at the beginning and the end of every important action."[116]

Overcoming Challenges to a Meaningful Prayer Life. There are many challenges to a meaningful prayer life. It takes an act of the will, supported by grace, to overcome those challenges and to form a healthy, disciplined prayer life. Mental distractions and worries plague everyone's prayer life, even the most holy of saints. One way to battle these is to give them to Jesus. Acknowledge their presence at the start of prayer. Then, in your imagination, place them at the feet of Jesus and step away from them. Prayers of praise and thanksgiving are also a good way to get our thoughts off ourselves and onto God.

What is true in human relations is true in spiritual relations: we grow from strangers to acquaintances, from acquaintances to friends as we spend time together. Truly, *he who loves God loves prayer.*

Holy Spirit, You who are the Artisan of Prayer, please awaken within me a strong desire for prayer. Please teach me how to pray as I ought and guide me into an ever more intimate relationship with Jesus, with yourself, and with the Father. Please fill me with a new joy and a new discipline for prayer. Thank you, Amen.

---

[114] Pope Benedict XVI, *Jesus of Nazareth*, Part I, Doubleday, 2007, pg 130.
[115] CCC section 2668.
[116] CCC section 2670.

6   Spirit of Holiness

Since the days of Creation, the Holy Spirit has been quietly preparing humanity for Jesus' coming – for Jesus' first coming two thousand years ago and for his second coming, which we presently await. The Holy Spirit prepares us to receive Jesus through his work of sanctification. To sanctify means to make holy.

In Moses' day, God commanded the people of Israel, "You shall be holy, for I the Lord your God am holy."[117] Centuries later, Peter taught, "As he who called you is holy, be holy yourselves in all your conduct."[118] Paul taught, "This is the will of God, your holiness."[119] This universal call to holiness applies to all people, in all generations.

For many of us, the call to holiness is undesirable. Holiness, we may think, lessens the human experience and deprives us of happiness. Others may think of it as prudish, old fashioned, boring, and even lifeless. True holiness is none of these things.

What then is holiness? Holiness has several meanings. It can mean: (1) to be set apart from a sinful world for God; (2) to be forgiven of sin; (3) to have the Spirit of God dwelling within us; (4) to have the Spirit of God freeing us of sin and growing us in virtue; or (5) to be in perfect relationship with God. This last definition is life in the Blessed Trinity unhindered by the corruption of sin.

Holiness is achieved in us only by the action of the Holy Spirit. The Catholic Church teaches that the Holy Spirit "is the source and giver of all holiness."[120] Holiness comes to us from the Holy Spirit, so that by his grace we become what God is by nature – holy! In the Book of Exodus, God amplifies this point saying, "[I]t is I, the Lord, who make(s) you holy."[121] If we understood, truly, what holiness is – *our sharing in God's divine nature* – we would pursue holiness with great desire, for in his holiness is the fulfillment of all we might rightly desire for ourselves, now and in eternity.

---

[117] Leviticus 19:2 (NRSV). Cf. Leviticus 11:44-45, 20:7-8, 26, Numbers 15:40.

[118] 1 Peter 1:15 (NRSV). Cf. Matthew 5:48, 1 John 3:3.

[119] 1 Thessalonians 4:3 (NAB). Cf. Romans 1:7, 1 Corinthians 1:2, 2 Corinthians 7:1, Ephesians 1:4, 1 Thessalonians 4:7, 2 Timothy 1:9, Hebrews 12:14.

[120] CCC section 749. Cf. *Roman Catechism* I, 10, 1; Hebrews 12:10; Pope John Paul II, GA, December 12, 1990.

[121] Exodus 31:13 (NAB). Cf. Leviticus 20:8, Ezekiel 20:12, 36:24-27, 37:28, Romans 15:16, 2 Corinthians 1:12, 1 Thessalonians 5:23, Jude 1:24.

The Holy Spirit's work of sanctification begins with the indwelling of the Spirit, which for most of us happens at Baptism. That is when we are set apart for God, forgiven of sin, and enabled by grace to know Jesus and believe in him.[122] As we allow the Holy Spirit to continue his work within us, we grow in holiness. The Spirit brings the holiness of Jesus into our lives through our faith in Jesus, which includes our loving obedience to Jesus' commands.[123] *As Jesus took on our guilt at Calvary, we take on his holiness through faith in him.* The Spirit's work of sanctification renews our hearts and minds, purges away our affection for sin, and transforms us over time into the persons God intends us to be.[124]

Through the depth of our ongoing relationship with Jesus, the Spirit infuses us with more and more of Jesus' holiness. Jesus' parable of the vine and the branches illustrates this point. Jesus is the vine and we are the branches.[125] As we remain connected to Jesus, his life-giving sap – *who is the Holy Spirit* – slowly transforms us, bringing the holiness of Jesus to maturity within us.[126]

What Holiness is Not. Christian holiness is not about self-discipline, enlightened philosophies of life, or high moralistic ideals.[127] It is not about good works done apart from a relationship with God. Nor is it about a will-power approach to fighting sin. We cannot will our way out of sin. Nor can we will our way into holiness. Human will, of its own, is not the solution. It is the problem. To be holy, we need what only God can give. Only God can cleanse our hearts and properly reset the direction of our lives, both morally and spiritually.[128]

Gift of Holiness to God. Though it is humanly impossible to make ourselves holy, we nevertheless have a role to play in our own

---

[122] Cf. CCC sections 1265-1266, 1987-1995.

[123] Cf. Acts 26:18, Romans 3:22-28, 5:17, 9:30-32, Galatians 2:16, Philippians 3:9, Colossians 1:22-23; CCC section 1991.

[124] Cf. CCC sections 1989-1991, 1993-1994.

[125] Cf. John 15:1-10. See also Romans 11:16.

[126] Cf. Romans 6:19, Ezekiel 36:27; CCC section 1108.

[127] The heresy of self-holiness is often called "Pelagianism," named for the heretic Pelagius, who believed holiness could be attained through human effort alone. St. Augustine, an ardent opponent of Pelagius, wrote extensively on the necessity of grace (Cf. Psalm 143:2, Ecclesiastes 7:20, Romans 3:20, 23, Philippians 3:9; CCC sections 406, 1987-2016). The Catholic Church denounced Pelagius' teachings on self-holiness at the Council of Carthage (418 AD).

[128] Cf. Psalm 51:7, 10, Proverbs 20:9; Pope John Paul II, GA, February 28, 1990, section 4.

holiness. Our role is to cooperate with the Holy Spirit in the conduct of our thoughts, words, and actions. Thus, St. Paul instructs us, "Let us purify ourselves . . . perfecting holiness out of reverence for God."[129] Pope John Paul II teaches that our holiness is achieved by allowing "ourselves to be made holy by him [the Holy Spirit] . . . by docilely cooperating with his transforming action."[130] The yielding of our will to the Holy Spirit is our gift to God. The more we yield various areas of our lives to God, the more the Spirit of Holiness flows within us.

In our effort to grow in holiness, our relationship with Jesus is of critical importance. Father Robert Barron aptly instructs, we must choose lives "unambiguously centered on Jesus."[131] We must love him above all things. We must allow him to be our best friend. Each of us must commit our whole life to him. This does not mean we all become clergy or join religious orders or become missionaries. What it does mean is that we become faithful and loving disciples of our Master. It means we strive to be authentic followers of Jesus, every day.

As mentioned in a previous chapter, our relationship with Jesus begins in earnest with sincere repentance of our sins and a firm commitment of our lives to Jesus. Perhaps you did that earlier in your life, or maybe you did this when you read the prayer at the end of chapter 2. *If not, consider doing so.*

Holiness and Spiritual Battles. Holiness is a process that plays out over time, a process of ongoing surrender and renewal. In this process, the rhythms of our lives are slowly harmonized with the rhythms of God's Spirit. For this process to achieve its purposes, we must "persevere in the faith"[132] through the various trials of life. Some trials will come from God to discipline us in the ways of holiness. As we hear in the Book of Hebrews, "[God] disciplines us for our good, in order that we may share his holiness."[133]

Our perseverance is a spiritual battle against the various forms of evil in our respective lives. We successfully struggle against the weaknesses of our own flesh, the temptations of sin, and the wickedness of the world only with the help of the Holy Spirit. St. John of the Cross referred to these struggles as the way of purgation

---

[129] 2 Corinthians 7:1 (NIV). Cf. 1 Thessalonians 4:7, Hebrews 12:14, 1 Peter 1:13-2:3.
[130] Pope John Paul II, GA, July 8, 1998, section 4.
[131] Father Robert Barron, *Untold Blessing: Three Paths to Holiness*, DVD, Part 1.
[132] Colossians 1:23 (NAB).
[133] Hebrews 12:10 (NRSV).

whereby the fires of the Spirit's love drive sin and our affection for sin out of us.[134] This is the refiner's fire referenced throughout Sacred Scripture that burns away the evil hiding in the depths of our being.[135] As these fires burn away darkness and imperfections, they make room for a greater infilling of the Spirit's grace.

Without the Holy Spirit's aid, we cannot see most of the imperfections that litter our souls. Sins, such as pride, envy, and anger, hide in our interior blind spots. As we journey closer to God, the Spirit's light makes our sins more visible. As we become more aware of our hidden sins, we may feel discouraged. This growing awareness may feel like failure. Truly, though, it is a positive development. Such awareness helps us to more deeply repent of our sins.

The battle for holiness is a struggle not only to avoid sinful words and deeds, but even more so to avoid sinful thoughts. We are all plagued with thoughts and feelings that are unholy, selfish, and disordered. Our misguided thoughts and feelings can lead us down wrong paths. We must be vigilant in defending our minds and hearts against such thoughts and feelings that come our way every day. We do so not merely by pushing them away with our will and trying to focus our mind on other things. More importantly, we can bring those negative thoughts and feelings "into captivity and obedience to Christ."[136] We must, in faith, shine the light of Christ on them and beckon the Holy Spirit to take them away.[137]

Practically speaking, how might we take our negative thoughts and feelings *into captivity and obedience to Christ*? First, by acknowledging to God their presence and asking him to remove them. Sometimes we may need to sit with God in prayer for some time until they leave us. Second, by turning to God in the moment of temptation with prayers of praise and thanksgiving. These prayers may include the singing of Church hymns or songs from Christian radio. Through such prayers, we invite God's grace to wash away our negative thoughts. Third, by anticipating possible struggles and asking God to bless us and to protect our purity. Fourth, by prayerfully allowing God's wisdom to guide us. His guidance will help us avoid places, situations,

---

[134] Cf. St. John of the Cross, *The Living Flame of Love*, Cosimo Classics, 2007, pages 15, 16, 50.

[135] Cf. Psalm 12:7, 66:10, Wisdom 3:5-7, Job 23:10, Sirach 3:1-5, Isaiah 4:3-4, 48:10, Zechariah 13:9, 1 Peter 1:6-7.

[136] 2 Corinthians 10:5 (NJB).

[137] Cf. Romans 8:13.

persons, lines of discussion, and forms of entertainment that feed unclean thoughts. We must obey the wisdom of God which teaches us, "Above all else, guard your heart, for it is the wellspring of life."[138]

In the battle for holiness, we must resist the influence of demonic forces. These forces are real and very much active in our world. They fuel many of our disordered thoughts and sins. Yet in this battle, the Apostle John teaches us, "[H]e who is in you" – a reference to the Holy Spirit – "is greater than he who is in the world"[139] – a reference to Satan. We must learn to apply this truth in our spiritual battles and avail ourselves of the Spirit's grace.

All spiritual progress involves cooperation with the Holy Spirit's work of sanctification. It most certainly involves struggle, difficult choices, and many new beginnings. It takes every believer, repeatedly, by way of the Cross, where we repent of our sins and we are renewed by the Spirit who comes "to help us in our weakness."[140] This progress is not merely about the stripping away of sin, but also the building up of virtue. Through it all, we never outgrow our need of the Spirit's grace. Quite the opposite, we grow more and more dependent on it.

Holiness and Joy. While the pathways of holiness involve struggle, they also bring joy. True holiness delights in the Lord. That may not always be the emotion we feel in times of trial and disappointment, but it is the overriding reality of our salvation. For this reason, St. Augustine prayed for the grace to delight in the Lord more than in the "fruitless joys" of sin. As he experienced victory over various sins in his life, God filled him with divine joy. He prayed: "How sweet it suddenly became for me to do without . . . [the pleasures of sin], and it was now a joy to put aside those things which I had been afraid of losing. For, Thou didst cast them out from me . . . and Thou didst enter in their place. . . . my Brightness, my Wealth, and my Salvation, O Lord, my God."[141]

St. Paul exhorted early Christians to pursue holiness, for as they did so, they would grow closer to God and experience a divine peace and joy that come only from the Holy Spirit.[142] As we seek the

---

[138] Proverbs 4:23 (NIV).

[139] 1 John 4:4 (NJB).

[140] Romans 8:26 (NJB).

[141] St. Augustine, *Confessions*, Book 9, chapter 1. Bourke, Vernon J. (translator), *The Fathers of the Church*, The Fathers of the Church, Inc. (1953), Vol. 21, page 228.

[142] Cf. Romans 14:17, 15:13, Galatians 5:22, Philippians 4:7.

kingdom of God in true earnestness, the pleasures of the world mean less to us, and the peace and joy of God increasingly bless us.

Disciplines of a Holy Life. The struggle for holiness becomes easier as we adopt the worthy disciplines of a holy life. These disciplines include the following:

- Daily prayer
- Frequent Bible study
- Sacraments
- Christian community

- Obedience to God's commands
- Works of love and justice
- Fasting and almsgiving
- Openness to the Spirit's charisms

The disciplines of a holy life help our relationship with the Father, with Jesus, and with the Holy Spirit grow more personal and more intimate. Moreover, these disciplines, St. Seraphim taught, are "a means of acquiring the Holy Spirit" to ever greater depths, so long as they are done for love of Jesus. The "true aim of our Christian life," he wrote, is "the acquisition of the Holy Spirit of God."[143]

The disciplines of a holy life open us up to an ever greater flow of the Spirit's living waters, which restore God's likeness within us. These waters flow out from the Holy Spirit dwelling in our spirit, quietly irrigating and renewing our hearts and minds. The Holy Spirit takes the holiness of Jesus, and carefully weaves it into the fabric of our lives. Over time, we experience profound changes in our character, our attitudes, our desires, our worldview, and the overall trajectory of our lives. Conversely, lapses in these disciplines deprive us of spiritual nourishment and weaken us in our spiritual battles.

Embracing the disciplines of a holy life is not easy, particularly at first. However, as we persevere in faith, activities that once seemed difficult, uncomfortable, or boring, become second nature, and filled with joy. Our challenge is to let holiness happen, to let it become a lifestyle, to let it become a joy.

Whether due to ignorance, prejudice, or fear, many Christians habitually reject what could be a greater flow of the Spirit's grace into their lives. We commonly resist the Spirit's grace with attitudes such as, "I go to church on Sundays, I don't need the Bible." "I read my Bible, I don't need to pray prayers of praise and thanksgiving." "I pray my rosary, I don't need to serve in ministry." "I'm a good person by

---

[143] St. Seraphim, *The Acquisition of the Holy Spirit.*

society's standard, I don't need the Sacrament of Reconciliation." "I have Holy Eucharist, I don't need the Spirit's charismatic grace." "I live a busy life, I don't have time for . . ." The reality is, all Christians should be proactive in the pursuit of the Holy Spirit's many graces.

The writer of the Book of Hebrews encourages us to pursue holiness and not drift away from our commitment to Christ. He exhorts readers to persevere and warns that those who fall back will face the wrath of God.[144] If we reject the Spirit's gift of holiness, it is to our own peril. Those who shrink back, trample on the body of Jesus, and they insult the Spirit of Grace.[145]

Being a Saint. To be holy is to be saintly. While the Catholic Church formally recognizes only a few persons as canonized saints, "all God's beloved ... are called to be saints."[146] We are called to be saints not only in the *after*-life, but also in the *present*-life. That may seem intimidating, but it should be exciting, since each of us is capable of being a great saint. We are capable of being great saints not by our own strength, but by the Spirit's grace. Whoever we are, the Holy Spirit will form us as saints, if we let him. St. Peter aptly teaches, "His divine power has given us everything we need for life and godliness ... So that through them [we] may participate in the divine nature and escape the corruption in the world caused by evil desires."[147]

For Christians, the call to be saints is not a call to become saints; it is a call to remain saints.[148] In Baptism, we became saints. As we persevere in the faith, we remain saints and grow in saintliness, even as we struggle with sin. If we are not saintly, then we are not truly Christians. This is important, because only saints go to heaven. Léon Bloy, the 19th century French novelist and noted Catholic, appreciated this point. He poignantly wrote: "There is only one real tragedy in life, not to be a saint."[149]

The Book of Revelation describes saints as persons "who keep God's commandments and their faith in Jesus."[150] We mature as saints

---

[144] Cf. Hebrews 10:26-31, 12:10-14.
[145] Cf. Hebrews 10:19.
[146] Romans 1:7 (NRSV).
[147] 2 Peter 1:3-4 (NIV).
[148] Cf. Suenens, Cardinal Leon-Joseph, *Ecumenism and Charismatic Renewal: Theological and Pastoral Orientations,* Servant Books, 1978, page 38.
[149] Léon Bloy, from his novel *The Woman who was Poor.*
[150] Revelation 14:12 (NAB).

as our wills more closely conform to God's will. Realizing all this, we can then look upon the Feast of All Saints, on the first day of November each year, perhaps with new eyes. It is a time to celebrate not only the saints in heaven, but all God's saints: in heaven, on earth, and in Purgatory.

Living Life to the Fullest. How wonderful it is to live life to the fullest. Yet what does that mean? For a worldly person, that might mean engaging in many exhilarating activities. For God's saints, it means living lives of holiness and virtue for love of Jesus, animated by the Spirit of Jesus. It is only by his holiness that we are truly alive; and we are "fully alive" only as his holiness is brought to perfection within us. Understanding this, we can then understand St. Irenaeus when he wrote, "The glory of God is man fully alive."[151]

Making All Things New. In the Book of Revelation, Jesus revealed to St. John, "Behold, I make all things new."[152] How does Jesus accomplish this work of newness? Through his gift of the Holy Spirit. As Pope Francis teaches, "This is the work of the Holy Spirit: he brings us the new things of God. He comes to us and makes all things new; he changes us. The Spirit changes us! . . . God is even now making all things new; the Holy Spirit is truly transforming us, and through us he also wants to transform the world in which we live."[153]

This is good news for every sinner. By God's grace, even the worst of us can be forgiven and made new. Addicts, prostitutes, murderers, racists, those whose hearts are filled with pride or greed or anger, or those trapped in a lifestyle of sexual sin can be made new by the Holy Spirit. Impediments to spiritual growth that once seemed so deeply ingrained into our psyche and essential to our personality or our way of life can be totally annihilated. That may seem like an impossible task. But, truly, all things are possible with God.

Being made new by the Holy Spirit entails a healing process – spiritual healing first and foremost, but also psychological healing, emotional healing, physical healing, and healing of relationships. Pope John Paul II accentuates the role of the Holy Spirit in this healing process: "Humanity must let itself be touched and pervaded by the Spirit given to it by the risen Christ. It is the Spirit who heals the

---

[151] St. Irenaeus, *Against Heresies*, 4.20.7.
[152] Revelation 21:5 (NAB).
[153] Pope Francis, homily, April 28, 2013. Cf. 2 Corinthians 5:17.

wounds of the heart, pulls down the barriers that separate us from God and divide us from one another, and at the same time, restores the joy of the Father's love and of fraternal unity."[154]

Holiness and Salvation. The writer of the Book of Hebrews teaches that holiness is essential to attaining the fruit of salvation: "Strive ... for that holiness without which no one will see the Lord."[155] Similarly, Paul teaches, we are "saved through the sanctifying work of the Spirit."[156] Peter draws a similar connection between holiness and salvation: "You ought to live holy and godly lives as you look forward to the day of God . . . make every effort to be found spotless, blameless and at peace with him. Bear in mind that our Lord's patience means salvation."[157]

Holiness and the Sabbath Command. The Bible first mentions holiness in the Book of Genesis: "God blessed the seventh day and made it holy."[158] The Book of Exodus likewise associates holiness with the seventh day of the week. One of the Ten Commandments God gave Moses directs Israel, "Remember to keep holy the Sabbath day. Six days you shall labor and do all your work, but the seventh day is a Sabbath to the Lord your God. On it you shall not do any work, neither you, nor your son or daughter, nor your manservant or maidservant, nor your animals, nor the alien in your gates."[159]

The Bible also commands us, "[T]he seventh day is . . . a day of sacred assembly, on which you shall do no work. The Sabbath shall belong to the Lord wherever you dwell."[160] "[E]ven during the plowing season and harvest [season] you must rest."[161] "[A]ll who keep the Sabbath, and do not profane it, and hold fast [to] my covenant – these I will bring to my holy mountain, and make them joyful in my house of prayer."[162]

Jews fulfill this command by celebrating the Sabbath on Saturdays (from Friday at sundown to Saturday at sundown), to honor

---

[154] Pope John Paul II, homily, April 30, 2000.
[155] Hebrews 12:14 (NAB). Cf. Psalm 24:3-4, Isaiah 35:8-10, Romans 6:22, Revelation 21:27.
[156] 2 Thessalonians 2:13 (NIV). Cf. Romans 6:22.
[157] 2 Peter 3:11-12, 14-15 (NIV).
[158] Genesis 2:3 (NIV).
[159] Exodus 20:8-10 (NIV). Cf. Exodus 31:12-17, Deuteronomy 5:12-15.
[160] Leviticus 23:3 (NAB).
[161] Exodus 34:21 (NIV). Cf. Nehemiah 10:31.
[162] Isaiah 56:6-7 (NRSV). Cf. Ezekiel 20:19-20, Jeremiah 17:19-27.

the seventh day of creation when God rested. Christians fulfill this command by celebrating "the Lord's Day" on Sundays, to honor the new creation made possible by Jesus' resurrection on Easter Sunday.[163] The Catholic Church teaches that the Lord's Day "is to be observed as the foremost holy day of obligation . . . [On this day] the faithful are bound to participate in the Mass."[164] "Those who deliberately fail in this obligation commit a grave sin."[165]

Rest on the Lord's Day is critical to every Christian's pursuit of holiness. This day is not about leisure and recreation, but about holiness and re-creation. It is not a day to do as we please, but to do as God pleases.[166] It is about friendship with God, in and through the Spirit of God. The Lord's Day is a thread of grace sewn into the fabric of time for our good. However, this gift only blesses us if we cooperate. God makes the day holy. Only as we honor the Lord's Day pursuant to God's prescriptions, do we allow the special graces associated with the day to bless our lives.

Pursuing holiness on the Lord's Day requires that we rest, physically and mentally. More importantly, it requires that we rest spiritually from the many distractions of the week. It is a time to worship God in sacred assembly, in which the People of God "strengthen one another under the guidance of the Holy Spirit."[167] It is a time for peaceful, quiet, contemplative rest in the Lord. It is also a time for wholesome fellowship with family and friends. It is a time to welcome strangers and to visit the sick, the elderly, and the homebound. It is a time to reconcile with enemies.

Jesus teaches us to view the Sabbath command as a gift from God, not as the legislation of men. In fact, he criticized the religious leaders of his day for over-regulating the Sabbath.[168] When Jesus declared, "The Sabbath was made for man, not man for the Sabbath,"[169] he was emphasizing how integral Sabbath rest is to the fulfillment of humanity's greatest aspiration – friendship with God. He also showed that while God forbade the work of everyday life, he did not forbid

---

[163] Cf. CCC sections 345-349, 1166-1167, 2168-2195.
[164] CCC section 2192.
[165] CCC section 2181.
[166] Cf. Isaiah 58:13.
[167] CCC section 2182.
[168] Cf. Matthew 12:1-13, Mark 2:23-3:6, Luke 6:1-11, 14:1-6, 13:10-17, John 5:1-14; CCC sections 2185-2186.
[169] Mark 2:27 (NAB).

works of mercy. Not only are works of mercy allowed on the Sabbath, sometimes they are required.[170]

The Old Testament recounts many occasions on which God's prophets rebuked the people of Israel for not keeping the Sabbath holy. The prophets understood that rejecting the Sabbath meant rejecting intimacy with God. As a result, many Jews and the nation of Israel as a whole, repeatedly fell out of relationship with God. For Christians today, it is no different. If our weeks are so busy with secular activities that we push those activities into the Lord's Day, then we should reduce or better manage those activities. Rather than pushing our secular activities into the Lord's Day, we should "push" the peace, holiness, and joy of the Lord's Day into the fullness of our weeks. The grace of this day is meant not merely for our own good, but also for the good of our families, local communities, nations, and the world.

> *Spirit of Holiness, I adore you. You are wonderful, you are mighty, you are beautiful. Spirit of God, please stir within me. Please bathe me in your light and robe me with your love. Please free me from the influence of all evil – all sin, all fear, all worldliness, all lies, and all demonic oppression. I ask this in Jesus' name. Amen.*
>
> *Spirit of Truth, Please show me my sins and aid me in the way of ongoing conversion. Help me find true freedom from sin. Please fill the depths of my heart with the flames of your love and with the holiness of Jesus. Inspire me, I beg you, to desire and live holiness in all areas of my life. Please teach me the ways of virtue.*
>
> *Holy Spirit, I want to be a saint. I want to be a great saint who gladly accepts the tasks that you choose for me, no matter how high or how low they may seem in the eyes of the world. Please help me in this noble aim. In my pursuit of increasing holiness, teach me to cheerfully embrace the gift of the Lord's Day. Open my heart and mind to the fullness of grace offered, each week, in this sacred moment in time. In Jesus' name I pray, Amen.*

---

[170] Cf. Matthew 12:11-13, Mark 3:4-5, Luke 6:9-10; CCC section 2173.

7   Power from on High

Throughout the Bible, from Genesis to Revelation, the Holy Spirit intervenes in human history as a supernatural power who changes lives and performs wonderful miracles. Not surprisingly, Biblical titles for the Holy Spirit include "Power of God," "Power of the Most High," "Power from on High," "Power of Christ," and "Power of the Resurrection."

The Book of Genesis depicts the Holy Spirit as the power who brings forth the beauty and order of Creation and gives life to all living things. In the Book of Exodus, he is the power manifested as fire and cloud, who covers Mount Sinai and gives Moses the Ten Commandments. Throughout the Old Testament, the Holy Spirit is the power who speaks through Israel's prophets illuminating for Israel the pathway of freedom.

In Luke's Gospel, the Holy Spirit is the power who overshadows Mary at the Incarnation placing Jesus in her womb. All four Gospels describe how the Holy Spirit descends upon Jesus at the Jordan River and anoints Jesus' humanity with supernatural power to proclaim the gospel, heal the sick, and cast out demons. In his letter to the Philippians, Paul teaches that the Holy Spirit is the Power of the Resurrection who raised Jesus from the dead. John's Gospel describes how Jesus appeared to his Apostles on Easter Day and breathed the Holy Spirit upon them, imparting to them, as priests of the New Covenant, power and authority to forgive sins in God's name.

Jesus Promises to Send the Holy Spirit. Luke's Gospel and his Book of Acts recount Jesus' final words to his disciples on the day he ascended into heaven. That day, Jesus made three important promises. First, Jesus promised to send the Holy Spirit, who is the *power from on high*: "I am going to send you what my Father has promised; but stay in [Jerusalem] until you have been clothed with power from on high."[171] Second, Jesus promised that the disciples would be baptized with the Spirit: "[W]ait for the promise of the Father about which you have heard me speak; for John baptized with water, but in a few days you will be baptized with the Holy Spirit."[172] Third, Jesus promised that the disciples would receive power when the Holy Spirit came upon

---

[171] Luke 24:49 (NIV).
[172] Acts 1:4-5 (NAB).

them: Jesus told them, "[Y]ou will receive power when the Holy Spirit comes upon you; and you will be my witnesses in Jerusalem, throughout Judea and Samaria, and to the ends of the earth."[173]

Fulfillment of these promises empowered Jesus' disciples to be extraordinarily effective evangelists for Jesus in many lands. When Jesus spoke of "power," he used the Greek word "*dunamis*" from which we get the English words dynamism, dynamic, and dynamite. Luke used this same word to explain the means by which Jesus performed his healings: "[T]he power [*dunamis*] of the Lord was present for [Jesus] to heal the sick."[174] This power went out from Jesus to effect the healings.[175] The Catholic Church teaches that this power was the Holy Spirit.[176]

Jesus' promise to empower his disciples through the Holy Spirit should be understood as an increasing empowerment of the Spirit's grace in their lives and not as an initial empowerment. The Spirit was present in their lives as they came to know Jesus, as they performed miraculous healings prior to Jesus' death, and as Jesus breathed the Spirit upon them, a few weeks earlier at Easter, for a ministry of forgiveness. Jesus' promise to send "power" truly was a promise to send "more power."

The Decent of the Holy Spirit. Ten days after Jesus' Ascension into heaven, on the Jewish feast of Pentecost, the Holy Spirit came upon Jesus' disciples, as he foretold. The disciples, some one hundred and twenty in all, including Mary and the Apostles, were gathered in the upper room for prayer. While they were praying, the Spirit manifested as wind and fire came upon them, and "All of them were filled with the Holy Spirit."[177] These followers of Jesus were radically changed as the Spirit filled them. Their faith was no longer the timid faith of unsure disciples. Because of the Holy Spirit, their faith was courageous, filled with purpose and power.

Just as the Holy Spirit had anointed Jesus at the Jordan for ministry, the Spirit now anointed the Apostles and others in their community for ministry. The Spirit released within each of them unique spiritual gifts for their respective roles of service in the early

---

[173] Acts 1:8 (NAB).
[174] Luke 6:19 (NIV). Cf. Luke 5:17, 8:46.
[175] Cf. Luke 5:17.
[176] Cf. CCC section 695.
[177] Acts 2:4 (NRSV).

Church. For example, Peter, an uneducated fisherman who loved Jesus but had struggled in his faith prior to Pentecost, was very much a changed man that day. Over time, the Spirit's power was manifested in him through gifts of leadership, prophecy, understanding, teaching, and healing. On that first Christian Pentecost, he preached a powerful sermon about Jesus. He spoke of repentance and interpreted the Jewish scriptures with authority. In response to Peter's preaching, some three thousand skeptics became believers and were baptized.[178]

All the wonderful stories we read in the Acts of the Apostles concerning the Apostles and the early Church, the miracles, and the growth of communities, are truly a work of the Holy Spirit in them and through them. We hear of people filled with a new boldness to live lives of holiness and service, lives conformed not to the ways of the world, but to the ways of heaven.

Two Outpourings of the Holy Spirit at Pentecost. In the Biblical account of Pentecost, we hear of two different outpourings of the Holy Spirit. The Bible uses forms of the word "baptize" to refer to both experiences. One of these experiences is the Sacrament of Baptism, by which a person receives the indwelling of the Holy Spirit. This sacrament was administered by Jesus' disciples to the three thousand converts who accepted the message that Peter preached.

The other outpouring of the Holy Spirit that Pentecost day fulfilled a prophecy spoken by John the Baptist three years earlier. John prophesied of Jesus: "He will baptize you with the Holy Spirit and fire."[179] Indeed, at Pentecost, the Spirit came upon Jesus' disciples as tongues of fire, filling them with himself and with a holy boldness by which they sang God's praises and proclaimed the good news of Jesus to others. Based on John the Baptist's prophesy and Jesus' own promise to send the Holy Spirit, some people today refer to Jesus as "the baptizer in the Holy Spirit."

The Experience of Pentecost is Offered to all Christians. Christians today can have experiences of God that are similar to what the Apostles experienced at Pentecost. We can experience a new and vibrant movement of God's grace that profoundly equips us for service in God's kingdom. Many of these graces may have been received in the Sacrament of Baptism, but with this later experience, those

---

[178] Cf. Acts 2:41.
[179] Mathew 3:11 (NJB). Cf. Mark 1:8, Luke 3:16, 24:49, John 1:33, 15:26.

dormant graces are awakened. If, in the Sacrament of Baptism, these graces were implanted into our hearts in seedling form, then in this later experience, those seeds begin flowering forth with new life and purpose. This later experience is commonly called being "baptized in the Holy Spirit." It is not the Sacrament of Baptism, but a later release of divine power received in the sacrament.

The experience of being "baptized in the Holy Spirit" expands our capacity to know, love, and serve God. Our faith becomes more courageous, filled with greater joy, purpose, and power. It is more than the power to become Christian or to live in holiness. It is the power by which Christians engage in wonderful acts of service for God's kingdom with the strength of the Holy Spirit that comes to us through charisms. It is an experience that manifests differently with each person, as the Spirit wills. Some Christians believe that for this experience of the Holy Spirit to be truly manifested in a person's life, a person must experience the gift of tongues. The Catholic Church does not hold this view. Many may indeed receive the gift of tongues, but that is not the litmus test for being baptized in the Holy Spirit.

If, in the Sacrament of Baptism, the Holy Spirit is poured into our hearts, with this later experience, the Spirit pours out from our hearts. If we have been living the disciplines of a holy life, then the Spirit of God has been flowing through us already. However, when we are "baptized in the Holy Spirit" that grace begins to flow with greater intensity. A 2009 Vatican report estimated that nearly 600 million Christians world-wide have been baptized in the Holy Spirit, including an estimated 120 million Catholics (approximately 10% of all Catholics).[180] More recent estimates suggest that over 150 million Catholics have been baptized in the Holy Spirit.[181]

For Christians who received the Sacrament of Baptism as infants, this more intense movement of God's grace ideally happens at Confirmation, which is offered as a "Pentecostal" experience.[182] However, too often this is not the experience of those receiving Confirmation. Grace may be imparted, but something – perhaps a lack of faith, a lack of personal commitment to Jesus, a lack of preparation

---

[180] Cf. Catholic/Pentecostal International Dialogue, *On Becoming a Christian: Insights from Scripture and the Patristic Writings*, 2009, sections 239 and 260.

[181] Cf. *Pentecost Today*, National Service Committee of the Catholic Charismatic Renewal, Fall 2013, page 5.

[182] Cf. CCC section 1302.

for the sacrament, or a lack of knowledge or expectation concerning the Spirit's spiritual gifts – obstructs an "on fire" experience.

For those who have not had an "on fire" experience, Pope Benedict XVI provides the following guidance: "I would like to extend [an] invitation to all: let us rediscover, dear brothers and sisters, the beauty of being baptized in the Holy Spirit; let us recover awareness of our Baptism and Confirmation, ever timely sources of grace."[183] This is an important message, because graces received in times past, which may be lying dormant within us, can be awakened by the Spirit today. Then, over time, through prayer, study, and service, those graces may grow and develop within us. Jesus said he came that we may have life and have it more abundantly.[184] The Holy Spirit's sanctifying grace is *that life*. The Spirit's sanctifying grace coupled with his charismatic grace flowing freely and vibrantly within us is *that life in abundance*.

Being "baptized in the Holy Spirit" is not necessary for our salvation, but it is essential in our faith journey if we are to fulfill many of the purposes God has for our lives. God desires not only that we know him and live in his holiness, but that we also perform various forms of service in the power of the Spirit's charismatic grace. Charismatic grace is power beyond our natural abilities, talents, and learned skills. The following analogy may be useful in understanding the Spirit's charismatic grace and its relationship to sanctifying grace.

The power of the Holy Spirit can be likened to electricity and the Sacrament of Baptism to the attachment of electrical lines from a central Power Plant to our homes (to our lives). The connection of our homes to the Power Plant does not, of itself, give rise to an ongoing flow of power within us. Great resources of power may be available to us, but until the right switches are turned on, the power does not flow. The disciplines of a holy life are the means by which we access the Spirit's sanctifying grace, the power that lights each room and circulates fresh air, the power that dispels darkness and mustiness, the power that restores within us the likeness of Christ. As we surrender each aspect of our lives to Jesus, one by one, they become electrified with the gift of the Holy Spirit. When we are baptized in the Holy Spirit, it is as though a more intense current of power flows through us. It is the Spirit's charismatic grace empowering the appliances in various rooms, bringing forth new and surprising calls to service.

---

[183] Pope Benedict XVI, RC, May 11, 2008.
[184] John 10:10.

Where does being baptized in the Holy Spirit fit in the normal progression of the Christian faith? The chart below presents seven steps to Christian perfection. The baptism in the Holy Spirit usually occurs after we have committed our lives to Jesus and we are purposefully pursing the disciplines of a holy life. Our challenge is not merely to have this "on fire" experience, but to let it take hold of us, change us, and give new direction to our lives. These steps are not always sequential, and some of them we revisit over and over again throughout our lives.

Seven Steps to Christian Perfection

Step 1. Receiving the Sacrament of Baptism. Our souls are cleansed. We become a new creation as the Spirit comes to dwell within us. We are given a capacity for faith. Refer to chapters 2, 15, and 23.

Step 2. Learning the Faith. With this step, we learn about the Christian faith through teachings, readings from the Bible and other spiritual books, prayer, and service to others. Chapters 2 and 5.

Step 3. Repenting from Sin / Committing our Lives to Jesus. Here, our adult relationship with God begins in earnest as we seek and receive forgiveness of our sins and as we dedicate our lives to Jesus. Our relationship with God is personal. Chapters 2 and 17.

Step 4. Practicing the Disciplines of a Holy Life. The Holy Spirit helps us to grow in our relationship with God and live our faith through prayer, the sacraments, Bible study, obedience to God's commands, and service. With increasing measure, we grow in faith, hope, love, and the fruit of the Spirit. Chapters 6, 15-21, 23-25.

Step 5. Being Baptized in the Holy Spirit. The Holy Spirit empowers us for more effective service in God's kingdom. The Spirit awakens us to the charismatic dimension of our own lives. A new phase in our life begins, if we let it. Chapters 7, 8, 18, and 22.

Step 6. Being Led by the Spirit. As we continue practicing the disciplines of a holy life and grow more obedient to the Spirit's inspirations, the Holy Spirit brings the holiness of Jesus to perfection within us. Charisms and the fruit of the Spirit mature within us. Chapters 9, 10, 11, and 22.

Step 7. Final Purification of God's Elect. In the Final Judgment, God's elect are purified by grace for entry into heaven. Chapter 14.

Not only in Apostolic times, but throughout Church history, stories abound of persons being baptized in the Spirit and experiencing wonderful spiritual transformations and an awakening of the Spirit's charismatic grace. Here are four remarkable examples: St. Philip Neri, St. Thérèse of Lisieux, Fr. Michael Scanlan, and Mother Angelica.

St. Philip Neri Baptized in the Holy Spirit. St. Philip Neri lived in 16th century Rome during the time of the Catholic and Protestant Reformations. St. Philip's achievements include the founding of a confraternity of servants who ministered to the thousands of poor pilgrims who flocked to Rome each year and to people released from hospitals who were still too weak to work. He also founded a religious order (the Orations) that was devoted to the preaching of the gospel and the reform of secular arts and entertainment. Philip was a man of deep prayer, an insightful confessor, a spiritual director to many clergy, and, interestingly, a jokester. He was an enormously popular person who aided the faith journey of many souls, earning him the title "Apostle of Rome."

Early in his faith journey, Philip formed a special devotion to the Holy Spirit. He prayed daily to the Holy Spirit, asking for the Spirit's graces to be manifested in his life. After several years of a deepening prayer life and various forms of service in the Church, the Holy Spirit filled Philip in an intense moment of spiritual ecstasy. This occurred on the eve of Pentecost in 1544 when he was 28 years old. While in prayer, he experienced a ball of fire entering his mouth and filling his chest, which he understood to be the fire of the Holy Spirit. The force and power of the Spirit inflamed his heart with a heavenly love and joy, so much so, that during his prayer time that evening, he eventually prayed, "Enough, Lord, enough! I cannot take anymore!"[185]

Philip's personal experience of Pentecost strengthened his faith in God and his pursuit of holiness. It also awakened charisms within him, enabling him for more effective service in God's kingdom, eventually as a priest. The charisms of evangelization, compassion for the sick, healing, and an irresistible joy filled his heart and his ministry.

St. Thérèse of Lisieux Baptized in the Holy Spirit. St. Thérèse ("The Little Flower") is one of the most interesting of saints. Though her life was short, her deep insights into prayer and the struggle for holiness are extraordinary, earning her millions of admirers.

---

[185] Türks, Paul, *Philip Neri, The Fire of Joy,* Alba House 1995, page 17.

St. Thérèse was born in Alencon France, in 1873. From an early age she enjoyed an intense love for Jesus, his Church, and Mary. At the age of nine, she became seriously ill with tremors, but was miraculously healed a year later on the feast of Pentecost. At age eleven, Thérèse received her first Holy Communion and at that time was intimately aware of Jesus' presence. She attributed her experiences that day to the previous three months of prayerful and studious preparation, which included a retreat at an Abbey of nuns. Regarding the experience of her first Holy Communion, she said, it was as if "Heaven itself dwelt in my soul . . . [as I received] a visit from Our Divine Lord."[186] Weeks later, Thérèse received the Sacrament of Confirmation. In the weeks leading up to her Confirmation, she had more studies and preparations, which she took very seriously. She said of her Confirmation, "I did not feel the mighty wind of the first Pentecost, but rather the gentle breeze which the prophet Elias heard on Mount Horeb."[187] With gentleness, Thérèse was baptized in the Holy Spirit at Confirmation.

At age 15, the Holy Spirit guided Thérèse to her vocation as a cloistered Carmelite nun. Her journey of faith included a strong desire for Bible study and other spiritual reading, devotions to Jesus and Mary, and much self-reflection on the struggle for holiness. Among the charisms that manifested in her life was teaching on spiritual matters, divine wisdom, and an intense power for intercessory prayer. She felt particularly called to pray for the conversion of sinners and for blessings upon missionaries in foreign lands. In 1897, at the age 24, Thérèse succumbed to tuberculosis. In 1997, Pope John Paul II bestowed on her the distinguished title, Doctor of the Church.

Father Michael Scanlan Baptized in the Holy Spirit. Father Michael Scanlan's life provides a noteworthy example of a person whose life was greatly transformed when he was baptized in the Holy Spirit. Prior to this experience, Father Scanlan had a wonderfully successful life by worldly standards. His achievements included degrees from Williams College and Harvard Law School, service as a lawyer in the Judge Advocate Corps of the United States Air Force, ordination as a Franciscan priest and rector of a seminary.

As a young man prior to being baptized in the Holy Spirit, Fr. Scanlan experienced the presence of God in profound ways that led

---

[186] St. Thérèse of Lisieux, *Story of a Soul*, chapter 4.
[187] St. Thérèse of Lisieux, *Story of a Soul*, chapter 4.

him to the priesthood. Nevertheless, a few years into his priesthood, he knew there was a deeper experience of God that he was missing. He realized that he was engaging in his many duties on his own strength and was beginning to feel burned out. He knew he needed more of God's grace, but how was he to acquire it? He had heard about people being baptized in the Spirit and decided to seek this experience. One evening, as he joined with others in prayer, he allowed a fellow priest and others to pray for him to be baptized in the Holy Spirit. As they prayed, Fr. Scanlan felt tremendous peace, a desire to know God, and an irresistible desire to praise God. Words of praise joyfully poured forth from his lips. Moments later, while praying for someone else, he suddenly experienced the gift of tongues.

Later that night, after he had gone to bed, he repeatedly awoke from his sleep in prayer. In his own words, "Prayer had been going on in me while I slept. I awakened and joined God's prayer in me. In the morning I wrote this sentence down on the pad I kept next to my bed: 'I know the presence of the risen Lord Jesus as I have never known it before.'. . . I also wrote this sentence on my pad: 'I can never deny the truth of what has happened.' I knew this experience would not last in its current intensity. I was sure troubles and trials would come in such number that they would threaten to turn the truth of what I was experiencing inside out. I wanted a reminder close at hand."[188]

Years later Fr. Scanlan wrote, "I know the baptism in the Spirit is real because it brought about lasting changes in me. It has also brought about changes in hundreds of men and women I know well."[189] The graces manifested in Fr. Scanlan's life would not only help him become a better priest, but also an extraordinarily capable leader as president and chancellor of Franciscan University of Steubenville. The immediate changes he experienced after being baptized in the Holy Spirit included a new zeal for prayer and Bible study. Over time, he also experienced the Holy Spirit work through him in new ways, through charisms of preaching, prophecy, miraculous healings, and power to command demonic spirits to flee.

Mother Angelica Baptized in the Holy Spirit. Mother Angelica is a remarkable woman. Much can be said about her life-long journey of faith. She founded two monasteries, a cable television empire (EWTN – Eternal Word Television Network), and a television show that she

---

[188] Scanlan, Fr. Michael, *Let the Fire Fall*, Franciscan Univ. Press, 1986, page 92.
[189] Scanlan, Fr. Michael, *Let the Fire Fall*, Franciscan Univ. Press, 1986, page 93.

hosted for twenty years – "Mother Angelica Live." As a result of these accomplishments, she became a major voice within the Catholic Church during the last two decades of the 20th century. Pope Benedict XVI awarded her the Pro Ecclesia et Pontifice Medal in recognition of her distinguished service to the Catholic Church.

In 1971, long before she established EWTN, Mother Angelica and her fellow nuns lived in a cloistered community outside Birmingham, Alabama. In those days, they were frequently visited by a young priest, Fr. Robert DeGrandis. With each visit, Fr. DeGrandis spoke of the Holy Spirit and offered to pray with the nuns, that they might be baptized in the Spirit. Mother repeatedly ignored his offer, sarcastically telling him that she already received the Holy Spirit in Confirmation. She followed a very rigorous spiritual discipline and had experienced many miraculous movements of grace in her life up to that time. What could she be missing in her spiritual walk? She was also suspicious of the charismatic renewal of which Fr. DeGrandis was a part.

Mother Angelica's thinking changed when Fr. DeGrandis brought a colleague of his to their community to pray for a sick nun. Touched by the depth of love in their prayers, Mother Angelica privately asked them to pray for her that she might be baptized in the Holy Spirit – *whatever that might mean*. As Fr. DeGrandis prayed for her, Mother Angelica felt nothing noteworthy, just peace. However, while reading a week or so later, she unexpectedly began speaking in tongues. A new language poured from her lips, a language she did not recognize. This would be the start of the Holy Spirit's power moving through her in new ways. This awakening of the Holy Spirit's charismatic grace within her included a thirst for Bible study that she had previously never known. Over time, the Spirit also brought forth a gift of prophetic messages and visions. If before, she was naturally endowed with talents of evangelization, teaching, and fortitude – now she was supernaturally endowed with charisms by the same names, which would become quite apparent over the next three decades.

A few weeks after this experience, Mother Angelica and Fr. DeGrandis prayed with each of the nuns in the community that they would be baptized in the Holy Spirit. All the sisters were blessed, and most of them immediately began experiencing the Spirit's charismatic grace in profound ways. The gift of tongues flourished among them as well as other spiritual gifts. Most striking, all were filled with an enthusiasm for Bible study. Mother later reflected on this moment as "really the beginning" of EWTN.[190] Years later, while visiting Rome, she briefly met with Pope John Paul II. His comments as he greeted her were prophetic in nature: "Mother Angelica, strong woman, courageous woman, charismatic woman" and, a moment later, "Mother Angelica, weak in body, strong in spirit. Charismatic woman, charismatic woman."[191] The wonderful accomplishments of Mother, her fellow sisters, and the EWTN community have not been their own, but that of the Spirit of God working through them. He is the secret of their success. Not by human might nor by human power, "but by my Spirit, says the Lord Almighty."[192]

A Special Blessing Meant for All. The experience of being baptized in the Holy Spirit is not meant merely for the Apostles and great saints of the Church, or for priests and religious only. It is meant for every believer in Christ, a normal part of the Christian experience. It is a form of spiritual refreshment that aids us in our faith journeys, our pursuits of holiness, and our service in God's kingdom.

Most Christians who have been baptized in the Holy Spirit are well aware of it; the event is quite memorable. Still, it is entirely possible to have this experience without being consciously aware of it – because it happened gently, or because the nature of the Spirit's grace awakened seems less dramatic. A person's particular charisms may blossom almost unnoticed, as they humbly serve in roles such as caring for the sick, working with the poor, praying for others, or teaching children. Though the charisms associated with these and other roles may seem less dramatic (compared to prophecy, tongues, or healing), they are no less supernatural and no less important.

As individuals and communities, we can live a full Christian life only if the Holy Spirit's sanctifying graces (power for holiness) and charismatic graces (power for service) flow freely within us. These graces are our spiritual legs, the means by which we walk the journey of faith. We are weak, or even crippled, in our journey if either of these is weak or crippled within us. In our Church work, absent the Holy Spirit's graces, we will go about tasks as we see fit, using only our natural talents and learned skills, and we will miss an awakening of grace that might make all the difference.

---

[190] Cf. Arroyo, Raymond, *Mother Angelica*, Doubleday, 2005, pages 119-123.
[191] Arroyo, Raymond, *Mother Angelica*, Doubleday, 2005, page 254.
[192] Zechariah 4:6 (NIV).

Generally speaking, when helping Christians find a place to serve in parish life, spiritual directors and staff in our local parishes consider a person's natural strengths, their personal interests, and what are the perceived needs of the community. If this analysis ignores the Spirit's supernatural gifts, then it will be less likely to yield an answer consistent with God's perfect will. How much better it is for people to be baptized in the Holy Spirit and experience an awakening of God's supernatural graces, and, based in part on that awakening, to discern their involvement in Church life. Throughout the universal Church, in the denominations, local parish communities, and in countless parish programs, the Church suffers under the very heavy weight of individuals working in their own vision and strength, and not God's.

Thriving Church communities are those that are open to the fullness of Pentecost, where the Holy Spirit's sanctifying and charismatic graces are nurtured and lived vibrantly by all in the community. Even if some in the community have been baptized in the Holy Spirit and are experiencing an awakening of charisms, there is a fullness they are missing if others have not had the expereince. There is a sharing of graces that is not happening and should be. How much better it is when a whole community is baptized in the Holy Spirit. We can look to the first Christian community, to Mary, the Apostles, and other disciples and the amazing effect this community-wide sharing in the gift of the Holy Spirit had on them.

Since the Second Vatican Council, the experience of being baptized in the Holy Spirit has generally manifested among Catholics through three channels: (1) the Catholic Charismatic Renewal, (2) Life in the Spirit seminars, and (3) foreign missions.

Catholic Charismatic Renewal. The Catholic Charismatic Renewal (CCR) is a collection of thousands of prayer groups, covenant communities, schools of evangelization, and healing ministries throughout the world. CCR prayer groups focus on praise of God, prayer that includes praying in tongues and prophecy, and teachings on the Holy Spirit and the Spirit's charismatic grace. The CCR is part of a larger movement of God's grace that began among Pentecostals in 1900, main-line Protestants in 1960, and Catholics in 1967.

The CCR enjoys the support of the Catholic Church's modern-day leadership, including Popes Paul VI, John Paul II, Benedict XVI, and Francis. Each of these popes has frequently met with leaders of the CCR and with large gatherings of CCR members. Fr. Raniero

Cantalamessa, preacher to the papal household for Popes John Paul II, Benedict XVI, and Francis, has been an important spokesperson for the CCR and a Vatican liaison to Pentecostal churches.

In a Pentecost homily in 2004, Pope John Paul II affirmed the work of the CCR saying, "Thanks to the Charismatic Movement [that has developed since the Second Vatican Council], a multitude of Christians, men and women, young people and adults have rediscovered Pentecost as a living reality in their daily lives. I hope that the spirituality of Pentecost will spread in the Church as a renewed incentive to prayer, holiness, communion and proclamation."[193] On other occasions, he said of the CCR, it "is a sign of the Spirit's action . . . [and] a very important component in the total renewal of the Church."[194] The CCR "is an eloquent manifestation of [the Church's youthful] vitality today, a bold statement of what 'the Spirit is saying to the churches'" in our day.[195]

Pope Benedict XVI commented on the more intense flow of grace that is celebrated in the CCR, "Christ's entire mission is summed up in this: to baptize us in the Holy Spirit, to free us from the slavery of death and to open heaven to us."[196] Moreover, he taught that "one of the positive elements . . . of the Catholic Charismatic Renewal is precisely their emphasis on the charisms or gifts of the Holy Spirit."[197]

As a young priest in the 1970s, Pope Francis was initially skeptical of the CCR, which was new to the Catholic Church at that time. However, he later became very supportive of it. As cardinal, he even participated in joint Catholic-Protestant-Pentecostal charismatic prayer services. At one such service, attended by some 7,000 people, he asked the attendees to pray for him. Surrounded by Catholic and Protestant clergy, he knelt down to be prayed over, that the Holy Spirit would bring new blessing upon his ministry.[198] In July of 2013, while on a flight from Brazil to Rome after World Youth Day, Pope Francis

---

[193] Pope John Paul II, homily, May 29, 2004, section 3.

[194] Pope John Paul II, 1979 meeting with CCR representatives, as quoted by the National Conference of Catholic Bishops, *Grace for the New Springtime*, 1997.

[195] Pope John Paul II, Address to an International Assembly of the Charismatic Renewal, May 15, 1987.

[196] Pope Benedict XVI, AN, Jan. 13, 2008.

[197] Pope Benedict XVI, Address to an International Assembly of Charismatic Covenant Communities, October 31, 2008.

[198] Cardinal Jorge Bergoglio and Rabbi Abraham Skorka, *On Heaven and Earth*, Image, 2013 (English translation), pages 219-220.

reaffirmed his support of the CCR: "I think [the CCR] does much good for the Church . . . [As a bishop,] I met frequently with them . . . I have always supported them, after I was *converted*, after I saw the good they were doing. . . . [The CCR] is a service to the Church herself! It renews us. Everyone seeks his own [involvement in Church life], according to his own charism, where the Holy Spirit draws him or her."[199]

The National Conference of Catholic Bishops (predecessor to the U.S. Conference of Catholic Bishops) expressed their support of the CCR in their statement *Grace for the New Springtime*. The bishops spoke of the "baptism in the Holy Spirit" as a special grace of the CCR. "We believe that the renewed outpouring of the Spirit of Pentecost in our times is particularly present in the Catholic Charismatic Renewal and in the grace of baptism in the Holy Spirit. ... As experienced in the Catholic Charismatic Renewal baptism in the Holy Spirit makes Jesus Christ known and loved as Lord and Savior, establishes or reestablishes an immediacy of relationship with all those persons of the Trinity, and through inner transformation affects the whole of the Christian's life. There is new life and a new conscious awareness of God's power and presence. . . . We encourage the whole Church to look into and embrace baptism in the Holy Spirit"[200]

Despite such support, many Catholics are apprehensive about the CCR. They resist teachings on the Holy Spirit, manifestations of the Spirit's charismatic graces, and more expressive forms of worship that are celebrated within the CCR. While all forms of legitimate worship may not be meant for everyone, we should emphasize here that the baptism in the Holy Spirit is meant for everyone. Moreover, all Christians should be open to the fullness of the Spirit's sanctifying and charismatic graces, *as the Spirit wills* for each of us.

Life in the Spirit Seminars. The Life in the Spirit seminars are tools by which the Catholic Church's teachings on the Holy Spirit, charisms, and a Spirit-filled life are taught. These seminars, which are usually offered in a parish setting, help participants renew their commitment to Christ, achieve a deeper prayer life, experience the baptism in the Holy Spirit, and become more actively engaged in parish life. Life in the Spirit seminars are designed to be the first step in a completely new way of life. These seminars are commonly led by prayer groups active in the CCR.

---

[199] Pope Francis, press conference, July 28, 2013.
[200] National Conference of Catholic Bishops, *Grace for the New Springtime,* 1997.

Catholic Missions. The reach of Catholic missions throughout the world is enormous. It includes over 300,000 full-time lay missionaries, priests, deacons, and religious in nearly every country in the world (and millions of part-time volunteers, including parish mission trips). They bring the good news of Jesus to every land along with education, medical assistance, food, child-care assistance, and works for justice. They run schools, hospitals, orphanages, and food distribution programs. No doubt, most of these workers are laboring with the strength of the Holy Spirit helping them, but some of these are also laborring with the full strength of the Spirit's charismatic grace.

Many Catholic missions, particularly in South America and Africa, include teams that are part of the CCR and who have been baptized in the Holy Spirit. They proclaim the power of the Holy Spirit as part of the basic gospel message. Their teams include ministers of healing and exorcism, who bring the Spirit's loving touch and miracles to persons who are suffering. Many of these teams also pray for believers in these regions to be baptized in the Holy Spirit.

We Need the Holy Spirit! Mary and the Apostles were the first charismatic Christians. They needed the vibrant action of the Holy Spirit in their lives to be holy and to carry out the tasks assigned to them. We need the Holy Spirit at work in us for the same reasons. The good news is, the same Holy Spirit is available to us today. We too can experience Pentecost and be clothed with power from on high. In the next chapter we will discuss how best to dispose ourselves to receive this deeper movement of the Holy Spirit in our lives.

Jesus, By your suffering and death on the Cross, you opened the door for my salvation. Thank you. I recognize that faith in you is everything. I want to be fully committed to you. Please help me. Please increase my faith. Please reign in my heart as Lord and Savior.

Jesus, You are the baptizer in the Holy Spirit. I beg you, please baptize me with the Holy Spirit and with fire. May the Holy Spirit fill me with heavenly light, heavenly love, and heavenly power as he filled the Apostles at Pentecost. May he enliven the graces of my Baptism and Confirmation. May those graces bloom forth with new and vibrant colors, a glorious aroma, and much pleasing fruit. May Pentecost be a living reality in my life. And may a new Pentecost fill the Church throughout the world. In your holy name I pray. Amen.

Living in the Spirit

You, however, live not by your natural inclinations, but by the Spirit, since the Spirit of God has made a home in you. Indeed, anyone who does not have the Spirit of Christ does not belong to him.

Romans 8:9 (NJB)

8   Be Filled with the Spirit

In his epistle to the Ephesians, Paul exhorts believers, "[B]e filled with the Spirit."[201] He does so realizing that this is the essence of being Christian, to be filled with the very life of God, who makes us holy and prepares us for every good work. Being filled with the Holy Spirit can be thought of in two ways: as a distinct, momentary experience or as a way of life.

Filled with the Spirit As a Momentary Experience. In our Christian journey, we are frequently touched by God's grace as we receive a variety of blessings. However, there can be times when we are literally drenched in the living waters of God's own Spirit. The New Testament mentions this phenomenon on several occasions with slightly different forms of speech. It mentions people being filled with the Spirit, or with grace, or being overshadowed by the Spirit, or having the Spirit come upon them. These expressions describe personal encounters with the Holy Spirit that are tangible, refreshing, and real.

To be baptized in the Holy Spirit as we discussed in the previous chapter is but one "filled with the Spirit" moment in a person's life. It is that experience that first gives rise to a vibrant movement of the Spirit's charismatic grace within us. However, we can be filled with the Spirit on many occasions.

At Pentecost, the Bible tells us that Jesus' disciples were "filled with the Holy Spirit and began to speak in other tongues as the Spirit enabled them."[202] We hear of this again, sometime later, after Jewish authorities reprimanded Peter and John for preaching about Jesus. Immediately afterward, they and the other Apostles gathered for prayer. After they finished praying, the place where they were gathered shook, and "they were filled with the Holy Spirit and spoke the word of God with boldness."[203]

Later, we hear of Christians from Ephesus having this experience. They had received the baptism of John, heard of Jesus and became believers, but they had never heard of the Holy Spirit. Paul taught them about the Holy Spirit, and he baptized them. Then, "When Paul had laid his hands on them, the Holy Spirit came upon them, and they

---

[201] Ephesians 5:18 (NAB).
[202] Acts 2:4 (NIV).
[203] Acts 4:31 (NRSV).

spoke in tongues and prophesied."[204] We also hear of Gentiles in Caesarea having this experience. Until that time, the Holy Spirit's known works in the early Church were in the lives of the Apostles and other Jewish converts to Christianity. Thus, Peter and his companions were astonished to see the Holy Spirit coming upon Cornelius, a non-Jew, and his whole household.[205] While Peter was sharing the Good News of Jesus, "the Holy Spirit came on all who heard the message . . . [and they began] speaking in tongues and praising God."[206]

These scenes were not isolated events but circumstances common to the Apostolic era. They have occurred throughout the centuries. They occur today. The experience of being filled with the Holy Spirit varies by person and situation. What people feel in the moment can include one or more of the following:

- profound awareness of God's presence
- increased faith in Jesus, a heart full of praise to Jesus
- deep sense of peace, warm glow of God's love, irresistible joy
- a sense of freedom; burdens, sins, or addictions lifted away
- revelation about God or about one's own life
- healing from an illness, infirmity, or wounded heart
- tears of joy, tears of sorrow, or tears of an awakening in faith
- a sensation of a divine fire filling the heart, mind, or body
- a physical fainting or relaxing of the body
- a manifestation of spiritual gifts (such as tongues or prophecy)
- a call to service

When filled with the Spirit, some people feel nothing, which does not mean nothing is happening, just that the depth of the experience is not revealed in that moment. The experience of being filled with the Spirit commonly lasts for a few minutes. Generally speaking, this experience will last longer and be more meaningful if we cooperate with faith, accompanying it with praise, thanksgiving, or quiet adoration. This experience can happen many times in our respective lives. It can even become a regular part of our prayer life. It can

---

[204] Acts 19:5-6 (NRSV). Essentially, they received the Sacraments of Baptism and Confirmation together, which is common in the Orthodox tradition.
[205] Cf. Acts 10:44-46.
[206] Acts 10:44, 46 (NIV).

happen at church, at home, in bed, in nature, or on a retreat. It can happen in a group setting or when we are alone. How often the Spirit fills us depends, in part, on our efforts to pursue an ever deeper relationship with Jesus.

For those of us who allow the Holy Spirit to intervene in our lives, Pope John Paul II promised, the Spirit "leaves [us] astonished. He brings about events of amazing newness, He radically changes persons and history."[207] This promise is for everyone, even the worst of sinners. It is an invitation into the fullness of the Christian experience.

While some "filled with the Spirit" experiences will seem more intense to our physical and psychological senses and other ones less so, we must never discount any Holy Spirit experience because what we feel is but a portion of what is actually happening. Whatever the experience, felt or not, it is all a gift from God. Often these moments are like a gentle rain of grace that slowly strengthens the virtues in our lives. This can happen daily, perhaps with little or no fanfare, as we rest prayerfully with the Lord. In God's wisdom, as we progress in faith, the Spirit may provide fewer consolations when he fills us. Regardless, every time he touches our lives, he changes us.

The extended effects of being filled with the Holy Spirit concern the ongoing strengthening of our relationship with Jesus, with an increased desire for prayer, holiness, and the sacraments, and with a new hunger to study Sacred Scripture, serve others, and participate in Christian community. Moreover, gifts of the Spirit become a meaningful part of our lives. If we cooperate with the Spirit's work, these experiences bring increased awareness and power to live an authentic Christian life. We will experience a keener awareness of sin, particularly in our own lives, an awareness that helps us in our spiritual battles. We also become aware of evil at work in various situations. Thankfully, we also become more aware of how we can access God's grace in our battles against evil.

If we cooperate, invariably the experience of the Spirit filling us brings profound changes to our lives. We become different people, more loving, joyful, gentle, and patient, not only at Church, but at home, at work, with friends, and with strangers. We have new interests, attitudes, perspectives, and a new nature.

---

[207] Pope John Paul II, address to ecclesial movements, May 30, 1998 section 4.

Author's Personal Testimony on Being Filled with the Holy Spirit

In my own life, I have had many experiences of being filled with the Holy Spirit. The first that I can recall was at age 36. It came as others prayed over me at a Life in the Spirit seminar held at my local parish. The year prior to the seminar, I began to seriously re-engage my Catholic faith after many years of going through the motions.

The seminar was one evening a week, for seven weeks. During the seminar, the speakers taught about the workings of the Holy Spirit in our lives, they explained the Spirit's sanctifying and charismatic graces, and they shared many engaging personal testimonies. During that seminar, my prayer life was strengthened, I came to appreciate for the first time the value of praising God, I returned to the Sacrament of Reconciliation, and I re-dedicated my life to Jesus.

During the seminar, a team of people prayed over me and I was baptized in the Holy Spirit. In the moment, I felt a warmth and a peace fill my body, nothing terribly dramatic, but it was real and pleasing. Then, over the next several weeks, I experienced a new interest in Bible study. The Word of God held fresh meaning to me and I began to see practical applications of what I read for my own life. I also awakened to the wonderful gift of Holy Eucharist. No longer was the real presence of Christ in the Eucharist a mere teaching, it was a reality that I could encounter. I could encounter this reality not only at Mass, but also in Eucharistic Adoration.

Not long after the seminar, I was at a singles meeting at our parish and a priest asked for more adults to volunteer as leaders in the parish's youth ministry program. When he began to pray for God to anoint persons for this task, I felt the Spirit of God come upon me like a lightning bolt, energy filled my body, tears poured out of my eyes, and I had a strong awareness of God's presence. I knew that God was calling me to serve, which I did.

Over time, I believe the Spirit has brought forth in me charisms of teaching, intercessory prayer, wisdom, and prophecy. He has also helped me to be more loving and less judgmental. I have thankfully been part of prayer groups where others with a variety of different charisms have blessed my life. Together we have mutually encouraged each other to walk and grow stronger in the gifts we have received. I have also experienced the Spirit's calling as it relates to the formation of a men's ministry at our parish and the writing of this book.

Over the years since being baptized in the Holy Spirit, I have had many special moments of prayer, at which time I felt the presence of the Holy Spirit stir within me and flow out from me with power. I have come to realize my need of being regularly refreshed by the Spirit's grace, through prayer, the sacraments, and active ministry. Also, I have learned that as we mature in the Lord, his consolations change. While there might be wonderful excitement and joy when we first come to know him and later when we are baptized in his Spirit, as we mature, the consolations change. Joy is still there, but that joy is manifest not so much in the excitement of new experiences. Instead, it manifests more frequently through a greater knowledge of God and in the privilege of serving others.

How Can We Be Filled with the Holy Spirit? Jesus taught that the Father "does not ration his gift of the Spirit."[208] The Father gives the Spirit in abundance. At issue is whether we are open to receive his gift and to receive it in abundance? Or are we closed to this gift, receiving it in limited supply or not at all?

St. Thomas Aquinas referred to a person's openness or lack of openness, as "the mode of the receiver."[209] We are open only as much as we truly desire and pursue a deeper relationship with Jesus. There are, of course, degrees of openness and, thus, degrees of "being filled." For example, we may experience an infilling of the Spirit when we repent of certain sins, yet we may still have areas of our lives plagued with other sins. That infilling, then, is only partial. As we repent of other sins and surrender other areas of our lives to God, we expand our capacity to receive the Spirit's grace.[210] The more we are emptied of sin and worldliness, the more we are opened to receive the gift of the Holy Spirit and his many graces.

The Holy Spirit comes into our lives as he pleases. Yet, there are ways we can open ourselves to his action. St. John of Avila, rightly encourages us: "[T]he coming of the Holy Spirit will have exactly the same effect on your soul today, as it had in the time of the apostles: take care that you receive Him well."[211] How do we receive him well?

---

[208] John 3:34 (NAB).
[209] Cf. St. Thomas Aquinas, *Summa Theologica*, Part I, question 84, article 1.
[210] Cf. St. Cyril, *Catechetical Lecture,* 17:37.
[211] St John of Avila, *The Holy Spirit Within,* Scepter Publishers, 2012, page 1.

In addition to the disciplines of a holy life discussed in a previous chapter, we may also do the following:

- (re)dedicate our lives to Jesus
- repent of our sins based on a deeper awareness of our sins
- meditate on the passion of Jesus, thank him for his sacrifice
- pray prayers of praise, thanksgiving, and contemplation
- form a special devotion to the Holy Spirit, pray to him
- allow others to pray for us with the laying on of hands
- faithfully serve God within a Church community
- endure painful trials with a resilient faith
- ask to be baptized in the Holy Spirit.

The gift of the Holy Spirit comes to us from Jesus and the Father, often through a human intermediary. This may be an evangelist proclaiming the Word of God, or a bishop administering the Sacrament of Confirmation, or fellow Christians praying for us in a prayer group setting. Or, as at the first Christian Pentecost, the Holy Spirit may come upon us with no human intermediary.

Some, like Mother Angelica, are prayed over for this experience, and the grace begins to flow in a more noticeable manner sometime later. In her case, days later, while reading. A person may be prayed over in one moment, and then experience the manifestation of new spiritual gifts days later while in Eucharistic Adoration, while in bed when they are suddenly awakened from their sleep, or while in the shower. I know of two men who had this experience while driving their car. When they pulled over and parked their cars, for the first time in each of their lives, they began speaking in tongues.

We should all consider these important questions: Do I desire intimacy with Jesus? Do I desire holiness? Do I desire freedom from the sins that plague my life? If offered the choice between a million dollars in cash or being filled with the Holy Spirit, do I desire the Spirit of God more? If so, we should express that desire to the Holy Spirit, to Jesus, and to the Father in prayer. We should prepare our hearts to "receive the Spirit well" by discarding sin and worldly cares and filling our hearts with goodness. We should preoccupy our thoughts with things that are true, holy, honorable, and just.[212] This may mean that

---

[212] Cf. Philippians 4:8.

we reject various activities and forms of entertainment (certain TV shows, movies, books, internet websites, hobbies, games) that we previously enjoyed. We sacrifice these pleasures of the flesh because of our growing love of God.

Prayer is Key. It is no coincidence that the Holy Spirit descended upon Jesus at the Jordan River as Jesus prayed, and he descended upon the Apostles at Pentecost after several days of prayer.[213] So also with us, prayer is key, particularly prayers of praise and thanksgiving to God. Such prayers open us up to the flow of God's grace.

Openness to God's Word is Key. Many experience being touched by or even filled with the Spirit while listening to a bold proclamation of God's Word – at church, on a retreat, at a parish mission, or at a religious crusade. This was the experience of Cornelius and his household when "the Holy Spirit fell upon all who were listening to the word"[214] that Peter preached.

Asking is Key / Desire is Key. If we have not been filled with the Holy Spirit, we should ask God for this experience. We should ask with a sincere motive and not for casual or curious reasons, or self-indulgent, or vain reasons. We should ask with a true desire to know God more deeply and to serve him more diligently.

In the Gospel of Luke, Jesus conveys this message saying, "Ask, and it will be given to you; search, and you will find; knock, and the door will be opened to you. . . . If you then, evil as you are, know how to give your children what is good, how much more will the heavenly Father give the Holy Spirit to those who ask him!"[215]

Avoiding Obstacles. The following are common obstacles to being filled with the Holy Spirit.

- lack of commitment to Jesus
- lack of knowledge of the Spirit
- lack of prayer
- feelings of inadequacy
- unrepented sin
- worldliness / materialism
- fears / insecurities
- skepticism about charisms

Identifying and clearing away these obstacles is important not only as it relates to being filled with the Spirit, but also as it relates to

---

[213] Cf. Luke 3:21-22 (Jesus at the Jordan); Luke 24:53, Acts 1:14 (Pentecost).
[214] Acts 10:44 (NAB).
[215] Luke 11:9, 13.

other matters of faith and holiness. Perhaps feelings of inadequacy are one of the most common obstacles to being filled with the Holy Spirit. We may think we are not good enough for God to bless us. We may think he does not love us. But who is good enough for God's blessing? No one. That is why it comes as a gift.

Lack of knowledge concerning the Holy Spirit, the filled with the Spirit experience, and the charismatic dimension of our Christian lives is also an obstacle. If we don't know of this experience or its purposes in our lives or if we have fears or apprehensions about it, then we will not seek it out. We will not welcome it. We will be satisfied with what we know of Christianity, missing out on a wonderful gift.

After being filled with the Spirit, other obstacles can impede the blossoming forth of God's graces. We might begin to feel embarrassed by it all. Some people might reject our experience, put it down, ignore us, or ridicule us. Or we might shrink back due to fears that God will push us more and more out of our comfort zones.

Filled with the Spirit as the Christian Way of Life. When Paul, in his letter to the Ephesians, instructs us to "be filled with the Spirit," he is not suggesting that we "get filled" but instead that we "remain filled." He is encouraging us to live life always open to the Holy Spirit, allowing his grace to flow continuously within us and through us. He said, "[B]e filled with the Spirit. Sing psalms and hymns and inspired songs among yourselves, singing and chanting to the Lord in your hearts, always and everywhere giving thanks to God."[216] Paul's teaching here was not a suggestion but an imperative for Christian living, so that holiness and wonderful works of service may abound. Paul exhorts us to live life constantly in the presence of God.

Spiritually speaking, only as we are filled up with the Spirit of Jesus are we healthy. Truly, it is a prerequiste for the abundant Christian life. The Father's gift of the Spirit is the pearl of great price of which Jesus spoke.[217] It is the kingdom of God flourishing within us and among us. "For the kingdom of God is . . . righteousness, peace, and joy in the Holy Spirit."[218]

In the abundant Christian life, we need to be replinished daily with the Spirit's grace. A preacher once emphasized the need of going

---

[216] Ephesians 5:18-20 (NJB).
[217] Cf. Matthew 13:45-46.
[218] Romans 14:17 (NIV).

to God daily to be "filled-up" with the Holy Spirit. We need to do so, he said, even if we were filled-up the day before, because we leak. Our sins are like holes in the wineskins of our hearts, and until our hearts are completely healed, we leak.

Communities Filled with the Spirit. We might also ask, how can Christian communities today – be they parish communities, religious communities, ministry teams, prayer groups, a deanary of priests, a synod of bishops, or a family – be filled with the Spirit? Together, how can we enjoy an abundance of grace, unity, and power as did the Apostles? The simplest answer is: imitate the Apostolic community.

When Jesus engaged in his public ministry, many tens of thousands of people heard his preaching and saw his miracles, but it was a much smaller number of persons that made the commitment to follow him closely. For the three years prior to Jesus' death and resurrection, they journeyed about together. They formed new relationships with one another, relationships that were centered on their common relationship with Jesus. Together, they listened to Jesus' teachings. Together, they ate meals, enjoyed fellowship, and shared one another's burdens. Together, they went out and served others. Together, they prayed. They were not half-hearted in their commitment to the Lord or their community. Their commitment to Jesus was their chief priority in life. And God blessed them. If we, individually and collectively, also make Jesus our chief priority, why should the Father's blessing on us be any less?

Holy Spirit, Spirit of Life and of Love, you are awe-inspiring. You are wonderful. You are holy. Thank you for all your many forms of grace. Thank you for your presence in my life, even as I have ignored you. Please continue your good work in me. Please flow within me with ever greater intensity. I beg you, please wash away my sins and my desire for sin. Please fill me with holy desires. Please help me to form the disciplines of a holy life. Please give me a heart oriented for worship of God the Father, Jesus, and yourself. I pray not only for myself, but also for my family, friends, and Church community – awaken us sweet Spirit. Revive us with your love. Bring forth a new Pentecost in our lives and in our communities. In the name of Jesus I pray, Amen.

9   Be Led by the Spirit

St. Paul taught, "Since we are living in the Spirit, let our behavior be guided by the Spirit."[219] Other translations suggest we are to "walk by the Spirit" or "be led by the Spirit." What is Paul suggesting? What is a Spirit-led life all about? In short, it is a life permeated by the Spirit's love and wisdom whereby the Spirit guides the overall trajectory of our lives and its moment-to-moment details. It is the Holy Spirit working within us "to will and to act according to his good purpose."[220] Toward that end, Pope Benedict XVI stated, "[I]t is important that each one of us know the Spirit, establish a relationship with Him, and allow ourselves to be guided by Him."[221]

Our Lives are not Our Own. The prophet Jeremiah tells us that "a man's life is not his own; it is not for man to direct his [own] steps."[222] Similarly, St. Paul tells us, "[W]e are God's workmanship, created in Christ Jesus to do good works, which God prepared in advance for us to do."[223] These thoughts run counter to much of what many of us in our modern society might think. Truly, though, our lives are not our own. We are God's creatures. Our lives belong to him. He is to direct our steps, for his good purposes. When we do not cooperate, whether due to defiance or ignorance, we are in rebellion against God.

God's General Will. The Spirit-led life begins with God's general will for everyone. It is God's general will for all people to believe in Jesus, inherit salvation, live holy lives, and be people of prayer.[224] Obedience to God's general will leads to increasing intimacy with Jesus and the Father. As Jesus said, "[W]hoever does the will of my Father in heaven is my brother and sister and mother."[225] Such obedience also leads us to our eternal reward in heaven: "Not everyone who says to me, 'Lord, Lord,' will enter the kingdom of heaven, but only the one who does the will of my Father in heaven."[226]

---

[219] Galatians 5:25 (NJB). Cf. Jeremiah 10:23.
[220] Philippians 2:13 (NIV).
[221] Pope Benedict XVI, Letter in Anticipation of World Youth Day 2008, July 20, 2007, section 5.
[222] Jeremiah 10:23 (NIV).
[223] Ephesians 2:10 (NIV).
[224] Cf. John 6:40, 1 Timothy 2:4, 1 Thessalonians 4:3, 5:16-18.
[225] Matthew 12:50 (NIV).
[226] Matthew 7:21 (NRSV).

The Ten Commandments, Jesus' Sermon on the Mount, and the great commands of love are expressions of God's general will for us. Study of the Bible and Church teachings help us understand and live God's general will. Such studies ground our hearts and minds in God's eternal truth. In our studies, the Spirit is our unseen Helper, assisting us not only in learning but also living God's general will.

God's Perfect Will. Beyond God's general will for all people, God also has a perfect will for each person's life, a definite purpose and plan. God's perfect will concerns our overall vocation, whether to marriage, chaste singlehood, the priesthood, or religious life. It also includes areas of service in our faith communities. Whatever may be the conditions or circumstances of our lives, God has a perfect will for each of us. Paul makes this point: "[E]veryone should live as the Lord has assigned, just as God called each one."[227] God's perfect will for each of us concerns not merely the broad direction of our lives. It also includes many of life's little details that arise each day.

God's Permissive Will. Most of life is not lived in God's perfect will, but rather in his permissive will. God gave us freedom to live our lives as we choose. His permissive will covers all aspects of human life from good to evil. For God's saints, often our choices are not merely between good and evil, but between God's perfect will and several lesser, but still good, alternatives. God often blesses us even as we are outside his perfect will, when we have chosen a good, just not the specific good he is calling us to in a given situation. God enjoys blessing us, but how much more when we strive to live his perfect will.

Listening to the Holy Spirit. Jesus said of his followers, "my sheep . . . listen to my voice."[228] Jesus speaks to us through the Holy Spirit. The Spirit speaks to us through the Bible, through the Church, through prayer, and through others (a priest, a spiritual director, a friend, or a stranger). He may speak to us through nature or through an inspiration in the moment. True followers make it a habit to listen for the Holy Spirit and obey. Often, the Spirit speaks with a still, soft voice in our hearts and with gentle nudges. Or he may speak to us through a well-formed conscience, bringing to our thoughts a scripture verse, or a virtue, or knowledge needed in a specific moment.

---

[227] 1 Corinthians 7:17 (NAB).
[228] John 10:14, 16 (NIV).

Other times the Holy Spirit may impress his will with great force and clarity, as impressive as a lightning bolt. The "lightning bolt" may be something we feel physically. It may also be a great sense of conviction in our hearts or clarity in our minds. We may hear a voice or see a vision or experience something that is unmistakably miraculous and we understand its meaning to our situation. To some, the Holy Spirit speaks with very specific instructions that a believer clearly hears in their mind or heart, by way of a prophetic gift.

In later chapters, we will discuss more in depth the charismatic dimension of the Christian faith. Here, it is important to note that one of the ways the Spirit speaks is through the charisms he gives us. He gives us charisms to use for his kingdom. Each charism is a message of sorts: *Here is one of the ways I want you to serve.*

However the Holy Spirit speaks to us, we must learn to listen. We must be docile in the presence of God, letting him form our consciences and guide us in the moment. As the Holy Spirit inspires us, we do not forgo our own capacity to think, feel, or make choices. We can obey him or ignore him.

Sometimes the Holy Spirit opens or closes doors in our lives to slowly draw us forward – perhaps to our vocation, to a new season of our lives, to a situation he wants us to experience, or to a place he wants us to serve. Other times he may curb our spirits in a given moment, helping us to avoid doing some action. For example, he may prompt us to keep our mouths shut, when we might otherwise want to speak. Or, he might prompt us to refrain from some activity that others are doing or that we are accustomed to doing.

Sometimes the Holy Spirit leads us and we are fully aware of his guidance, his inspirations, his revelations. Other times we are not. Sometimes he leads us quietly through our thoughts, helping us to observe situations from a particular perspective, and placing before our thoughts his will, and we do not realize he is speaking, but he is. Almost instinctively, we know what is the right thing to do, as the Holy Spirit speaks to us through the reasoning of our mind.

Sometimes it may seem that the Holy Spirit has gone silent, that he is not communicating with us, that he is not there. And yet he is there. We may be going through a very difficult trial or having to make an important decision and he seems to be ignoring us. Despite what we may be feeling in our emotions, we should strive to trust that Holy Spirit is indeed present and will guide us. We must be patient.

Depending on the circumstances, we may need to make a decision, and then take a first or second step in regards to the decision. We should do so trusting the Lord to be with us and if we make the wrong decision, we must be open to his inspirations to redirect us onto the right path.

As the Holy Spirit reveals his instructions, we must not prejudge such matters or the cost. And yes, there is a cost to following the Spirit of God. We will need to let go of three things: our love of the sins and distractions that find a home in us, our love of control, and our love of worldly gratification. For all of us, this letting go comes in increments over time. It is not easy. Thankfully, the Spirit is there to help us.

In the moment, most of us are aware of the many urges that arise each day from our mind, our emotions, our memories, our body, from others, or from circumstances. However, we can be totally clueless as to inspirations that come from the Holy Spirit. This is because we have the habit of living life from our wounded soul.[229]

By our own way of thinking, the Holy Spirit's inspirations may often seem quite difficult, or even impossible. On our own, many of his commands may indeed be impossible. But by grace, each of his inspirations is possible. Often his will for us is fulfilled, in part, by his grace at work in others, of which we may be totally unaware. Our challenge is to have faith, follow his lead, and do our part. The more we are persons of prayer, the more we study God's Word, the more we experience God's healing graces, the more we will be able to live from our spirit, attentive to the Holy Spirit dwelling within us.

A tough lesson we must learn in our spiritual growth is this: *In the kingdom of God, there is no such thing as a self-made man or a self-made woman.* Rugged independence, personal ambition, and libertine thinking may be prized traits among the children of the world, but not for the children of God. In God's kingdom, we are called to be Spirit-made and Spirit-led persons. As the psalmist proclaims, "[H]e made us, we belong to him."[230] If we belong to him, we need to follow him.

Importance of Grace. The Spirit-led life is all about grace. In a discussion of the "primacy of grace" Pope John Paul II taught, "There is a temptation which perennially besets every spiritual journey and pastoral work: that of thinking that the results depend on our ability to

---

[229] Cf. Bennett, Dennis, *How to Pray for the Release of the Holy Spirit*, Bridge-Logos, 1985, page 7.
[230] Psalm 100:3 (NJB).

act and to plan. . . . [I]t is fatal to forget that 'without Christ we can do nothing.' . . . When [the primacy of grace] is not respected, is it any wonder that [our works of service so often] come to nothing and leave us with a disheartening sense of frustration?"[231]

In our spiritual struggles, St. Ignatius encourages us, "Pray as if everything depends on you, act as if everything depends on God."[232] *Pray as if everything depends on you*, realizing that absent the Spirit's grace, tasks assigned to you will not fulfill the Father's plan no matter how good the result may seem to our human eyes. *Act as if everything depends on God*, realizing that we can walk in confidence, without fear, when things are truly in his hands. Yes we have to work hard, and do our part, and go the extra mile if need be. We are his servants. Yet the results of our efforts belong to him.

Spiritual Maturity. Spiritual maturity is never about growing so wise as to be independent and on our own. Instead, it is about becoming increasingly dependent on God. It is learning to rely not on our own human intelligence, strength, plans, or worldly resources, but on the Holy Spirit's grace.[233] We must learn to do everything with the Spirit's help, cultivating the various spiritual gifts he gives us and working in a mutually respectful fashion with those around us.

The life of the mature Christian is ordered by the indwelling of the Holy Spirit. The Spirit's action in our lives and our cooperation with the Spirit, consciously and unconsciously, is the substance of all spiritual progress. Apart from the Holy Spirit, there is no spiritual progress, there is no spiritual maturity, only decay.

For all that God calls us to do, he provides the grace to do it. However, in many circumstances, his will is not that we be successful as humans might define success. Instead, his will is that we be faithful. Success as we might hope it to be, may or may not come, for a variety of reasons. And, as a practical matter, we don't always know what

---

[231] Pope John Paul II, NMI, section 38. Interior quote is from John 15:5.

[232] Cf. Scanlan, Fr. Michael, *Appointment with God*, Apostolate of Family Consecration, 1987, page 12. This maxim of St. Ignatius is often quoted, incorrectly, as "Pray as if everything depends on God, act as if everything depends on you." Fr. Scanlan notes that this transposition error was originally made by early biographers of St. Ignatius as they translated his writings. The errant wording can lead us to sin. To act *as if everything depends on me* is a breeding ground for the sins of pride, self-sufficiency, and self-importance.

[233] Cf. Proverbs 3:5, Zechariah 4:6.

success actually looks like. For all who were there that day, the Cross seemed a great defeat for Jesus and his followers. Ironically, it was singularly the greatest victory of all human history. The lives of the Apostles were also filled with many worldly failures. But in the midst of their apparent failures, their faithfulness produced much fruit for God's kingdom. The blood of every holy martyr advances the kingdom of God. No matter the extent of any evil, God can bring forth good. Think of St. Maximilian Kolbe living a heroic and faith-filled life in a Nazi concentration camp during World War II. Surrounded by great evil, his heart was filled with joy and peace and strength. Through his faithfulness amid much suffering and death, God's grace brought forth much goodness and life.

As Christians, we must come to understand and accept our innate weakness and uselessness apart from the Holy Spirit and his grace. We must realize that hidden in our weakness is the mystery of Christian fulfillment. As St. Paul said of himself, "[W]hen I am weak, then I am strong."[234] Think of Mary. In her day, she was so very insignificant from the world's perspective. But she was far greater and more powerful than Caesar Augustus and all his armies and all his material wealth because she was filled with the grace of the Holy Spirit.

Toward the goal of spiritual maturity, it is right that we literally beg the Holy Spirit, daily, to continue his good work within us, guiding us in all matters. With him, we must make the spiritual condition of our souls a priority. We must make our relationship with Jesus a priority. We must make prayer, and the other disciplines of a holy life a priority – not in some rigid legalistic way, but with loving trust.

St. Faustina taught that the "shortest route" to spiritual maturity is "faithfulness to the inspirations of the Holy Spirit."[235] Such faithfulness demands that we be alert to the Spirit's inspirations that come to us each day. Toward that end, it behooves us, as Pope Benedict XVI taught, to "establish a relationship with Him."

The Holy Spirit Disturbs Us. Sometimes the Holy Spirit will lead us by disturbing us. He will disturb us to get our attention. Other times he may humiliate us to correct our bad behavior. His Sacred Word is one of the common ways he disturbs or humiliates us. We may be

---

[234] 2 Corinthians 12:10 (NAB).

[235] Sister Faustina, *Diary of Sister Maria Faustina Kowalska*, Marian Press, 2004, page 137.

studying the Bible one day or listening to a sermon, and a Word of truth strikes us, a truth we may be resisting. In that moment, we know that Word is meant for us that day. It makes us feel uncomfortable. It commands us to repent.

The Spirit of God may disturb us by letting us see the true ugliness of our own sins or of some injustice or sin in society. He may disturb us so that we might, in some way, help bring an end to some societal evil or at least no longer be complicit in it. This is the convicting power of the Spirit of Truth at work within us, leading us out of the darkness of sin into the light and the love of Christ.

History is filled with many inspiring stories of the Holy Spirit disturbing believers in the course of their Christian walk, helping them grow in holiness and become an agent of reform in society. It should be no surprise that in U.S. history, for example, many of the great social reformers were men and women of God. In many cases, no doubt, some of these persons were disturbed by the Holy Spirit and then led by the Spirit to various actions. The anti-slavery, women's suffrage, and the civil rights movements, and so many initiatives for the poor, elderly and sick in society all find their origins among the people of God. Think of Martin Luther King: he was indeed a great civil rights leader, but more importantly, he was a man of God who was sensitive to the Spirit of God. He spoke a prophetic word to a nation that resisted the ways of God regarding race relations; and that prophetic word had effect, it did not return void.

The Holy Spirit can also disturb non-believers and bring forth conversion and renewal in them and through them. Consider the story of Dr. Bernard Nathanson. In the 1970s, Nathanson ran the largest abortion clinic in the world. He was also a social activist who helped form NARAL (the National Abortion Rights Action League). With the development of ultrasound technology, Dr. Nathanson saw the grave errors of his ways. Through this technology, we might say, the Holy Spirit disturbed him, and helped him come to realize the true sanctity of unborn human babies and the evils of abortion. Having been enlightened, Nathanson ended his career as an abortion provider, and he became a pro-life leader and lecturer. He also produced an influential pro-life film, "The Silent Scream."

In 1996, Nathanson converted to Christianity through the Catholic Church. He was baptized by Cardinal John O'Connor of New York and his sins were washed away. Through repentance and baptism, he received God's forgiveness. Despite his many horrible sins, the Spirit brought forth conversion in him and used him as a force for social justice. His story is a story of hope for all peoples. No matter how complicit we are in the evils of our day, no matter how filthy our hearts, minds, and bodies may be due to sin, we can come to the truth, find freedom, renewed purity, and true purpose.

Thy Will Be Done. Saint Alphonsus Liguori describes the path we should follow as disciples of Jesus: "The accomplishment of the divine will should be the sole object of all our thoughts . . . To this end, we should direct all our devotions, our meditations . . . and all our prayers. We should constantly beg of God to teach and help us to do his will. . . . Let us always have in our mouths the petition from the Our Father – 'thy will be done.' Let us frequently repeat it in the day, with all the affection of our hearts."[236]

As we learn to follow the Holy Spirit, there is a reward. St Paul explains this reward: "[T]hose who are led by the Spirit of God are children of God."[237] Our reward is our identity in Christ through whom we are transformed into children of God.[238] *For we are children of God not by virtue of our existence, but instead by virtue our willingness to be enlivened and led by the Spirit of God.*

To be led by the Spirit, we must be people of prayer. We must truly begin and live our days in prayer. I am not sure, but I believe St. Francis de Sales is credited with saying, "Everyone should pray at least 30 minutes at the start of each day, and persons with busy lives and heavy responsibilities should pray at least 60 minutes." Without prayer filling our souls with purpose, direction, and power, we will go about our days on our own strength and in our own judgments. No matter how well intended we may be, we will miss the mark if our efforts are not led by the Holy Spirit through prayer. We must also learn that the purpose of our prayers is not to change God's mind to support our plans, but to allow God to change our minds to support his plans.

Divine Appointments. Being led by the Spirit means serving God in the many divine appointments that come our way. To those of us open to the Spirit's lead, he will give us opportunities to serve in

---

[236] *Sermons of St. Alphonsus Liguori*, TAN Books and Publishers, Inc., page 216. Inner quotes refer to Psalm 143:10, Matthew 6:10.
[237] Romans 8:14 (NAB).
[238] Cf. John 1:12.

precise moments with little or no advanced notice. The Spirit will put people in our paths or direct our steps to certain situations and when we are there, he wants us to serve. We must be attentive to these opportunities, no matter how insignificant they may seem.

Sometimes, we may wonder why certain changes come to our lives. For example, some change in circumstances might significantly free up our daily work schedule, then suddenly there is a need (perhaps an ailing family member needs help). We go to serve and while serving, an awareness comes over us (an epiphany, if you will) that we are precisely where God wants us. Then we realize he was arranging things well in advance of that moment because he wanted us to serve.

Faithful servants pray each morning: "*Use me Lord! May I be a blessing to others, today.*" Faithful servants do so surrendering their plans and desires to the Lord. They start each day as seems proper, but they are open to altering their plans as the Spirit directs.

Divine appointments are not just about us serving others. Sometimes the appointment is for us to receive God's blessings. God may bless us through the service of others or through a set of circumstances. Often what in life we call wonderful coincidences are in fact gifts of the Spirit – *God instances*. Our challenge is to receive and appreciate these moments as they come, giving thanks to Whom thanks are due.

Author's Personal Testimony of a Divine Appointment

An example of a divine appointment in my own life occurred one evening when I awoke from my sleep around 1:00 AM. I felt a strong inspiration to go to a friend's home – immediately. I got dressed and as I headed to the door, I sensed the Lord say, "Bring a rosary," which I did. When I arrived at my friend's condominium complex, I didn't know what to do. I could see the lights were out to her unit. I went around the building and sat on the back steps. Then I felt inspired to pray a Divine Mercy chaplet on the rosary beads – which I did with a fervent heart. Afterward, I went home.

The next day, I called my friend and learned that her ailing father, who had been staying with her family, died during the night – at approximately the same time I was praying on the back steps. She had gone to bed exhausted around midnight. She told me that she tried to pray a Divine Mercy chaplet with him, but did not have the strength. She placed on his chest a Divine Mercy image (a picture of Jesus with red and white rays coming from his heart) and she prayed "Jesus, I trust in you." As she described her experience, grace flooded my heart. I learned that the inspiration I had felt the night before was not a fluke. The Lord had used me to bless her father.

On many occasions, I have heard the Spirit call me to a task, usually small things, and hopefully in most of those cases I have responded accordingly. I dare say, the Spirit speaks to me more often than I know, and I have no doubt missed many more opportunities to serve because I failed to hear his call or I heard his call and said "no" – I was either lazy and failed to act, or I did not like the call and chose not to act. I think God wants to use all of us, daily, to bless others, and that he is speaking constantly, in different ways. But we rarely realize it because we have not learned to hear his voice.

Fruit of the Spirit. As we let the Holy Spirit reign in us, letting his grace fill and guide us, the fruit of the Spirit is able to blossom more freely in our lives. This blossoming includes the fruit listed by Paul in his letter to the Galatians: love, joy, peace, patience, kindness, goodness, faithfulness, gentleness, and self-control.[239] The more our lives are rooted in Christ, the more we are led by the Spirit, the more the fruit of the Spirit matures within us. This fruit is a sure mark of a maturing faith.

Working in the Present Toward the Future. We may speak of the Spirit-led life as living in the present, constantly open to the Spirit's moment-to-moment inspirations. However, such openness does not negate the setting of forward-looking goals and making plans for the future. Often, the Holy Spirit will place on our hearts matters that relate to the future, matters we are to work towards in obedience to the Spirit. In the Old Testament, the lives of Noah, Abraham, Joseph, Moses, Joshua, David, and Solomon involved Spirit-led projects that were fulfilled over long periods of time after much planning and effort. In New Testament times, we see this very much in Paul's life. He was given the long-term mission of evangelizing many nations. By no means was Paul passive or indifferent to his vocation. He was committed to it, led by the Spirit. He applied his natural and supernatural talents, his creativity, and hard work to the task. He planned his trips but was always open to the Spirit's adjustments. So should we be toward the callings the Lord has on our lives.

---

[239] Cf. Galatians 5:22-23.

There is also planning that is appropriate to our station in life – a farmer plants, a student studies, an engineer designs, a builder lays a foundation, a writer outlines her thoughts, an expectant mother prepares for the needs of her unborn child, a priest prepares his Sunday homily – all with a goal in mind. Such planning, within the boundaries of God's perfect will for us, is proper. Yet planning born of pride, vanity, greed, or any vice is not of the Holy Spirit. We must prayerfully discern what spirit is motivating our plans, our actions, and our inactions – even as it relates to our Church work.

Sometimes our walk with God includes times of spiritual dryness when it seems God is far away. This dryness comes to many believers. John of the Cross described it as "the dark night of the soul." For example, in the Old Testament, Joseph, Job, and Daniel had this experience; their abandonment to God felt as though God had abandoned them. In those periods of dryness, a believer roots himself ever deeper into his faith just as an oak tree, in periods of drought, sinks its roots deeper into the soil searching for water. In these periods, we experience the Spirit of God in the unconscious regions of our spirit. Though it may feel as if our faith is crumbling, as we persevere, we are actually growing stronger in faith.

Spontaneity and the Spirit. Many people with outgoing personalities are spontaneous. Thoughts come to mind, and they impulsively express those thoughts or act on them. For persons who live life quickly responding to urges that spring up from their *psyche* (that is, from their intellect, will, or emotions) or from their body (such as the sexual urge, eating, or an addiction), their spontaneity is worldly in character, even as they engage in good works. The Spirit-led person is spontaneous too, but in a very different way. He or she is responsive not to the inner urges of their psyche or body, but to the inspirations of the Holy Spirit. Such persons may be quiet as a mouse and unseen by others, but their lives are filled with divine spontaneity.

Jesus compared the Holy Spirit to the wind, which "blows where it wills."[240] Spirit-led persons are sails who move about in that wind, letting the wind take them where the Spirit wants them to go, letting the Holy Spirit be the pilot. This means we must wait upon the Holy Spirit to lead us. Often the Spirit, for reasons we are unaware of, may not move or direct our steps as quickly as we might hope. Still, we must learn to wait upon the Lord, prayerfully, joyfully, and faithfully.

---

[240] John 3:8 (NAB).

75

The Necessity of Humility. To hear what God is actually saying to us, to hear it in its proper context, and to respond according to God's perfect will requires a believer to assume a proper posture. Before God, the proper posture is that of creature, small and weak, loyal and true. This posture before God is called humility.

In everyday speech, the words "humility" or "meekness" are often understood as weak character traits, words that describe someone who is easily manipulated by other people. Some use these terms in a more positive sense to refer to persons who are gentle, quiet, or mild mannered. Neither of these is the essence of Christian humility. Christian humility is a term that refers to persons who are teachable by God, persons who are open to and led by the Spirit of God. Humility is the gateway to intimate fellowship with God.

The most distinguishing mark of Moses' character, ancient Israel's greatest leader, was his humility. As the Bible tells us, "Moses was extremely humble, the humblest man on earth."[241] For this precise reason, God chose him to lead Israel.[242]

Humility was also a distinguishing feature of Jesus' humanity. He was totally open to and led by the Holy Spirit. He was focused on the Father's will, led by the Spirit, and empowered by the Spirit. As Jesus said, "[L]earn from me, for I am meek and humble of heart; and you will find rest for yourselves."[243] What an awesome promise for those who learn humility – "you will find rest."

Rightly understood, humility is a great strength. It is our choice to allow the Holy Spirit to give vitality, purpose, and direction to our lives. It is the antithesis of pride, arrogance, selfishness, and self-sufficiency. The humble person learns to see with the eyes of Jesus, to hear with the ears of Jesus, and to love with the heart of Jesus. At times, this may require us to be gentle and kind, and other times courageous and bold. Sometimes it may mean we quietly suffer humiliation. Other times, we may need to confront evil head on.

As we allow ourselves to be guided in each moment by the Spirit's inspirations, we have what Paul called a mind "controlled by the Holy Spirit."[244] He tells us, "[T]hose who live in accordance with

---

[241] Numbers 12:3 (NJB).
[242] Cf. Sirach 45:4.
[243] Matthew 11:29 (NAB).
[244] Romans 8:6 (NIV). Cf. Galatians 5:25, Philippians 2:13.

the Spirit have their minds set on what the Spirit desires."[245] In time, a person can attain "the permanent disposition to live and act in keeping with God's call."[246] Such "habitual grace" flows in and through us as we become increasingly obedient to the Spirit's inspirations. Even in the storms of life, surrounded by much evil, the humble soul lives holiness. At times, the Spirit of God may lead us through "dark valleys" as indicated in the 23rd Psalm, nevertheless he is always at our side.[247]

According to Saint Thomas Aquinas, "True humility consists in not presuming on our own strength, but in trusting to obtain all things from the power of God."[248] It means we learn to depend on the Holy Spirit, daily, for direction, assistance, strength, and protection.

Humility and Freedom. The battle for humility, for openness to the Spirit of God, is a fight for freedom, for "where the Spirit of the Lord is, there is freedom."[249] *And what is freedom?* It is not the license to sin, nor is it the license to do as we please. Truly, all sin is bondage and the desire to do as we please is the sin of pride. *Freedom is to be who God created us to be, filled with heavenly peace and love, holiness and joy, come what may.*

The Holy Spirit is the Spirit of Freedom who can free us from fears, lies, hurts, patterns of sin, addictions, mental and emotional illnesses, and demonic oppression. The Holy Spirit can take the dirtiest of sinners and transform us into the cleanest of saints. He can get inside us and restore our lost innocence. With him, we find the only true freedom in life, which is in Christ.

Learning Humility. Mother Teresa taught that we "learn humility only by accepting humiliation . . . The greatest humiliation is to know that you are nothing."[250] Such humiliation makes us intensely aware of our frailty as humans, that apart from God we are literally nothing. Our pride, our sense of self-importance deplores this thought. Yet, we are creatures, mere specs in the great expanse of the universe. When this

---

[245] Romans 8:5 (NIV).

[246] CCC section 2000.

[247] Cf. Psalm 23:4, 66:11-12.

[248] Aquinas, Thomas, *The Aquinas Catechism*, Sophia Institute Press, 2000, page 106. Cf. Proverbs 3:5-6, Jeremiah 17:5.

[249] 2 Corinthians 3:17 (NAB).

[250] Mother Teresa, *Everything Starts with Prayer*, White Cloud Press, Ashland Oregon, 1998, page 60.

understanding seeps deep within, it helps to frees us from the bitter root of our pride. As for daily humiliations that may arise in our human interactions, we are to accept them with grace, not retaliating, not grumbling, not resorting to anger or despair.

One way we can grow in humility is to purposefully consecrate each day to God. Every morning, we should come to him in prayer, acknowledge his sovereignty over us, and ask for the grace to do his will. On our knees, if we can vocalize this prayer aloud with reverence, we will likely go about the rest of our day with a divinely altered perspective. We should re-enforce this prayer throughout the day with spontaneous words of praise or simple pleas: *Jesus, you are Lord. Father, Thy will be done. Holy Spirit come.*

Communities Led by the Spirit. We can discuss the Spirit-led life in a personal context, but in God's vision, the Spirit-led life is communal. Just as individuals are to be humble and open to the Spirit's lead, so also communities be they marriages, families, friendships, ministries, parishes, schools, businesses, nations, or the universal Church. The Father gives the Holy Spirit not only to persons, but also to whole communities for our common good. As communities, we must seek first to serve God's purpose and promote his glory. We must appreciate the wonder of God's plan to involve all persons in pursuit of his goals. We must learn to be open not only to the Spirit moving in my life, but also his movements in the lives of others.

Heavenly Father, I stand in total weakness before you. I give you all that I am. I trust in your mercy, your wisdom, and your love. Please send your Holy Spirit to renew my mind and my life. May the Holy Spirit fill my heart with his graces and teach me your ways.

Holy Spirit, Please show me the areas of my life I have not yielded to you, and help me do so. Please disturb me as it concerns the injustices of society that I deny or ignore. Please teach me to be a witness for truth. Please give me the courage to change my mind, and to speak up and act with a holy boldness and with love. Please order my steps to fulfill the Father's perfect will for my life. Please protect me from evil. I ask these things in Jesus' name, Amen.

10   Worship in Spirit & Truth

Jesus taught that "the hour is coming – indeed is already here – when true worshippers will worship the Father in spirit and truth: that is the kind of worshipper the Father seeks. God is spirit, and those who worship [him] must worship in spirit and truth."[251] Worship of God is all the ways we express our love of and loyalty to God. It can take many forms, but whatever form it takes, it is a work of the Holy Spirit in us, a work of the Holy Spirit in whom we learn to delight and with whom we cooperate.

Whether we realize it or not, a basic element of our humanity is the capacity and inclination for worship, which is the excitement or reverence or devotion we feel or show to persons or things we greatly admire. Every human being is wired for worship, and most of us do it. We commonly worship celebrities, politicians, artists, athletes, sports teams, or bands. Some worship their work, ambitions, activism, dreams, hobbies, family, special memories, or a treasured object. Some worship the latest cultural trends or technology. Some worship success, power, and control. Some worship money and the things money buys; others worship sex, alcohol, and the party life style.

All worship, whether to God or to someone else or to something else, involves sacrifice. It involves the sacrifice of time, resources, and attention we might give to other interests. The disturbing truth, all worship not directed toward God is the sin of idolatry. And with each form of worship, we open our hearts to the spirits associated with the object of our worship. All true worship of God is an outgrowth of the humility we discussed in the previous chapter. True worship is the lever by which we open our hearts to the flow of God's love, holiness, and power.

Jesus taught, "The Lord, your God, shall you worship and him alone shall you serve."[252] Such worship was at the heart of God's covenant with ancient Israel: "I will be your God and you will be my people. . . . You shall have no other gods before me. . . . Worship the Lord with gladness . . . Worship the Lord in the splendor of his holiness."[253]

---

[251] John 4:23-24 (NJB).
[252] Matthew 4:10 (NAB).
[253] Jeremiah 7:23, Exodus 20:3, Psalm 100:2, 1 Chronicles 16:29 (NIV).

In the days of Moses, God's principal purpose for Israel's Exodus from Egypt was <u>not</u> to lead the people home, in a physical sense, to the Promised Land. It was to lead them home, in a spiritual sense. The pathway home was all about worship. As Moses said to Pharaoh, speaking on God's behalf, "Let my people go, so that they may worship me in the wilderness."[254] For Israel then and for us today, worship of God rightly orients us for our faith journey home. It orients us for intimacy with the one, true, living God.

The Wilderness? Every journey in life takes us from someplace to someplace. God called the Israelites to journey out of Egypt, that place of slavery, into the wilderness, that place of worship. What is the wilderness? Somewhere away from slavery. The Israelites were to journey three days into the wilderness: a journey away from the old life they knew in the direction of a new life God had planned for them. For us, that journey is away from our slavery to sin, to a new life with God.

For Christians today, what more can we say of the wilderness? It is a place of silence. It is a place free from the pretensions, distractions, busyness, and confusions of worldly life. It is place where, because of the silence, it is easier to pray to God and to hear God speak to us. It is a place to grow in knowledge of God and of self, a knowledge born not of scientific, medical, social, or psychological analysis. Instead, this knowledge comes by way of special encounters with God, who allows us to see him, ourselves, and the world around us as we truly are.

The wilderness is a place to lighten our load, to be stripped of sin, and worldly cares. It is a place of poverty, a place where the world's provision is slight and believers must rely on God's provision.

The wilderness is also a place of safety, where people run when they are pursued by enemies. It is where Moses ran early in his life when Pharaoh wanted to arrest him; it is where David ran when Saul's army was chasing him; it is where Elijah ran when Jezebel threatened his life; and in the Book of Revelation, it is where "the Woman" fled when pursued by the dragon.[255] In this sense, the wilderness is our prayer life, where we can find protection from the evils that are pursuing us.

---

[254] Exodus 7:16 (NRSV). Cf. Exodus 8:1, 20, 9:1, 13, 10:3; Joseph Cardinal Ratzinger, *The Spirit of the Liturgy*, Ignatius Press, 2000, pages 15-16.

[255] Cf. Exodus 2:15 (Moses); 1 Samuel 23:14 (David); 1 Kings 17:3, 19:4, 8 (Elijah); Matthew 2:13-15, Revelation 12:6 (the woman).

The wilderness is a place where God's living waters flow – the River of Life, which is a Biblical metaphor for the Holy Spirit. It is a river that refreshes and heals as it flows through the desert's parched land bringing forth newness of life. The wilderness is also the place where God prepares his people for his promises and his purposes. The Spirit of God led the Israelites into the desert preparing them for entry into the Promised Land. The Spirit of God drove Jesus into the wilderness to prepare him for his public ministry. He does the same with us, if we let him.

Let us now consider some important means of worship: praise and thanksgiving, meditative and contemplative prayer, and obedience. In each of these, the Holy Spirit is our strength, our guide, and our solace.

Praise and Thanksgiving. Praise is prayer that joyfully acknowledges God for who he is, his greatness, his power, his wisdom, or his love. It is the language of heaven. For that reason, it fills the Church's liturgy. It is a style of prayer (spoken, sung, or meditated within our hearts) that purifies our intellect, our will, and our emotions. It does so by focusing our minds on God, allowing the innocence of our new birth to breathe and expand. Praise fosters intimacy with God.

The Psalmists teaches that praise of God invites God's presence, for the Lord inhabits the praises of his people.[256] Pope John Paul II spoke of man's "duty of praise." He said praise is "the starting point for every genuine response of faith to the revelation of God in Christ."[257] Pope Benedict XVI referred to praise as the means by which we discover God. "God," he said, "is found above all in praising him."[258] Ponder that thought, *God is found above all in praising him.*

Our willingness, our desire, our effort to praise God is one of the best barometers of each person's spiritual health. Saints and angels enjoy praising God. That which any of us gets enthusiastic about, we enjoy praising. But it is praise of God that lasts into eternity.

Songs can be a form of praise – whether to God or to persons, groups, ideas, or things to which we are loyal. Most of us enjoy singing secular songs. In certain venues, most of us enjoy singing – at home, in the car, at a party, a concert, or a ballgame. But what about singing at church? What about church songs? And if you sing at

---

[256] Cf. Psalm 22:3.
[257] Pope John Paul II, NMI, January 6, 2001, section 4.
[258] Pope Benedict XVI, GA, May 14, 2008.

church, is it because you enjoy singing generally, or because others are doing it and you want to fit in, or is it because you are in love with God and you enjoy serenading him? Saints and angels are in love with God and enjoy serenading him. This is worship.

Prayers of praise are a choice we need to make, daily, to honor God. Such prayers are a sacrifice of time, ego, and our false idols. While our praise of God adds nothing to his greatness, our praise opens us up to a deeper awareness of his greatness, allowing his greatness to more deeply touch our lives. Fr. Gabriele Amorth, Chief Exorcist of Rome, tells us, when resisting evil, "[T]he most efficacious prayers are those of adoration and praise to God."[259] Demons are irritated when we praise God and their influence over us is weakened. Knowing this, Satan is glad when we find such prayers boring.

To those who have never done it, praising God may seem dull or awkward at first. Yet we must remember, heaven is an eternity of praise. If we truly desire heaven, then now is the time to begin praising God. If we truly desire intimacy with God, we must praise him. Even in the midst of confusion, hurt, and disappointment, we must learn the power of praise whereby we invite the God of the Universe into our lives and into our struggles. Whether the words of our praise are directed to God, or the Father, or Jesus, or the Holy Spirit, the Spirit of God is at work fanning the embers of our hearts. He is the Lord inhabiting our praises.

I love you Jesus, you are the Son of God and the Son of Man . . . You are the Eternal Word . . . the Alpha and the Omega . . . the King of kings and the Lord of lords . . . I thank you Jesus, you are the Good Shepherd . . . the Lamb of God . . . the Bread of Life . . . You are My Savior . . . My Teacher . . . My Friend. I love you. You are Lord!

If praise is the rejoicing in God for who he is, thanksgiving is the rejoicing in God for what he has done, is doing, or has promised to do. The Psalmist instructs us to "Enter [God's] gates with thanksgiving, and his courts with praise. Give thanks to him, bless his name."[260] Paul encourages us, "Sing and make music in your heart to the Lord, always giving thanks to God the Father for everything."[261] "And whatever you do, in word or deed, do everything in the name of the Lord Jesus,

---

[259] Amorth, Father Gabriele, *An Exorcist: More Stories*, Ignatius Press, 2002, page 97.
[260] Psalm 100:4 (NRSV).
[261] Ephesians 5:20 (NIV). Cf. Ephesians 5:4, Philippians 4:4-6.

giving thanks to God the Father through him."[262] "[F]or all things give thanks; this is the will of God for you in Christ Jesus."[263] Truly, it is "right and just . . . always and everywhere"[264] to give God thanks.

Thanksgiving is a critically important form of prayer. St Paul taught that failure to give God the thanks he deserves is an age-old sin that has horrible consequences. It is a form of foolishness that leads to a darkened heart.[265] It is a breach of the great command to love God with our whole heart and mind. Those who love God, thank God.

Meditative and Contemplative Prayer. Two important forms of worship are meditation and contemplation. Each of these forms of prayer is a collaborative communion with the Holy Spirit that draw us deeper into the mystery of Christ. We must note that in everyday speech, the words "contemplate" and "meditate" are synonyms. Yet, as forms of prayer, they are quite different. Meditative prayer is quiet pondering of a matter with God. It is not about mere human reasoning, but reasoning purposefully done with the Spirit of God, so as to grow in divine wisdom, holiness, love, or some other virtue.

In the Bible, the psalmist offers several examples of meditative prayer, when he reflects on the Law of God, or God's majesty, or his mighty works done in times past. Mary is an excellent example of a person who engages in meditative prayer. In the infancy narrative of Luke's Gospel, we learn that she struggled to understand the events that were taking place in her life and she "pondered [these things] in her heart."[266] Generally, meditation will be about Jesus, an event in his life, a scripture verse or Biblical event, an attribute of God, a virtue, or maybe a problem in our own lives. Our meditations may engage our imaginations as we, in our mind's eye, gaze upon a situation with God. The rosary is offered as a meditative prayer that reflects on various mysterious as we pray each decade.

Whereas meditative prayer is a quest of the mind quietly pondering a matter before God, contemplative prayer is a quest of the spirit quietly resting in the mystery of God. As the Bible tells us, "Be still and know that I am God."[267] "Be still before the Lord; wait for

---

[262] Colossians 3:17 (NRSV). Cf. Colossians 2:7.
[263] 1 Thessalonians 5:18 (NJB). Cf. Hebrews 12:28.
[264] The Roman Missal (2010), preface to the Eucharistic prayer.
[265] Cf. Romans 1:21.
[266] Luke 2:19 (NIV). Cf. Luke 2:51.
[267] Psalm 46:10 (NRSV).

God."[268] "[T]he Lord waits to be gracious to you . . . blessed are all those who wait for him."[269]

In contemplative prayer, our minds rest as the Holy Spirit intimately communes with our spirits. Contemplative prayer bypasses our intellects as the Holy Spirit embraces us in holy silence. In such moments, a person absorbs God's grace, much the way a grassy meadow absorbs a gentle, soaking rain. The Holy Spirit dwelling in our spirit softly flows out from our heart and refreshes our soul. We can experience this at home, in Church, in nature, or wherever we can be alone with God and rest in his presence.

If praise may be likened to the joy of children running out to greet a parent returning home from a trip, then contemplation is the warm and quiet curling-up of the children in their parent's arms. The Holy Spirit is the love in both these instances, flowing freely between parent and child. With respect to contemplative prayer, St. John of the Cross tells us that the Holy Spirit is "the principal agent here, and the real guide of souls."[270] In contemplative prayer, the Holy Spirit tenderly infuses our souls with his grace, wisdom, and love.

To enter contemplation, we must quiet our interior thoughts and focus on God's divine presence. We might begin by softly repeating a word or phrase to cast out distracting thoughts. When a distracting thought comes to our mind, we softly push it away with a chant of our word or phrase. For example, "Jesus, Jesus, Jesus" or "Jesus, I love you" or "thank you Jesus." St. Francis de Sales, in a sermon on prayer, talked of contemplation in the lives of Saints Francis of Assisi, Bruno, and Augustine and how they followed this method of disposing their hearts to the work of the Spirit in contemplation. "Saint Francis passed an entire night repeating: You are 'my All.' . . . St. Bruno was content to say, 'O Goodness!' And St. Augustine: 'O Beauty ever ancient and ever new!'"[271] A 14th English spiritual director whose name has been lost to history, suggests, "A one-syllable word such as 'God' or 'love' is best. But choose one that is meaningful to you. Then fix it in your

---

[268] Psalm 37:7 (NAB). Cf. Psalm 27:14, 130:5-6, Isaiah 8:17.

[269] Isaiah 30:18 (NRSV). Cf. Psalm 33:20, Isaiah 30:15, 64:4, Lamentations 3:25-26, Daniel 12:12.

[270] St. John of the Cross, *The Living Flame of Love*, (stanza III, section 47), Cosimo Classics, 2007, page 87.

[271] St. Francis de Sales, sermon, April 12, 1615. De Sales, Francis, *On Prayer, The Sermons of St. Francis de Sales*, Tan Books and Publishers, 1985, page 26. Cf. St. Augustine, Confessions, book IX, chapter 10.

mind so that it will remain there come what may. . . . Use it . . . to subdue all distractions."[272]

Alternatively, we might silently gaze upon Jesus in the Sacrament of Holy Eucharist, or gaze upon a piece of religious art, or in our imagination gaze into a mystery in the life of Jesus. Or, we might begin with another form of prayer – a prayer of praise, a hymn, or a rosary – and at some point, in the "silent love"[273] of the moment, drift into contemplation. Or we might be reading Scripture, and then pause in meditation, and then slowly enter contemplation.

We may enter contemplation in a prayer group setting when others pray over us, and we rest in the Spirit's grace. Today, some Christian songs may go for ten minutes or so softly repeating a Biblical verse or chorus of praise; then, in the repetition, we might experience a clearing of our mind as the Holy Spirit engages us in contemplation.

In the moment of contemplation, as the Spirit mysteriously fills the temples of our hearts, most people experience peace. Some may experience an elevated consciousness. The greater experience, though, is within our spirits, where we do not know with any specificity what is happening, we only trust it is all good and all of God. The Spirit's love, his holiness, and his power are being poured into the inner most depths of our being, healing us, restoring us, and building us up in faith. This time with God allows our spirits to be strengthened so that they may properly direct the activities of our minds and bodies.

For some, contemplation may involve visions and other mystical experiences. For others, this can be a time of dryness, when the finiteness of our beings trembles before the majesty of God. For all, contemplative prayer is a time to grow in knowledge of God, not through our intellect, but through our spirit.

It is important to note that the silence of Christian contemplation is not the silence of the Buddhist prayer of self-emptying or the semi-hypnotic prayer exercises of Hinduism, Transcendental Meditation, or the New Age Movement, which also focus on silence and may use words (or "mantras") to dispel distracting thoughts. In the case of the Buddhist, he does not believe in God. In silence, he seeks a higher awareness of self. The Christian seeks to encounter God. Others seek

---

[272] William Johnson, ed., *The Cloud of Unknowing*, Doubleday, 1973, page 56.
[273] Cf. St. John of the Cross, *Maxims and Counsels*, section 53.

union with the false gods of their religion. Christians should avoid the prayer regiments of these non-Christian groups as well as Christian clergy who dabble in these and other forms of the occult.[274] This caution, though, should not dissuade anyone from rightly seeking God in authentic Christian contemplation.

The Catholic Church teaches that contemplative prayer, is "the pre-eminently *intense time* of prayer. In it the Father strengthens our inner being with power through his Spirit 'that Christ may dwell in [our] hearts through faith' and we may be 'grounded in love.'"[275] "One does not undertake contemplative prayer only when one has the time: one makes time for the Lord, with the firm determination not to give up, no matter what trials and dryness one may encounter."[276]

On Obedience. Obedience is another form of worship. In a non-religious sense, we see this form of worship in people's following of fads, styles, ways of acting, or advice from those they idolize. In a religious context, our obedience is a form of worship when we purposefully follow God's commands for love of him. Moses understood this when he asked God, "Teach me your ways so I may know you and continue to find favor with you."[277] Similarly, Paul talked about the importance of being "completely obedient"[278] to God. Peter taught that the Holy Spirit is "given to those who obey him."[279]

Obedience is a sacrificial offering of our will to God: *not my will be done, but yours O Lord*. Our challenge is not merely to obey dutifully, but to obey joyfully. Our challenge is not merely to give God the minimum of what he asks, but to give him the best of what we have. When we obey his commands for love of him, we honor him.

Godly worship feeds the soul. For this reason, Jesus could say of his own obedience, "My food is to do the will of the one who sent me and to finish his work."[280] At the Last Supper, Jesus connected the themes of love, obedience, and the gift of the Holy Spirit when he said,

---

[274] Some Christians promote a "centering prayer" regiment that is consistent with Christian contemplation. However, other proponents of centering prayer co-mingle Christian teaching with ideas and practices from the New Age movement, eastern religions, and the occult. It is advisable to avoid these other persons.

[275] CCC section 2714. Internal quotes from Ephesians 3:16-17.

[276] CCC section 2710.

[277] Exodus 33:13 (NIV).

[278] 2 Corinthians 2:9 (NJB).

[279] Acts 5:32 (NAB).

[280] John 4:34 (NAB). Cf. Isaiah 1:19

"If you love me, you will keep my commandments. And I will ask the Father, and he will give you . . . the Spirit of truth."[281] Not only does obedience invite the Spirit, but the Spirit enables obedience.[282]

Christian Worship. What is Christian worship? It is rightly acknowledging God for who he is. It is the choice to give him our full attention and respect. That reality calls us to praise and thanksgiving and to quiet meditation and contemplation. That reality calls us to loving obedience, service, and works of charity. That reality calls us to repentance, Bible study, and the joyful singing of hymns. All of this is worship, a work of the Holy Spirit within us, with whom we choose to cooperate. As Pope Benedict XVI aptly said, the more our "whole existence is directed toward God – the more [we] accomplish true worship."[283] If we learn to worship in the Spirit daily, we will experience an increasing intimacy with God that leads to true friendship. Where do we find the right motivation for our worship? In an increasing awareness of God's majesty, power, and love, and an increasing appreciation that we are forgiven.

Dear God, You alone are worthy of worship. You alone are worthy of praise. You are wonderful. You are everything. Blessed be the name Abba, Father, the name Jesus, and the name Holy Spirit.

Thank you Lord for my life. Thank you for the gift of faith, which enables me to know you. Thank you for the beauty of Creation. Thank you for all the ways your grace touches my life. Thank you for the gift of Sacred Scripture and your Church. Jesus, thank you for your death on the Cross. Thank you for your forgiveness and mercy in my life.

Come Holy Spirit and lead me into the stillness of the desert to honor the Father my Creator, Jesus my Redeemer, and you my Friend. Please quiet my heart and mind, and help me to rest. Help to rest with you in the silence of this moment. Instead of continuing my reading or getting lost in my own thoughts, I choose to rest with you. I choose to dispel distracting thoughts by softly chanting the name of my Savior. Jesus, Jesus, Jesus. Please fill me with reverence and awe for Jesus.

[Rest for 10 minutes in silence, softly chanting the name of Jesus.]

---

[281] John 14:15-16 (NAB). Cf. 1 John 2:3-5.
[282] Cf. Luke 1:74-75.
[283] Pope Benedict XVI, *Jesus of Nazareth*, Part II, Ignatius Press, 2011, page 234.

11   Gift of Trials

Trials and hardships provide some of the most valuable encounters we can have with the Holy Spirit. We all experience them, big ones and little ones, some that last minutes or hours, others that last days or weeks, and still others that last years or even a lifetime. All trials, all sufferings, all hardships of whatever kind God permits, and a few he actually sends our way. Whether we realize it or not, these times are the proving ground of our faith and each is an opportunity to grow in faith.

Some of our trials are truly small, but they can seem large in the moment: a flat tire, someone's unkind remarks, a computer crash, a headache, a worry, or a temptation to sin. Our tougher trials commonly relate to broken relationships, loneliness, an addiction, finances, aging, a serious illness, or the death of a loved one. Most trials come against believers in the same way they come against all humanity. They are just a part of life.

Yet some trials come upon us as Christians because we are Christians. Says the ancient sage, "when you come to serve the Lord, prepare yourself for trials."[284] Some of our trials come in the form of persecution. As Jesus told his Apostles, "If they persecuted me, they will also persecute you."[285] As Paul reminded Timothy, "[A]nybody who tries to live in devotion to Christ is certain to be persecuted."[286] In our modern day, such persecution can be physical attacks, imprisonment, and even murder as some Christians might experience in certain areas of Asia and Africa. In western countries, the persecution that devout Christians often experience is ridicule, gossip, social out-casting, and being overlooked for jobs.

What may surprise many of us is that some of life's trials are actually sent by God. We rarely realize it at the time or at all, but each trial from God is truly a blessing in disguise. They are opportunities to realize, more deeply, our need of God. Trials sent by God usually expose what is actually in our hearts. God often puts trials in our path to break down our pride, our sense of self-sufficiency, and our desire to

---

[284] Sirach 2:1 (NAB).

[285] John 15:20 (NAB). Cf. Matthew 5:10-11, 10:22, Luke 6:22, John 16:33, Acts 5:41, 2 Corinthians 6:3-10, Philippians 1:29, James 1:2, 1 Peter 4:14-16.

[286] 2 Timothy 3:12 (NJB). Cf. Acts 14:22, 1 Thessalonians 3:3-4, 1 Peter 1:6, 2:4, 5:10, Psalm 34:19.

be in control. A trial can often be that which provokes a person to seek God for the first time or after a long time away. Trials, if we let them, teach us dependency on God, "to trust not in ourselves but in God."[287]

Very often trials have a purpose that only God understands. In the Old Testament, Joseph's trials are a good example. His brothers sold him into slavery where he endured thirteen years of hardship, much of it in jail. God let this misfortune happen as part of his plan to bring Joseph to Egypt in advance of a famine. What Joseph's brothers meant for ill, God used for good. During this long hardship, God transformed an overconfident boy into a humble, wise, and holy leader.

Regarding trials that involve God's correction, Jesus tells us, "I reprove and discipline those whom I love."[288] Similarly, the writer of Hebrews says, "My son, do not make light of the Lord's discipline, and do not lose heart when he rebukes you, because the Lord disciplines those he loves . . . God disciplines us for our good, that we might share in his holiness. No discipline seems pleasing at the time, but painful. Later on, however, it produces a harvest of righteousness and peace for those who have been trained by it."[289]

Some things come to us in our faith journey, particularly at the beginning, that seem a trial and later become a joy. For example, if we are not accustomed to prayer, Bible study, singing hymns, going to the Sacrament of Reconciliation, or serving others, these activities can initially be a trial. Yet as we continue in our faith journey, these can become a joy.

We often experience new beginnings solely because of hardships. What at first seems to be something that might break us can become that which makes us stronger. Or, it might be better said, the Holy Spirit working within us, through the circumstance, makes us stronger. Truly, the Spirit of God can use our deepest hurts and our greatest failures and defeats to bring forth good.

As Pope Francis teaches, "The journey of the Church, and our own personal journeys as Christians, are not always easy; they meet with difficulties and trials. To follow the Lord, to let his Spirit transform the shadowy parts of our lives, our ungodly ways of acting,

---

[287] 2 Corinthians 1:9 (NJB)

[288] Revelation 3:19 (NRSV). Cf. Deuteronomy 8:5, Job 5:17, Judith 8:27, Proverbs 3:12, 118:8, 1 Corinthians 11:32.

[289] Hebrews 12:5-7, 10-11 (NIV).

and cleanse us of our sins, is to set out on a path with many obstacles, both in the world around us but also within us, in the heart. But difficulties and trials are part of the path that leads to God's glory, just as they were for Jesus, who was glorified on the cross; we will always encounter them in life! Do not be discouraged! We have the power of the Holy Spirit to overcome these trials!"[290]

Some of life's trials are attacks by Satan or his demons. In this life, we have a clear enemy, whose works Jesus came to destroy.[291] On the night before Jesus' death, he spoke to Simon Peter saying, "Simon, Simon. Satan has asked to sift you[292] as wheat. But I have prayed for you,[293] Simon, that your faith may not fail. And when you have turned back, strengthen your brothers."[294] While Peter's faith stumbled in this trial, ultimately it did not fail. Thanks to Jesus' prayer, Peter did recover, turn back, and strengthen his brothers.

Demonic attacks come at all persons, Christians are not excluded. Such attacks commonly come in the form of a temptations to sin or as feelings of anxiety, sadness, fear, or rejection. Sometimes the evil one attacks those around us, so as to indirectly bring harm to us or trick us into sin. Our challenge is to see these ordeals for what they are and to resist impulses of our flesh to sin or to waste time and energy entertaining some negative emotion.

One of the more difficult trials of life is worldly success, because with it, it is so easy to forget our need of God. Satan tempts us to be impressed by our own accomplishments and excited by our personal ambitions. He tempts us to take credit for the goodness in our lives and seek fulfillment apart from God. We pray for worldly success, we work hard for it, and when it comes, it is often the last thing we truly need. St. John of Avila noted, "More strength is required to remain virtuous in success and prosperity than in adversity. You need more grace to prevent you from falling when you are in a position of importance than when you are brought low by misfortune."[295]

Father Henri Nouwen, one of the more renowned Catholic writers of the 20th century, taught at the most prestigious academic institutions

---

[290] Pope Francis, homily, April 28, 2013.

[291] Cf. 1 John 3:8.

[292] In Greek, the "you" here is plural, referring to all the Apostles.

[293] In Greek, the "you" here is singular, referring to Peter.

[294] Luke 22:31-32 (NIV).

[295] St. John of Avila, *The Holy Spirit Within,* Scepter Publishers, 2012, page 105.

in the United States. He authored many highly acclaimed books. Yet, he determined late in life, that he needed to seriously alter his career and assume a lowlier lifestyle. He did so, choosing to become the chaplain for a community of mentally disadvantaged adults. Writing about this decision, Nouwen said that at some point he began to wonder whether his achievements were bringing him closer to Jesus, or pushing him away: "Everyone was saying that I was doing really well, but something inside me was telling me that my success was putting my own soul in danger. I began to ask myself whether my lack of contemplative prayer, my loneliness, and my constantly changing involvement in what seemed most urgent were signs that the Spirit was gradually being suppressed. It was very hard for me to see clearly, and though I never spoke about hell or only jokingly so, I woke up one day with the realization that I was living in a very dark place and the term 'burnout' was a convenient psychological translation for spiritual death."[296]

Last, many of our trials deal with human relations, where our brokenness, woundedness, and character flaws bump into the brokenness, woundedness, and character flaws of others. So often we are quick to see, or think we see, the problems in others' lives that give rise to conflict and we are slow to realize our own problems. Here we must constantly seek the Spirit's grace to be patient, kind, and understanding as we deal with others and as we deal with our own brokenness.

Our Response to Trials. Trials touch everyone. What distinguishes faith-filled Christians is how we respond to trials. Our challenge is to joyfully persevere through our hardships, always drawing closer to God. We must come to realize that "all things work together for good for those who love God."[297] We should not be afraid of difficulties or suffering, nor should we foolishly seek these out. Rather, we should accept the challenges that come our way, learning to rely on the Spirit's help in the midst of it all.

In times of adversity, it is proper to feel and admit our pain, disappointments, and frustrations. In the case of a loss, it is right to grieve. If there are problems that need addressing, we should address them. But beyond this, we must not wallow in self pity, or grief, or

---

[296] Nouwen, Henri J. M., *In the Name of Jesus, Reflections on Christian Leadership*, The Crossroad Publishing Company, 1989, page 20.
[297] Romans 8:28 (NAB). Cf. Genesis 50:20.

worry, or anger. We must not grumble or complain. We must lean on the Holy Spirit who, as Paul tells us, "helps us in our weakness."[298] Our trials, then, become a chance for greater intimacy with God, a chance to grow stronger in faith as we rely more on him, a chance to focus on what really matters. Thus, Paul could boast, "[F]or Christ's sake, I delight in weaknesses, in insults, in hardships, in persecutions, in difficulties. For when I am weak, then I am strong."[299] He was strong because he depended more and more on the Holy Spirit.

In his own life, Paul experienced much hardship. He was often beaten by mobs, frequently arrested, flogged, imprisoned, and verbally maligned in city after city. When Paul asked God to heal an ailment that he thought was hindering his work, God told him, "My grace is sufficient for you, for [my] power is made perfect in weakness."[300]

To the extent we respond from our flesh to problems (from a place of insecurity, or frustration, or pride, or anger, etc.), we only make our problems worse. The wise know to give their problems to God and strive to obey God's commands. This requires prayer – not a worrisome prayer that gives God detailed instructions on how to fix things, but rather a prayer of faith that gives him the concern and trusts. If we are praying to Jesus, we can repeat over and over if necessary, *"Jesus, I trust in you."* The instinct to go to God in prayer, to give him our problems, to trust him in prayer, and to patiently wait is a work of the Holy Spirit, helping us to grow in faith and holiness.

It is certainly appropriate to pray that God deliver us from our sufferings, injustices, and any demonic attacks. But so long as a difficulty lasts, we should strive to endure it as Christ would, turning to the Holy Spirit, our divine Helper. As we rely on his graces, obeying his inspirations, we grow stronger. Truly, the Spirit is with us even in our darkest moments; our challenge is to realize that and let him comfort us. If we let him, he is our strength to continue forward, our joy despite unpleasant circumstances. If we let him, he provides support not only for us, but also for us to share with others.[301] Conversely, his grace often comes to us through others, which we must be open to receive.

---

[298] Romans 8:26 (NRSV).
[299] 2 Corinthians 12:10 (NIV).
[300] 2 Corinthians 12:9 (NAB).
[301] Cf. 2 Corinthians 1:3-5.

Author's Personal Testimony Responding to a Trial

In my own life, one trial in which I experienced a spiritual victory is worth sharing. I was working on a project with a team of colleagues, and a supervisor treated one of our team members in a disrespectful way and threatened to veto an idea that the team was excited about. I privately reached out to the supervisor and suggested that he reconcile with the person he mistreated. In the moment, the supervisor got quite angry. He bad mouthed the whole team, my colleague, and the idea that the team was excited about. Then he started making accusations against me and threatened to kick me off the team.

In the moment, I felt anger quickly rising up within me. I felt the urge to respond with uncharitable comments of my own. This was not a work environment where this supervisor could affect my livelihood. I could have easily responded to his bad behavior with my own bad behavior and felt quite justified in the moment. However, I was able to restrain myself. The Holy Spirit brought to my mind a quote of Mother Teresa. The quote suggested that one of the ways we grow in humility is by suffering humiliation with grace, responding to unpleasant situations with love and not anger.

In the moment, as I was being yelled at, I had the presence of mind to stay calm and pray in my heart for the other man. I prayed that God bless him and free him from his anger. After about ten minutes of a horrible encounter, the volcano of his anger burned out. His countenance immediately changed. He became reasonable. It was as though the prior ten minutes had never occurred. All the issues he had with our team seemed to disappear. The team was able to move forward on the planned activity without obstruction and he reconciled with the team member in his own way. This trial taught me that suffering humiliation with grace can change the direction of events. It allows the Holy Spirit to take charge.

Uniting Our Sufferings with the Sufferings of Christ. The French poet Paul Claudel appropriately observed, "Jesus did not come to explain suffering nor to take it away: he came to fill it with his presence."[302] While we tend to see suffering in the moment, God sees it in the expanse of eternity, when our lifetime on earth is but the blink

---

[302] As quoted by Leon Joseph Cardinal Suenens, *A New Pentecost?*, Seabury Press, 1975, page 67.

of an eye. Indeed, as St. Paul tells us, all "the sufferings of this present time are as nothing compared with the glory to be revealed for us."[303]

The Bible tells us that Jesus "learned obedience from what he suffered."[304] Similarly, with the help of the Holy Spirit, we can learn obedience from our sufferings. The Spirit teaches us to accept our trials, even as we ask God to remove them. We must learn from Jesus' example in the Garden of Gethsemane on the night before he died. That night, he prayed to the Father, asking him to remove the agony he was beginning to experience: "Father, if you are willing, take this cup away from me; still, not my will but yours be done."[305]

In our suffering, the Bible encourages us to prayerfully unite our distress with the sufferings of Jesus, to see them as a sharing in Jesus' passion.[306] As suggested in the *Imitation of Christ*, if we suffer, "It behooves [us] to suffer with Christ, and for Christ, if [one day we] would reign with Christ."[307]

St. John of the Cross taught that "[I]nterior trials and tribulations destroy and purge away the imperfect and evil habits of the soul. We are, therefore, to count it a great favor when our Lord sends us interior and exterior trials."[308] Such trials are opportunities to grow in holiness. As Paul and his companions proclaimed, "It is necessary for us to undergo many hardships to enter the kingdom of God."[309]

Truly, the less we worry about our problems and devote ourselves to God and his calling on our lives, the more we then give God permission to take care of us and our problems. We must release them into his care. If we are pre-occupied with worry, then we are in essence holding on to our problems and not trusting God. We are an obstacle to our own best interests.

Through all of our trials, through each and every one, even the ones we create and the ones we make worse because of our own sin,

---

[303] Romans 8:18 (NAB).

[304] Hebrews 5:8 (NIV).

[305] Luke 22:42 (NAB).

[306] Cf. Romans 8:17, 2 Corinthians 1:5, Colossians 1:24, 1 Peter 2:20-21, 4:13-19.

[307] *Imitation of Christ*, book 2; Thomas a' Kempis; Harold C. Gardner, translator, Doubleday, 1955, page 77.

[308] St. John of the Cross, *The Living Flame of Love*, (stanza II, section 34), Cosimo Classics, 2007, page 50.

[309] Acts 14:22 (NAB). Cf. St. John of the Cross, *The Living Flame of Love*, stanza II, section 25.

God is with us. He is very near, always. The more we are aware of this, the safer we will feel, and the better decisions we will then make. The more we turn to him and let his grace comfort, guide, and protect us – including the grace of his forgiveness, when we repent – the safer we will be. Such trust is not some sort of Pollyanna escape from reality. Instead, it is turning of our hearts and minds to God, who is the ultimate reality. As real as our problems seem, they are all passing. God is the ultimate reality, and he is near. We need to realize that and embrace the grace of his presence, come what may.

Rejoice, Give Thanks. In our trials, we are often tempted with a variety of negative emotions. Yet, the Bible tells us to rejoice in our suffering.[310] While he was in prison, Paul wrote to his disciples: "Rejoice in the Lord always. I shall say it again: rejoice! . . . The Lord is near. Have no anxiety at all, but in everything, by prayer and petition, with thanksgiving, make your requests known to God."[311] "God will not let you be put to the test beyond your strength, but with any trial will also provide a way out enabling you to put up with it."[312]

St. Peter similarly taught, "[R]ejoice to the extent that you share in the sufferings of Christ, so that when his glory is revealed you may also rejoice exultantly. If you are insulted for the name of Christ, blessed are you, for the Spirit of glory and of God rests upon you."[313] James made the same point this way, "[C]onsider it a great joy when trials of many kinds come upon you, for you well know that the testing of your faith produces perseverance, and perseverance must complete its work so that you be fully developed, complete, not deficient in any way."[314] "[G]ive thanks in all circumstances."[315]

Rejoice in our trials? Consider it a great joy? Give thanks? To most of us, these instructions may sound ridiculous. That is because we are spiritually immature. These instructions are pearls of wisdom. Praise and thanksgiving to God are acts of the will, not our feelings. They are acts of faith that God cares for us and is present in every situation accomplishing good, no matter how grim things seem. Learning to praise God in adversity is a key to greater spiritual and

---

[310] Cf. Matthew 5:12, Luke 6:22-23, Acts 5:41, 16:25, Romans 5:3, 1 Thessalonians 1:6, James 1:2, 1 Peter 4:13-19.

[311] Philippians 4:4-6 (NAB). Cf. 2 Corinthians 7:4.

[312] 1 Corinthians 10:13 (NJB).

[313] 1 Peter 4:13-14 (NAB). Cf. Acts 13:52.

[314] James 1:2-4 (NJB). Cf. Habakkuk 3:18-19, Romans 5:3-5.

[315] 1 Thessalonians 5:18 (NIV). Cf. Ephesians 5:20, Philippians 4:6, Colossians 4:2.

psychological freedom and it is one of the *ways out* of our hardships. In the storms of life, we are so easily distracted and confused by circumstances, other people, and our feelings. Yet, if we focus intently on Jesus with our praises, then miracles become possible. Think of Peter that stormy night when he walked on water. As long as he focused on Jesus, the wind, lighting, and waves did not harm him.

The Bible teaches us to give thanks to God in all situations,[316] even bad ones. We should thank God in our trials, whether it is the loss of a job, a struggle with an addiction, a financial setback, rejection from others, the death of a loved one, or an illness. *For all things work for the good of those who love God.*[317] When we thank God in our trials, everything in us begins to change, despite external problems that seem unchanging. Inside we change, our hearts change, all for the good, because of the Holy Spirit. Though outwardly we may be wasting away, inwardly we are being renewed.[318]

A former U.S. Army chaplain, Merlin Carothers, suggested that we should praise God not only in our trials, but also for our trials. "[T]o praise God for difficult situations, [such] as sickness or disaster, means literally that we accept its happening, as part of God's plan to reveal his perfect Love for us. . . . [It means] that we are accepting the fact that God is responsible for what is happening and will always make it work for our good. . . . We praise God, not for the expected results, but for the situation just as it is."[319] When we, in faith, thank God for our lives just as they are, with the hardships – our faith opens the floodgates of the Spirit's grace to work more dynamically within us and in the challenges we are facing. In such times, Pope John Paul II taught, the Holy Spirit can be our "remedy against sadness."[320]

Spiritual maturity consists in this, accepting adversity with Christian confidence, loving God and our fellow human beings through it all. Said St. Alphonsus Liguori, a Doctor of the Church, if we learn to accept trials as "from the hands of God with Christian resignation, they should be blessings and not evils. The jewels which give the greatest splendor to the crown of the saints in Heaven, are the

---

[316] Cf. 1 Thessalonians 5:18, Ephesians 5:20, Philippians 4:6, Colossians 4:2.
[317] Cf. Romans 8:23.
[318] Cf. 2 Corinthians 4:16.
[319] Carothers, Merlin, *Power in Praise,* Carothers, 1972, pages 2, 6.
[320] Pope John Paul II, GA, March 13, 1991, section 1.

tribulations which they bore with patience, as coming from the hands of the Lord."[321]

Experiencing Trials in Community. One of the blessings of a trial is the comfort of family and friends and the unexpected kindnesses of strangers. Trials can be times when people pull together. Our love becomes more real, more tangible in such moments. The Holy Spirit can use trials to heal wounds and to set matters straight in human relationships. Communities often define themselves or redefine themselves only through difficulties experienced together. If all we have are easy times, relationships will tend to be superficial and shallow. The supernatural closeness and love a community may experience during an unpleasant ordeal is a work of the Holy Spirit.

Dear God, I praise you. Father, Son, and Holy Spirit, I praise you. Blessed is your name, now and forever.

I thank you for my life and for those things that bring me joy and peace. I thank you for [list the blessings of life that make you happy]*.*

I also thank you for the difficulties in my life, the trials and the struggles. Specifically, I thank you for [list specific trials]*. I trust that you are present in all my struggles working all things for the good of those who love you. I pray for your perfect will to be accomplished in each of these matters. Please take over control of each of these matters and of my life. I thank you for my current situation.*

Holy Spirit, please help me to be more aware of your presence, to trust you, and to rejoice in you. Please make straight the crooked paths of my life. Please heal my heart and memories. Please increase the grace of divine love within me so that I might love God above and my neighbor here below more fully. In Jesus' name I pray, Amen.

---

[321] *Sermons of St. Alphonsus Liguori*, TAN Books and Publishers, page 213.

12 Do Not Stifle the Spirit

Frequently, the Bible uses the imagery of a stream or river to refer to the Holy Spirit. This stream flows through the wildernesses of life, the streets of heaven, and within the hearts of believers. In this stream, we find happiness, peace, and purpose. When we block or resist the stream's flow, we cause harm. Thus, Paul admonishes believers, "[D]o not stifle the Spirit."[322]

How do we stifle the Spirit? How do we obstruct the flow of God's grace in our lives and our world? The simplest answer is sin. Sin blocks the flow of grace. Sin clouds our minds and poisons our perspective. Wherever there is greed, gossip, impure sexual desires, racism, or anger, the Spirit is stifled. Wherever there is pride or vanity, envy or judgmental attitudes, a competitive spirit or the love of money, the Spirit is stifled.

When we choose not to repent of our sins and not to seek God in prayer, we stifle the Spirit. When we forgo the Sacraments, or avoid Bible study, we stifle the Spirit. When we are not open to the charismatic dimension of our Christian walk, we stifle the Spirit. Fear, worry, despair, and other negative feelings also stifle the Spirit.

For every Christian, there is a hidden war waged in our minds between the Spirit and the flesh. The battle, like so much of life itself, comes to us through our natural senses – seeing, hearing, touching, tasting, and smelling. From many directions, both good and evil enter our lives, seeking to form our thoughts and loyalties in a variety of different ways. We are also influenced by the interior life of our own thoughts, our memories, our hurts, our fears, our ambitions, etc. Some influences can be healthy for us. Increasingly, though, in our fallen world, these influences are negative and they stifle the Spirit.

By acts of the will, we open and close various gateways to our minds that allow different influences to have access. If we are to grow closer to Christ, we must close those gateways by which we receive the spiritual poisons of the world and open those gateways by which we receive God's grace. Our eyes and ears are gateways. What we allow to pass through them, what we allow our imagination and intellect to ruminate on, influences the direction of our lives.

---

[322] 1 Thessalonians 5:19 (NJB).

Old Self – Five Senses

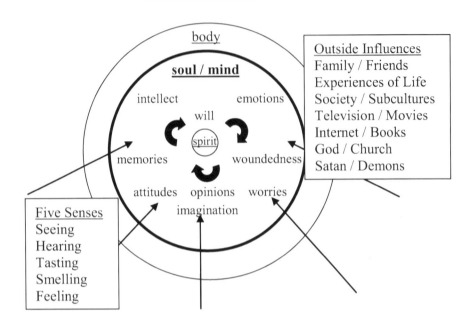

New Self – Flow of God's Grace

If we are open to the Spirit's streams of grace, our interior wounds begin to heal, our minds are awakened to truth, and evil is pushed away. Slowly, we are transformed into the saints we were created to be. Without the Holy Spirit flowing within us, our spirits are like dry, shriveled raisins. Only as the Holy Spirit flows within us, do our spirits moisten into grapes and, if we cooperate, the Holy Spirit brings forth in our lives a wonderful new wine.

As we sincerely seek Jesus and his dominion over us, the Spirit of God flows out from our heart to our mind – be it dramatically in a single moment as may occur in some cases or, in mosts cases, gradually each day. The Spirit flows out from our spirit not only to bless us, but also to bless others. The Spirit should not leak out due to sin or spiritual laziness, but instead flow out in service, obedience, and prayer. As the Spirit of Love flows out from us with purpose, he also flows in replinishing our reserves.

Jesus said of the Holy Spirit, "Out of the believer's heart shall flow rivers of living water."[323] This is life in the Spirit, a life filled with Godly purpose day-in and day-out. We are to leave behind the old self and its fondness for sin and allow our minds and our lives to be renewed, constantly, by the Holy Spirit.

Stifling the Spirit concerns not only the Spirit's movement in our own lives, but also how our actions or inactions stifle the Spirit in others. The way we treat other people, through harshness, or controlling ways, or indifference can stifle the Spirit in them. In our friendships and associations, we can stifle the Spirit by engaging in sin and knowingly and unknowingly baiting one another to sin. It is sad how often friends do grave harm to one another by encouraging them to engage in some form of sin.

Moreover, the social, political, economic, and moral trends of society that are in conflict with God's love, stifle the Spirit. When we participate in these trends, consume these poisons, or support institutions that are awash in spiritual or moral decay, we are part of the problem. From entertainment to business, from politics to sports, countless unseen cultural forces regulate society, many of which have no concern for obeying the will of God.

---

[323] John 7:38 (NRSV). Cf. Isaiah 58:11.

Do Not Grieve the Holy Spirit. Sin not only stifles the Spirit, it grieves the Spirit. In the Old Testament, Isaiah describes how the people of Israel, by repeatedly disobeying God's Law, were in outright rebellion against God – and their rebellion, he told us, "grieved" the Holy Spirit.[324] That is why Paul instructed Christians in his day and us in our day, "[D]o not grieve the Holy Spirit."[325]

It is hard to imagine that the God who created the universe can be grieved by something we might do, given how small and insignificant each of us is in the scheme of the whole universe. Nevertheless, this is so because God loves us and his offer of love, by its nature, makes him vulnerable to sorrow. Just as parents are grieved when children reject them or when they hurt one another, it grieves God when we reject or ignore him, and when we reject, ignore, or hurt one another. We were created for love and purity, not sin and rebellion.

Do Not Lie to the Holy Spirit. One of the more shocking events of the early Church occurred when a married couple, Ananias and Sapphira, sold their farm and gave a portion of the proceeds to the Church. Yet when Ananias presented this gift to Peter, he pretended that it was the full proceeds. While he and his wife were under no obligation to give the full proceeds to the Church, because they lied by pretending to do so, they were each struck dead by God. Though they spoke the lie to Peter, they were struck dead for lying to the Holy Spirit. Peter asked Ananias immediately before he died, "[W]hy has Satan filled your heart to lie to the Holy Spirit?"[326]

Though the Holy Spirit very rarely punishes liars this way, we see in this event how grave this crime is from God's perspective. Each of us in our own way lies to the Holy Spirit whenever we deliberately choose the pathways of sin, thinking it is no big deal. When we do so, we are acting as if we are gods ourselves. It is a return to the primal sin of Adam and Eve.

Do Not Blaspheme the Holy Spirit. Jesus tells us, "[E]very sin and blasphemy will be forgiven men, but the blasphemy against the Spirit will not be forgiven . . . either in this age, or in the age to come."[327] Usually we think of blasphemy as a form of improper

---

[324] Cf. Isaiah 43:10.
[325] Ephesians 4:30 (NRSV).
[326] Acts 5:3 (NRSV).
[327] Matthew 12:31-32 (NIV). Cf. Mark 3:29, Luke 12:10.

speech, such as using God's name when we curse. Certainly, such speech is a sin and a form of blasphemy. However, it is not the unforgiveable sin of which Jesus refers.

As Pope John Paul II taught, blasphemy against the Holy Spirit "does not properly consist in offending against the Holy Spirit in words; it consists rather in the refusal to accept the salvation which God offers to man through the Holy Spirit, working through the power of the Cross. . . . [B]lasphemy against the Holy Spirit consists precisely in the radical refusal to accept [God's] forgiveness, of which he [the Holy Spirit] is the intimate giver . . . If Jesus says that blasphemy against the Holy Spirit cannot be forgiven either in this life or in the next, it is because this 'non-forgiveness' is linked, as to its cause, to 'non-repentance,' . . . to the radical refusal to be converted. . . . Blasphemy against the Holy Spirit, then, is the sin committed by the person who claims to have a 'right' to persist in evil – in any sin at all – and who thus rejects Redemption."[328]

Truly, there are no limits to God's mercy. But if we reject his mercy, if we refuse his love by choosing not to repent, if we chose not to follow Jesus as the Holy Spirit prompts us to do, we in effect reject God's gift of salvation.[329]

Your Body is a Temple of the Holy Spirit. Paul, in a teaching on sexual purity asks believers, "Do you not know that your body is a temple of the Holy Spirit within you, whom you have from God, and you are not your own? For you have been purchased at a price. Therefore glorify God in your body."[330] In his epistles, Paul teaches against the sexual sins that flourished in the Mediterranean cultures of his day – adultery, fornication, homosexuality, prostitution, and lust of the mind – all of which grieve the Holy Spirit and do harm to our spirit, soul, and body. To this list we could rightly add pornography which is an epidemic today. Paul exhorts believers to keep away from these sins because "the body is not for sexual immorality; it is for the Lord, and the Lord is for the body."[331]

Throughout the Bible, sexual immorality in its various forms is condemned. Over and over again, it appears as a sin that overcomes

---

[328] Pope John Paul II, DeV, section 46.
[329] Cf. CCC section 1864; Pope John Paul II, DeV, section 46.
[330] 1 Corinthians 6:19-20 (NAB).
[331] 1 Corinthians 6:13-14 (NJB).

people and cultures, filling their lives with darkness. Then and today, people rationalize the acceptability of their sexual sins, never realizing how deeply they offend God. When we pollute our bodies with sexual sin, we pollute the Temple meant to house God's Spirit. In the brokenness of our pride, we falsely justify our sins claiming unnatural desires to be natural or normal. As a result, we do much harm to ourselves and others.

Every sexual sin is a form of violence that does harm. Even our lustful thoughts cause harm (as do prideful, angry, or racist thoughts). The disordered sexual mores of our day (vividly promoted through movies, television, internet, music, etc.) do grave harm. Sex has become a means by which we *use* others for our own broken purposes. Using people, even if they consent and are using us back, causes harm – to them and to us. We are called to live lives that do no harm.

Our bodies and our sexuality are gifts of God, who breathes his Spirit upon us for his purposes of holiness. Our challenge is to respect the gift of our sexuality and use it in the manner God prescribes; and the only sexual activity that truly is natural is that which is an expression of love between a husband and wife in marriage. To joyfully live the chastity to which we are called, we need the Holy Spirit.

Come Holy Spirit. Thank you for the gift of life and the gift of human sexuality. Please forgive me for all the ways I have violated the Bible's commands regarding sexual purity. Please free me from all sexual sin and related lies. I beg you, please heal those areas of my heart and my memories wounded by sexual sin. Please cleanse the temple of my body – and the temple of my heart and mind – as only you can. Please restore my lost innocence. Please fill me with desires for true holiness and love.

Holy Spirit, you are a consuming fire. Please fill my heart with your fire. Please purify my heart and cleanse me from within. Direct my ways. Help me to serve the kingdom of God with a holy boldness and love. In Jesus' name I pray. Amen.

13 Gift of Eternal Salvation

Salvation is the gift of eternal life with God in heaven. It is the paradise meant for humanity from the beginning. It is to know the Father, and Jesus Christ his Son, with the Holy Spirit, in the fullness of their glory.[332] As Pope Benedict XVI put it, "God is heaven. He is our destination, the destination and the eternal dwelling place from which we come and for which we are striving."[333]

Salvation can rightly be seen as gift of each Person of the Blessed Trinity. It is a gift of the Father, who "so loved the world that he gave his only Son, so that everyone who believes in him may not perish but may have eternal life."[334] It is also gift of the Son, who voluntarily died on the Cross as a "ransom for all."[335] He died so that we might "have life, and have it to the full."[336] Salvation is also gift of the Spirit who is at work within us, guiding us in the ways of our conversion, sanctification, and salvation in and through Jesus. Paul tells us, "[I]f you sow to the Spirit, you will reap eternal life from the Spirit."[337]

As it concerns the gift of salvation, the work done to atone for humanity's sins was done, once for all, by Jesus on the Cross. No one of his own effort can ever merit or attain the reward of heaven.[338] We are saved not because of any righteous things we do, but by God's grace and mercy.[339] It is all gift from God.[340] Because of sin, we are unworthy of this gift, but by God's grace we are made worthy.[341] Nevertheless, we have a role to play in our own salvation. *We must accept the gift of salvation on the Giver's terms.* We must repent and believe in Jesus; we must be baptized and live the Christian faith.[342]

While in some sense, we can talk of salvation as a moment in time – focusing on when it begins with the indwelling of the Holy Spirit or

---

[332] Cf. John 17:3.
[333] Pope Benedict XVI, homily, August 15, 2008.
[334] John 3:16 (NRSV). Cf. John 3:14-15.
[335] 1 Timothy 2:6 (NAB).
[336] John 10:10 (NIV). Cf. John 17:2.
[337] Galatians 6:8 (NRSV). Cf. 2 Corinthians 13:4.
[338] Cf. Romans 9:32, 11:6.
[339] Cf. Acts 15:11, Romans 3:28, 9:16, Ephesians 2:8, 2 Timothy 1:9, Titus 3:5.
[340] Cf. Romans 6:23, Ephesians 2:8, Philippians 2:12.
[341] Cf. Colossians 1:12.
[342] Cf. Acts 2:38, 3:19, Psalm 51:1, John 3:5-8, 14-15, 6:47, 8:24, Hebrews 11:6; CCC section 161.

when, as adults, it begins in earnest as we repent of our sins and invite Jesus into our hearts as Lord. However, it is more appropriate to think of it as a journey through time. In this journey, the Holy Spirit is our guide. Paul expresses this thought when he exhorts Christians to "work out your own salvation with fear and trembling; for it is God who is at work in you, enabling you both to will and to work for his good pleasure."[343] This journey is a process of renewal whereby we come into the fullness of our salvation over time. Thus Peter tells us, "[Y]ou are receiving the goal of your faith, the salvation of your soul"[344] and later he encourages us to drink spiritual milk "so that . . . you may grow into salvation."[345] We "work out" or "grow into" our salvation by cooperating with the Spirit's sanctifying graces. For salvation comes "through sanctification by the Spirit and through belief in the truth."[346]

On more than one occasion, a follower of Jesus asked him the question: "What must I do to inherit eternal life?" To one disciple, Jesus said, "If you wish to enter into life, keep the commandments."[347] On another occasion, Jesus talked about the importance of loving God and loving one's neighbor.[348] These and many other scriptures speak to some aspect of salvation and the Final Judgment, providing many meaningful indications of God's message to humanity. The Scriptures emphasize repentance from sin,[349] faith in Jesus,[350] the Sacrament of Baptism,[351] good works, particularly for the benefit of the less fortunate,[352] obedience to God's commands,[353] sound moral conduct,[354] learning to be childlike,[355] calling on the name of Jesus,[356] and acknowledging Jesus before others.[357]

---

[343] Philippians 2:12-13 (NRSV). Cf. 1 Corinthians 1:18, 15:2-3.
[344] 1 Peter 1:9 (NIV).
[345] 1 Peter 2:2 (NAB). Cf. Acts 2:47.
[346] 2 Thessalonians 2:13 (NRSV). Cf. Romans 6:22.
[347] Matthew 19:17 (NAB). Cf. Mark 10:17-30, Luke 18:18-30.
[348] Cf. Luke 10:25-37.
[349] Cf. Mark 16:16, Acts 2:38.
[350] Cf. John 3:16, 18, 36, 6:40, 11:25-26.
[351] Cf. John 3:5, Mark 16:16, Acts 2:38, 1 Peter 3:20-21, Titus 3:5.
[352] Cf. Matthew 25:31-46, Luke 16:19-31, John 15:2, James 2:14-17.
[353] Cf. Matthew 7:21, 19:17, Romans 2:13, 2 Timothy 2:5, Hebrews 5:9.
[354] Cf. John 5:29, Romans 2:6, 2 Corinthians 5:10, Revelation 20:12-13.
[355] Cf. Mark 10:15.
[356] Cf. Acts 2:21, Romans 10:9.
[357] Cf. Luke 12:8-9.

As for the command to "repent and believe in the good news!"[358] – truly it is all encompassing. This may not seem so at first, because many Christians have an inadequate understanding of what it means to "believe in" or "have faith in" Jesus. Faith is all about holiness, all about relationship with Jesus through which the Holy Spirit flows into our lives, cleanses and renews us, teaches us obedience, and otherwise works through us for his good purposes. Such faith is by no means passive intellectual agreement with Christian teaching, but one that involves doing the will of the Father, doing the good works he has preordained as our way of life, and doing those works with love.

Perhaps the most common misunderstanding among Christians in regards to salvation is the belief that salvation is about being a good person by society's standard or one's own standard. This is a lie that does grave harm, stunting the spiritual growth of many. We are called to be good persons by heaven's standard, which is all about faith in Jesus, love of God, obedience to God's commands, and love of our neighbor. It is about holiness. It is a work of the Holy Spirit within us.

Falling Away from the Faith. As we walk the journey of faith, we are, in a sense, saved because we are on the journey; but it is more accurate to say, with Paul, that we are "working out our salvation."[359] For indeed, one can and many do turn away from the faith. In the parable of the sower and the seed, Jesus prophesied as much. For many receive the truths of God with enthusiasm, make a profession of faith, recite a sinner's prayer, and receive various sacraments only to later turn away. This is the seed that fell upon the rocky path or amid the thorns.[360] Practically speaking, those who fall away include those who disown the faith and choose a pathway of life purposefully denying God's sovereignty. Others, in an outward sort of way seem to stay in the faith, but on the inside they are lukewarm and faithless.

In his letter to Titus, Paul speaks of the Holy Spirit who God has poured out on believers "so that, having been justified by his grace, we might become heirs according to the hope of eternal life."[361] Why, when speaking to believers who have been "saved . . . through the washing of rebirth and renewal by the Holy Spirit,"[362] does Paul say

---

[358] Mark 1:5 (NIV).
[359] Cf. Philippians 2:12.
[360] Cf. Luke 8:5-15 (emphasis on verses 13 and 14).
[361] Titus 3:7 (NRSV).
[362] Titus 3:5 (NIV).

they "might" become heirs? Or similarly, in a letter to Timothy, when speaking again of believers, why does Paul speak of his ongoing ministry to them so that they "may" obtain salvation in Christ?[363] Because of the issue of backsliding, which he and other Biblical writers counsel against throughout the New Testament. In his other letters, Paul exhorts believers not to wander from the faith, not to return to their prior ways of sin, for if you do, "you will die; but if by the Spirit you put to death the misdeeds of the body, you will live."[364]

Peter counsels fellow Christians not to lose "the firm ground that you are standing on, [not to be] carried away by the errors of unprincipled people. Instead, continue to grow in the grace and in the knowledge of our Lord and Savior Jesus Christ."[365] Speaking of those who have backslid, he says, "If they have escaped the corruption of the world by knowing our Lord and Savior Jesus Christ and are again entangled in it and overcome, they are worse off at the end than they were at the beginning. It would have been better for them not to have known the way of righteousness than to have known it and then to turn their backs on the sacred command that was passed on to them."[366]

The writer of Hebrews, addressing fellow Christians who have endured much suffering for their faith, offers similar counsel: "[W]e must pay greater attention to what we have heard, so that we do not drift away from it."[367] For some "who have once been enlightened, who have tasted the heavenly gift, who have shared in the Holy Spirit, who have tasted the goodness of the word of God, and the powers of the coming age"[368] will fall way. When they do, "they are crucifying again the Son of God and are holding him up to contempt. . . . My soul takes no pleasure in anyone who shrinks back."[369] When Jesus comes again, he will "bring salvation to those who are waiting for him."[370] The writer of Hebrews goes on to say, we must not be like Esau, "who sold his birthright for a single meal."[371] *As baptized believers in Christ, heaven is our birthright; yet if we turn from Jesus and stop following him, then we in essence give up our birthright.*

---

[363] Cf. 2 Timothy 2:10.
[364] Romans 8:13 (NIV). Cf. Galatians 1:6-7, 3:1-5.
[365] 2 Peter 3:17-18 (NJB).
[366] 2 Peter 2:20-21 (NIV).
[367] Hebrews 2:1 (NRSV).
[368] Hebrews 6:4-5 (NIV). Cf. Hebrews 3:12-14, 10:26-29, 35-39.
[369] Hebrews 6:6, 10:38 (NRSV).
[370] Hebrews 9:28 (NIV).
[371] Hebrews 12:16 (NAB).

In Jesus' parable of the vine and the branches, we hear that the Father, the gardener, will cut off from Jesus, the vine, "every branch that does not bear fruit."[372] In this parable, Jesus emphasizes the importance of not backsliding. We must persevere in faith. We must remain in him. "Remain in me, and I will remain in you. . . . If anyone does not remain in me, he is like a branch that is thrown away and withers; such branches are picked up, thrown into the fire and burned."[373] Jesus' figurative language in his parables of the sower and the seed, the ten virgins, and the watchful servants similarly warn believers of the perils that befall those who fall away from the faith.

During Jesus' own ministry, after his bread of life discourse, many of his disciples fell away; they "returned to their former way of life and no longer accompanied him."[374] They, who once followed Jesus, changed their mind. This happened frequently in the early Church, in many of the communities established by Paul. This has continued down through the ages and is prevalent today. Paul tells us, "The Spirit has explicitly said that during the last times some will desert the faith and pay attention to deceitful spirits and doctrines that come from devils."[375]

In the Book of Revelation, Jesus describes backsliders as persons who have "abandoned the love [they] had at first."[376] Speaking to others whose faith had grown lukewarm, he says, "I know your works; I know that you are neither cold nor hot. . . . So, because you are lukewarm, neither hot nor cold, I will spit you out of my mouth."[377] In a private revelation to Saint Faustina, Jesus said about lukewarm souls, "These souls wound My Heart most painfully. My soul suffered the most dreadful loathing in the Garden of Olives because of lukewarm souls. They were the reason I cried out: *Father, take this cup away from Me, if it be Your will.* For them, the last hope of salvation is to flee to My mercy."[378]

Persevering in the Faith. The walk of salvation requires us to stand firm in our faith, to persevere and not backslide, not grow

---

[372] John 15:2 (NRSV).

[373] John 15:4, 6 (NRSV). Cf. 1 John 2:24-25.

[374] John 6:66 (NAB).

[375] 1 Timothy 4:1 (NJB). Cf. 2 Timothy 2:12, 4:3-4.

[376] Revelation 2:4 (NRSV).

[377] Revelation 3:16 (NIV).

[378] Sister Faustina, diary entry for August 1, 1937, section 1228. *Diary of Sister Maria Faustina Kowalska*, Marian Press, 2004, page 442.

lukewarm. Jesus expressed this thought when speaking of the final days. He taught that there will be an increase in wickedness and the love in most people will grow cold, "but he who stands firm to the end will be saved."[379] "By your endurance you will gain your souls."[380] "He who overcomes will inherit all this [the kingdom], and I will be his God and he will be my son."[381] We persevere only with the help of the Holy Spirit.

An often misunderstood scripture that has bearing on this discussion comes from St. Paul's letter to the Romans. It reads, "[I]f you confess with your mouth that Jesus is Lord and believe in your heart that God raised him from the dead, you will be saved."[382] Some Christians use this scripture to support a theory of salvation that suggests that all we have to do to be eternally saved is have a faith experience some time in our life where we proclaim Jesus is Lord. According to this theory, if we have such an experience, our names are irrevocably placed in the book of life. This theory, "once saved, always saved," denies the many scriptures concerning backsliding and perseverance that we discuss in this chapter, and it greatly narrows the definition of faith to a momentary experience that a person may or may not live our over the remainder of their life. This teaching leads to false assurances of salvation and, for some, to religious arrogance.

Every faith experience is important but the mere occurrence of one is not all that salvation requires. We must also persevere in faith, living it not only with words in insolated moments of fervent desire, but also with our lives. Those moments of profound repentance and turning to Jesus as Lord, whether in a sinners prayer or in the Sacrament of Reconciliation are new beginnings of salvation. Those moments, though, are not the end. We must persevere. If not, we may fall from grace and lose our salvation.[383]

Paul also promises us that nothing can separate us from the love of God in Christ.[384] This promise is directed toward believing Christians who are living out their faith. It essentially means that no

---

[379] Matthew 24:13 (NIV). Cf. Matthew 10:22, Mark 13:13, Luke 21:19, Hebrews 11:6, James 1:12, Revelation 2:5-7, 10-11, 16-17, 25-28, 3:5, 11-12, 20-21, 21:7; *Didache* (Teaching of the Apostles) 16:5.

[380] Luke 21:19 (NRSV).

[381] Revelation 21:7 (NIV).

[382] Romans 10:9 (NAB).

[383] Cf. Romans 2:4-11, 11:22, Galatians 5:4, Colossians 1:22-23.

[384] Cf. Romans 8:39.

outside force can steal our salvation, so long as we remain in Christ. The only threat to our salvation as believers is ourselves, if by an act of our will we turn from Jesus and choose lifestyles of sin.

To Christians living in Colossae, Paul exhorts believers that it is not enough to have "received Christ Jesus as Lord," but we must "continue to live in him."[385] Paul tells them, Jesus has "reconciled [you] . . . through his death, [so as] to present you holy, without blemish [to the Father] . . . provided that you persevere in the faith . . . not shifting from the hope of the gospel."[386]

Paul reminds Christians living in Rome of both the kindness and the severity of God: "severity toward those who fell [away], but God's kindness to you, provided you remain in his kindness; otherwise you too will be cut off."[387] He spoke similarly in other letters, encouraging Christians to hold fast to the Gospel through which they are being saved.[388] And he rebuked some in Galatia, "Having started with the Spirit, are you now ending with the flesh? Did you experience so much for nothing?"[389] "Let us not become weary in doing good, for at the proper time we will reap a harvest if we do not give up."[390]

The writer of Hebrews tells us "Christ is trustworthy as a son is, over his household. And we are his household, as long as we fearlessly maintain the hope in which we glory. . . . [W]e have been granted a share with Christ only if we keep the grasp of our first confidence firm to the end. . . . You need perseverance if you are to . . . gain what he has promised."[391]

These Biblical passages emphasizing perseverance are not meant to intimidate believers, but to present critical truths. Those of us who are purposefully following Jesus need not be frightened by these warnings, for in the midst of our sins, God's Mercy is reclaiming us.

---

[385] Colossians 2:6 (NIV).

[386] Colossians 1:22-23 (NAB).

[387] Romans 11:22 (NAB). Cf. Romans 2:4-8.

[388] Cf. 1 Corinthians 15:1-2, Philippians 2:12-14, 3:12-16, 4:1, Galatians 5:1-12, 6:7-9, 1 Timothy 4:15-16, 2 Timothy 2:5, 11-13.

[389] Galatians 3:3 (NRSV). Cf. Galatians 1:6-7, 2 Corinthians 6:1. It is also interesting to note Jesus' comments in Matthew 7:23 concerning those who had exercised charismatic gifts, but who apparently fell away from God in their hearts. On the day of Judgment they will hear Jesus say "I never knew you; go away from me you evildoers."

[390] Galatians 6:9 (NIV).

[391] Hebrews 3:6, 14, 10:36 (NJB). Cf. James 1:2-4, 12.

Even as we periodically fall, the Spirit tenderly picks us up, forgives us, and by his grace helps us along. So long as we are truly in Christ Jesus, there is no condemnation.[392] However, to those who do fall away from the faith, or never truly began it, or who are lukewarmly going through the motions, these are stern warnings indeed.

Warnings Against Self-Deception. In our Christian walk, one of the things each believer must guard against is self-deception. A common form of this is the self-assessment of our faith. Human beings are not able to measure faith, whether it is our own faith or someone else's faith. God alone can assess a person's faith, for God alone knows the heart of those he created.[393] Likewise, concerning matters of salvation, we are not to judge our own eternal fate or that of others. Whether it be of a glorifying nature (heaven) or a condemning nature (hell), we are not to judge anyone's eternal fate.

Paul says, not only does he not judge others, but "I do not even judge myself. I am not aware of anything against myself, but I am not thereby acquitted. It is the Lord who judges me. Therefore do not pronounce judgment before the time, before the Lord comes, who will bring to light the things now hidden in darkness and will disclose the purposes of the heart."[394] "I beat my body and make it my slave so that after I have preached to others, I myself will not be disqualified of the prize."[395]

"Not that I have secured it already, nor yet reached my goal, but I am still pursuing it in the attempt to take hold of the prize for which Christ Jesus took hold of me. Brothers, I do not reckon myself as having taken hold of it; I can only say that forgetting all that lies behind me, and straining forward to what lies in front, I am racing towards the finishing-point to win the prize of God's heavenly call in Christ Jesus. So this is the way in which all of us who are mature should be thinking, and if you are still thinking differently in any way, then God has yet to make this matter clear to you."[396]

---

[392] Cf. Romans 8:1.

[393] Cf. 1 Samuel 16:7, 1 Kings 8:39, 2 Chronicles 6:30, Proverbs 21:2, 44:21, Jeremiah 17:9-10, 20:12, Revelation 2:23.

[394] 1 Corinthians 4:3-5 (NRSV). Cf. 1 Corinthians 9:16, 2 Corinthians 10:18, Romans 2:16; CCC section 678.

[395] 1 Corinthians 9:27 (NIV).

[396] Philippians 3:12-15 (NJB).

A practical application of this teaching concerns the death of our loved ones. It is right for us to hope for their salvation, but we truly do not know their fate. It may comfort us psychologically or emotionally to think of them as in heaven, but truly we do not know that. Only God can render these judgments.

Faith and Works. Most certainly, the Bible gives us powerful insights about matters of faith and salvation to guide our journey. Jesus connects these themes with love of neighbor making it clear that faith requires works.[397] Such works, of themselves, do not save us.[398] Yet when we engage in good works in loving obedience to God, those works are part and parcel of our faith, which does save us.

In the Book of James we are told, "What good is it my brothers, if someone says he has faith but does not have works? Can that faith save him? . . . [A] person is justified by works and not by faith alone . . . For just as a body without a spirit is dead, so also faith without works is dead."[399] The faith James rebukes is a false form of faith; he rebukes a faith that is nothing more than religious pride or the mere intellectual agreement with doctrines. Such false forms of faith lack an interior movement of the heart toward a living, loving, and obedient relationship with God.

In regards to the Final Judgment, Jesus taught that the Son of Man will divide humanity much as a sheepherder, at the end of the day, divides the sheep from the goats.[400] The sheep are those bound for heaven and the goats for hell. Jesus describes the sheep as those who, by their works, showed kindness to the Son of Man, giving him clothing, food, shelter, etc. The goats are those who, by their lack of works, showed contempt for the Son of Man denying him these things. When did the sheep do that for Jesus? When did the goats deny that to Jesus? Whenever they gave it or denied it to the least of humanity.

Here, we must pause and note a major difference between Catholic and some Protestant understandings of salvation. Some Protestant groups derive their teachings of salvation from the theories of Martin Luther. They point to this assertion of Luther, "Before all things, bear in mind . . . that faith alone without works, justifies, sets

---

[397] Cf. Luke 10:25-37, 16:19-31.
[398] Cf. Galatians 2:16, Romans 3:20.
[399] James 2:14, 24, 26 (NAB). Cf. Matthew 7:19-23.
[400] Cf. Matthew 25:31-46. See also James 2:14-17.

free, and saves."[401] In his German translation of the Bible, Luther added to the text of Romans 3:28 the word *"allein"* – in English "alone" – to make the text read *"a person is justified by faith alone"* – changing the meaning of the text. Obviously, Luther's personal views are in direct conflict with what the Holy Spirit proclaims through the Book of James (as well as Jesus' parable of the sheep and goats). Thus, to bolster his theories on salvation and other matters, Luther removed the Book of James from the canon of the Lutheran Bible along with Hebrews, Jude, Revelation, and seven Old Testament books.[402]

Predestination. Another significant difference between Catholic and some Protestant understandings of salvation concerns the topic of predestination. John Calvin, another major Protestant reformer, believed that before all time, God issued an unchangeable decree whereby he predetermined those humans who would be saved. To them, Calvin believed, God gave irresistible graces to accept him by faith. Everyone else, he believed, God predestined for hell. Said Calvin, "[S]alvation is freely offered to some while others are barred from access to it. . . . We call predestination God's eternal decree, by which he determined with himself what he willed to become of each man. For all are not created in equal condition; rather, eternal life is foreordained for some, eternal damnation for others."[403]

Calvin's theory of predestination conflicts with Biblical revelation that tells us, "God . . . wills everyone to be saved and to come to knowledge of the truth."[404] God does not want "any to perish, but all to come to repentance."[405] Jesus died on the cross as a "ransom for all."[406] Thus, the Catholic Church teaches, "God predestines no one to go to hell."[407] To suggest that God, from before Creation, rejected some of his creatures and foreordained them for damnation, attributes to God characteristics inconsistent with his nature, which is love. Hell is

---

[401] Cf. Luther, Martin, *On Christian Liberty*; Wace, Henry and Buchheim, C.A., ed., *Luther's Primary Works*, Hodder and Stoughton, 1896, page 260.

[402] After Luther 's death, Lutherans restored the four New Testament books to their canon, but not the seven Old Testament books (Tobit, Judith, 1&2 Maccabees, Wisdom, Sirach, and Baruch).

[403] John Calvin, *Institutes of the Christian Religion*, translated by Fred Lewis Battles, The Westminster Press, 1960, (Book III, chapter 21), pages 921, 926.

[404] 1 Timothy 2:4 (NAB). Cf. Titus 2:11.

[405] 2 Peter 3:9 (NSRV).

[406] 1 Timothy 2:6 (NAB). Cf. John 3:17.

[407] CCC section 1037. Cf. Council of Orange II (529): DS 397; Council of Trent (1547): 1567.

indeed a reality and there is a Final Judgment, which we will discuss in the next chapter, but God did not create any of us with hell in mind.

So then, what does St. Paul mean when he refers to predestination in his letters to the Romans and Ephesians?[408] In those letters, he refers to an eternal mystery stemming from both God's sovereignty and his omnipotence. In Creation, God has a purpose and plan for every created being. It is God's desire that everyone be saved. Yet, in giving us freewill, God knows that some of us will reject him. Though God did not create any of us for the purpose of hell, he foreknows that many in rejecting him, will choose that fate. He also foreknows that some will choose him and receive heaven's reward. Foreknowledge (what God knows in advance) and foreordination (what God determines unto himself in advance) are not the same thing.

But Am I Saved? There is a natural desire to want to know the unknown. Everyone would like to have his or her salvation ticket punched in advance. However, the trusting servant and the loving child does not ask such questions. Rather, he trusts. He obeys. He loves. He serves. She trusts. She obeys. She loves. She serves. As Christians, we take confidence in Jesus' victory on the Cross, which is our doorway to everlasting life. However, we must strive to live a faith-filled life whereby we walk through that doorway and not just talk about it. The gift of salvation is not for talkers, but for doers. For, as Jesus taught, the kingdom of God is open to "the one who does the will of my Father in heaven."[409] Jesus became "the source of eternal salvation for all who obey him."[410]

But am I saved? If I die tonight, do I know that I am bound for heaven? Like Paul, we must not seek judgments before their time.[411] Yet we need not panic. Instead, we must rest with confidence in the assurances of our faith, such confidence coming to us not from religious arguments but instead as a fruit of the Spirit's work in our lives. The Apostle John tells us that as we live in God's love, that love is brought to perfection in us, giving us "confidence on the day of judgment, because we are like him [Jesus]."[412] This assurance is not knowing the eternal judgment of God in advance, which as Paul told us

---

[408] Cf. Romans 8:28-30, Ephesians 1:3-6.
[409] Matthew 7:21 (NAB).
[410] Hebrews 5:9 (NAB).
[411] Cf. 1 Corinthians 4:3-5, Philippians 3:12-15.
[412] 1 John 4:17 (NIV). Similarly, Paul talks of a "confident hope" in Galatians 5:6.

we cannot know until that day. Instead, it is an intimate knowing and experiencing of God's love in our present lives that comforts us until that day. Toward the end of his own life, filled with such assurance, Paul talked of having "finished the race" and having "kept the faith" and awaiting the "crown of righteousness."[413]

What About People Who Never Heard of Jesus? It is common to wonder about the eternal fate of unborn babies, or small children who die never knowing Jesus, or persons who are mentally disabled, or who grew up in a society that had no Christians. The Catholic Church teaches that while faith is necessary for salvation, for persons who never come to know the Gospel of Christ, but they nevertheless seek God and his eternal truths with a sincere heart, and they do so moved by God's grace working through their consciences, they too may experience eternal salvation.[414] "God can lead those who, through no fault of their own, are ignorant of the Gospel, to that faith without which it is impossible to please him."[415] The Catholic Church hopes and prays for the eternal salvation of these and all persons, which comes *only* by way of Jesus' sacrifice on the Cross.

A Biblical basis for this hope comes first from Paul's teaching on the Final Judgment. Concerning those who never heard the Gospel or God's Law, yet had the Law written on their hearts. They will be judged by their compliance with that Law. Said Paul, "[I]t is not those who hear the law who are righteous in God's sight, but it is those who obey the law who will be declared righteous. Indeed, when Gentiles, who do not have the law, do by nature things required by the law, they are a law for themselves . . . since they show that the requirements of the law are written on their hearts."[416]

There is also the story of Cornelius, a Roman Centurion. Before he converted to Christianity, he was a pagan who nevertheless feared God. He prayed daily, lived an upright life, and was generous in his almsgiving. The Bible tells us that God heard his prayers.[417] Peter,

---

[413] Cf. 2 Timothy 4:7-8.
[414] Cf. Second Vatican Council, LG, section 16; CCC section 847; Romans 2:12-16, 1 Timothy 4:10, Hebrews 11:6; Martin, Ralph, *Is Jesus Coming Soon?*, Ignatius Press, 1997, pages 114-118.
[415] Second Vatican Council, AG, section 7 as quoted in CCC section 848. See also CCC 1260 concerning the fruits of Baptism in the life of those ignorant of the Gospel.
[416] Romans 2:13-15 (NIV).
[417] Cf. Acts 10:4.

upon meeting Cornelius and seeing the Holy Spirit come upon Cornelius as he heard the Gospel, exclaimed, "I truly understand that God shows no partiality, but in every nation anyone who fears him and does what is right is acceptable to him."[418] Of course, doing "what is right" involves acknowledging Jesus as Lord and seeking baptism when one hears the Gospel, which is what Cornelius did.

Dear God: Father, Son, and Holy Spirit. Thank you for the gift of life as I know it now. Thank you, as well, for the opportunity to enjoy eternal life with you in heaven. You offer me the gift of salvation on your terms – through faith in Jesus – an active faith, founded on a trusting relationship with you, prayer, obedience, and holy works.

Jesus, I profess to you now, with words from my own heart, that I believe you are the Son of God. You are the King of kings and the Lord of lords. You are Israel's long-awaited Messiah. You are worthy of praise. You are my Savior. I wish to be your disciple.

Holy Spirit, by your grace, may I henceforth boldly live the Christian faith with integrity. Please strengthen me. Help me to know Jesus, love him, and serve him as I ought. Help me to persevere in faith to the Day of Judgment with a loving joy in my heart, whatever trials and tribulations may come. Help me to be an extension of your love and kindness to other people. In Jesus' name I pray. Amen.

---

[418] Acts 10:34-35 (NRSV).

14 Final Things

Whether we give much attention to it or not, there are definite spiritual realities connected with the expressions: death, resurrection of the dead, the Final Judgment, heaven, hell, purgatory, and prayers for the dead. Let us explore these realities through the lens of our primary topic, the Holy Spirit.

Physical Death. With the exception of those alive at Jesus' Second Coming, all other human beings will die a physical death. Whether due to old age, cancer, a heart attack, an accident, war, disease, or malnutrition, our bodies will cease to function. At that moment, our spirit and soul will separate from our body.[419] While the body decays, the spirit and soul depart to await the Final Judgment. The Holy Spirit, who gave us life and who sustains us in life, will sustain our spirit and soul after death. Of the intermediate experience from physical death to the resurrection of the dead, little is known. Paul refers to this period as a time of sleeping.[420]

Resurrection of the Dead. At the end of the present age, all the dead will rise for the Final Judgment: those who have done good will rise to eternal life with God in heaven, and all others to final damnation.[421] The Bible mentions two resurrections: one at the end of time, associated with the Final Judgment[422] and an earlier resurrection of holy martyrs who participate in Jesus' millennial reign.[423]

---

[419] Cf. CCC section 366.

[420] Cf. 1 Thessalonians 4:13. See also John 11:11.

[421] Cf. John 5:28-29, Acts 24:15, Matthew 16:27, 25:31-32, 46, Daniel 12:2; CCC sections 998, 1038.

[422] Cf. John 5:28-29, Acts 24:15, Isaiah 26:9.

[423] Cf. Revelation 20:4-6. The Bible speaks very little of Jesus' millennial reign. What we know comes mainly from the 20th chapter of the Book of Revelation. During Jesus' millennial reign, Satan will be restrained by God, locked in an abyss (20:1-3). Jesus, with the assistance of certain holy martyrs, will reign together (20:4-6). Toward the end of this reign, Satan will be temporary released from imprisonment and wreak havoc upon the earth; this period of upheaval is the Tribulation (20:7-8). Satan will then be cast into the lake of fire (20:10). Then comes the resurrection of the dead and the Final Judgment (20:11-15). Jesus' Second Coming is not mentioned in this discussion of the millennial reign. Other scriptures place his Second Coming with the resurrection of the dead and the Final Judgment (Matthew 25:31-46, Mark 13:26, 1 Corinthians 15:23, 2 Thessalonians 2:8). The term "rapture" is used to refer to the rising of the saints to meet Jesus in the sky upon his return (cf. 1 Thess. 4:16-17). When this rapture occurs is a matter of dispute.

The raising of the dead is a ministry of the Holy Spirit. Paul tells us, "If the Spirit of him who raised Jesus from the dead dwells in you, he who raised Christ from the dead will give life to your mortal bodies also through his Spirit that dwells in you."[424] That resurrection will re-unite our spirit and soul with our resurrected body.[425] At the

There have been different theories on whether the millennial reign occurs before or after Jesus' Second Coming; whether it will last exactly 1,000 years or merely a long period of time; whether Jesus will reign on earth or from heaven during this period, and whether the millennial reign is presently occurring or is a future event. The Catholic Church has not issued a definitive interpretation on the millennial reign. Among Christians, there are three predominant theories for this reign.

The first theory is *premillennialism*. A version of this theory was popular in the 2nd and 3rd centuries, and was supported by St. Justin Martyr. Pursuant to this theory, the millennial reign is a future event here on earth, after Jesus' Second Coming. Then, after 1,000 years of Jesus reigning, comes the Tribulation, Final Judgment, and Jesus' eternal reign. Some versions of this theory place the Tribulation before the millennial reign. (Note, Revelation 20:1-8 places the Tribulation at the end of the millennial reign). A variant of this theory, developed by Rev. John Darby in the 1830s, involves a pre-Tribulation rapture associated with a second coming of Jesus in which he takes believers to heaven. Those left behind have to endure the Tribulation. Later, there is a third coming of Jesus and another rapture and then the Final Judgment. The Catholic Church rejects millennial theories that suggest Jesus will return to rule over a fallen earth; or that his Second Coming relates to anything other than the end of the ages (cf. CCC 676).

The second theory is *postmillennialism*. Pursuant to this theory, the millennial reign begins after the whole earth has been Christianized. As Christianity spreads, the forces of Satan are slowly defeated. Jesus will reign through his Church. It will be a period of peace, Christian unity, and virtue. Tertullian in the 3rd century, John Calvin in the Protestant Reformation, the Pilgrims of Plymouth Rock, and the 19th century revivalist Jonathan Edwards supported versions of this theory. They believed works of evangelization and social justice helped to usher in this reign. After this reign came Jesus' Second Coming and the Final Judgment.

The third theory is *amillennialism*. St. Augustine championed this theory in his work *City of God* (Book 20, section 9). Pursuant to this theory, the millennial reign is occurring now; it represents the span of history from Jesus' first coming to his Second Coming. Jesus reigns, by the power of the Holy Spirit, through the Church and through the lives of all believers – *I am with you always* (Mt 28:20). Here "the Church" refers to all of Christendom and not one denomination; it includes the grace of the sacraments, Bible study, preaching, prayer, works of social justice, etc. At the end of this reign comes the Tribulation, Jesus' Second Coming, the rapture of the Church, the Final Judgment, and Jesus' eternal reign.

If the millennial reign is presently occurring, the holy martyrs reigning with Jesus in heaven likely include those saints formally recognized by the Catholic Church. To these saints, we can pray and ask for assistance. Moreover, all active Christians are in some sense among the resurrected saints (Cf. Ephesians 2:6). We are resurrected through baptism and faith in Jesus. We reign with Christ even now.

[424] Romans 8:11 (NRSV). Cf. 1 Corinthians 15:42-49, 2 Corinthians 4:14, Philippians 3:10-11, 1 Thessalonians 4:14; CCC sections 988-1019.
[425] Cf. CCC sections 366, 997.

resurrection of the dead, it is not clear in what sense our resurrected bodies will be similar to our present earthly bodies. For those bound for heaven, what little we might speculate concerning our resurrected bodies begins with the Transfiguration. When Moses and Elijah appeared to Jesus, their bodies were visibly human. Then, on Easter morning, when Jesus appeared at the tomb and on the road to Emmaus, his body was also visibly human. And yet people very close to Jesus did not recognize him. Later that day, when Jesus appeared to ten of the Apostles, they did recognize him.

These encounters suggest that our resurrected bodies will be human, but they may look different from our current bodies.[426] It may also be safe to say that the resurrected bodies of God's saints will be free from disease, disability, and defects – more healthy and more beautiful than ever before. St. Augustine speculated that regardless of how young or old we were at death, at the resurrection, our bodies will appear to be about thirty years of age.[427]

During his resurrection appearances, Jesus walked about, ate food, drank liquids, and held conversations as we presently do. Perhaps that will be the same for us, only without sin and its ill effects. Perhaps it will be as it was for Adam and Eve before the fall – a time filled with innocence, joy, and peace with God.

Jesus said, at the resurrection, the saints will "neither marry nor be given in marriage; they will be like the angels in heaven."[428] We will not be like the angels in a physical sense, for we will have bodies and they do not. Instead, like them, we will be in the presence and peace of God, in unbroken fellowship with our Creator and fellow creatures.

The Final Judgment. There is a day of reckoning when Jesus will return to earth in glory "to judge the living and the dead,"[429] the just and the unjust.[430] No one can escape this judgment, which the Father has entrusted to Jesus.[431] Jesus said of himself, "I am the one who searches minds and hearts, and I will give to each of you as your works deserve."[432] At that time, "God will bring every deed into judgment,

---

[426] Cf. Luke 24:15-16, John 20:14-15; CCC section 999.
[427] Cf. St. Augustine, *City of God*, Book XXII.
[428] Mark 12:25 (NIV). Cf. Luke 20:36-36.
[429] Apostles Creed. Cf. John 5:22, 27, 9:39, Acts 10:42, 2 Timothy 4:1.
[430] Cf. Matthew 25:46, Acts 24:15, Daniel 12:2; CCC sections 1038-1041.
[431] Cf. John 5:22, 27, Matthew 16:27, 25:31, Acts 10:42, 17:31, 2 Corinthians 5:10.
[432] Revelation 2:23 (NRSV). Cf. CCC sections 678-682, 1039.

including every hidden thing, whether it is good or evil."[433] People often speak of this coming period as the "end times." However, we are in the end times now. The end times began with Jesus' first coming; his Second Coming will bring the end times to a close.

As to the timing of the Final Judgment, only the Father knows the day and hour.[434] When that time comes, God will reveal the ultimate meaning of Creation and his plan of salvation, and how by the Holy Spirit, he led his people throughout salvation history toward their final end in him.[435] Some will enjoy the eternal reward of heaven and others the eternal punishment of hell.[436] This time of judgment will not be a time to plead our case or offer excuses, but instead it will be a time for the Spirit to reveal with clarity the meaning and consequences of our various choices in life – most critically, our choices to follow Jesus or not. There is no repentance after death.[437] At death, the eternal fate of our soul is set, to heaven or to hell – often referred to as our "particular judgment."[438]

Heaven. Jesus tells us "eternal life is this: to know [the Father], the only true God, and Jesus Christ whom [the Father] sent."[439] That knowledge is born of our experience of God, with him and in him – wonderfully aware of his goodness, free from the ill effects of sin. Heaven is a never-ending "wow" experience of God. It is an eternal sharing of God's glory with all his angels and saints, united in love. It is an eternal gaze upon the glory that created the universe, from within that glory. "No eye has seen, no ear has heard, no mind has conceived what God has prepared for those who love him."[440]

Heaven is the New Jerusalem, the City of God, prepared for all who are loyal to God.[441] It is where God will dwell with humanity face-to-face and his saints will be completely pure, holy, and without blemish. The Holy Spirit will perpetually light this city and his grace

---

[433] Ecclesiastes 12:14 (NIV). Cf. Matthew 16:27, 25:31-46, Luke 12:2-3, John 5:26-30, Revelation 20:12-13, 22:12, Romans 2:6-8, 1 Corinthians 3:8, 12-13, 2 Corinthians 5:10, Colossians 3:25, Ephesians 5:1-5, Galatians 6:7-9, Psalm 62:12, Sirach 16:12-14, Jeremiah 17:10, 21:14, 32:19, Ezekiel 18:20.

[434] Cf. Matthew 24:36, Acts 1:7.

[435] Cf. CCC section 1040.

[436] Cf. Daniel 12:2, Matthew 25:31-46, John 5:28-29.

[437] Cf. Hebrews 9:27; CCC section 393.

[438] Cf. CCC section 1051.

[439] John 17:3 (NJB). Cf. CCC sections 1023-1029.

[440] 1 Corinthians 2:9 (NIV).

[441] Cf. Hebrews 12:22, Revelation 3:12, 21:2, 10, Galatians 4:26.

will flow through the city as a river of living water.[442] God will be "all in all"[443] and the universe will be restored to its original grandeur.[444]

Hell. As for those who reject the good news of Jesus, they will experience a consequence the Bible calls "hell." Jesus spoke of hell as eternal punishment, God's wrath, a second death, unquenchable fire, fire and brimstone, a place with much wailing, weeping, and the gnashing of teeth.[445]

St. Paul tells us that when Jesus comes "from heaven with his mighty angels, in blazing fire, [he will inflict] punishment on those who do not acknowledge God and on those who do not obey the gospel of our Lord Jesus. These will pay the penalty of eternal ruin, separated from the presence of the Lord and from the glory of his power."[446]

Jesus and Paul tell us that among the persons consigned to hell will be those indifferent to the plight of the poor, cowards, those who worshipped false gods, misers, murders, the sexually immoral (who regularly practiced adultery, fornication, homosexuality, or lust), those who participated in the occult, thieves, drunkards, those caught up in arguments, rivalries, and factions.[447] From this list, one that could be the most unsettling is "cowards." Who are the cowards sent to hell? Perhaps, they are Christians who weakly went along with the worldly culture of their day and did not acknowledge Jesus before others. They called themselves Christians, but their hearts went astray from him. They choose a life of disobedience and did not worship the Lord.[448]

The Catholic Church teaches, "The chief punishment of hell is eternal separation from God, in whom alone man can possess the life and happiness for which he was created and for which he longs."[449] Those in hell will experience the Spirit not as Love, but as the judgment of the One they rejected in this life. Their rejection of God in this life is their "self-selection" of hell in the next life.

---

[442] Cf. Revelation chapters 21 and 22.

[443] Cf. 1 Corinthians 5:28; CCC section 1050.

[444] Cf. CCC section 1047.

[445] Cf. Matthew 5:22, 29, 8:12, 13:41-42, 49-50; 18:9, 22:13; 24:51, 25:30, 41, Mark 9:43-48, Luke 13:28, 16:24. See also Deuteronomy 32:22, Psalm 21:10, 112:10, Judith 16:17, Isaiah 66:24, Romans 2:8-9, 2 Thessalonians 1:9, 2:12, 2 Peter 3:7, Jude 1:7, Revelation 20:14, 21:8.

[446] 2 Thessalonians 1:7-9 (NAB).

[447] Cf. Matthew 25:41-46, Revelation 21:8, 1 Corinthians 6:9-10, Galatians 5:19-21.

[448] Cf. Psalm 95:10-11, Hebrews 4.

[449] CCC section 1035. Cf. 2 Thessalonians 1:9.

Purgatory. The Catholic Church teaches that, "All who die in God's grace and friendship, but still imperfectly purified, are indeed assured of their eternal salvation; but after death they undergo purification, so as to achieve the holiness necessary to enter the joy of heaven. The Church gives the name *Purgatory* to this final purification of the elect."[450] Purgatory is not a second chance to be saved as some may suggest; nor is it a mini-hell. Instead, it is a process of purification that prepares already saved souls for entry into heaven.

The experience of Purgatory may indeed be painful, yet it is nevertheless a positive experience, for in it the Spirit purges from us all remaining vestiges of sin and infuses us with grace. The Scriptures that have guided the Church's understanding of this process include Jesus' words in the Book of Revelation that "nothing impure will ever enter [heaven], nor anyone who does that which is shameful or deceitful, but only those whose names are written in the Lamb's book of life."[451] *Nothing impure, that is to say, nothing unholy, will enter heaven.* The writer of Hebrews similarly tells us, "Pursue . . . the holiness without which no one will see the Lord."[452]

Yet most of God's saints, at death, are in many respects "impure" or "unholy." They are all holy in the sense that they are set apart, by faith, as children of God. However, that holiness is not yet perfected. While past sins may have been forgiven, most believers die still having an affection for certain sins. It is through the purifying flames of God's Judgment that the Holy Spirit removes our affections for sin.

Paul mentions the purifying flames of God's Judgment when he teaches, "If any man builds on this foundation [of faith] using gold, silver, costly stones, wood, hay or straw, his work will be shown for what it is, because the Day [of Judgment] will bring it to light. It will be revealed with fire, and the fire will test the quality of each man's work. If what he has built survives, he will receive his reward. If it is burned up, he will suffer loss; he himself will be saved, but only as one escaping through flames."[453] The prophet Malachi also spoke of a refiner's fire purifying God's people on the Day of Judgment.[454]

---

[450] CCC sections 1030, 1031.

[451] Revelation 21:27 (NIV). Cf. Isaiah 35:8-10.

[452] Hebrews 12:14 (NRSV).

[453] 1 Corinthians 3:12-15 (NIV). Cf. Wisdom 3:5-7.

[454] Cf. Malachi 2:17-3:5, 4:1-3. Zechariah and the psalmist use similar language to describe a purification of a God's people while they are still on earth (Zechariah

Those saints and mystics who have received special revelations of Purgatory (including saints Gertrude of Helfta, Catherine of Genoa, Faustina Kowalska of Poland, and Padre Pio), teach that although Purgatory is a positive experience that prepares souls for heaven, it is nevertheless not an enjoyable experience. All who experience Purgatory will, as Paul suggests, "suffer loss." This loss is the final purging of our spiritual imperfections. In a private revelation to Sister Faustina, Jesus said of Purgatory, "My mercy does not want this, but justice demands it."[455] We lessen the need for this purification by pursuing holiness in the present life. The wise heed this warning and pursue greater holiness now.

Prayers for the Dead. The Catholic Church's practice of praying for the dead follows an ancient Jewish practice of praying for the dead. The most celebrated of Jewish prayers for the dead is the *Kaddish*, a Hebrew term which means "to make holy." This prayer praises God and is offered for the benefit of a deceased person.[456] There is also a prayer called the *Yizkor*, which is recited by Jewish congregations four times a year (on *Yom Kippur* and on the last day of *Sukkot*, *Passover*, and *Shavuot*) for the benefit of deceased relatives.[457]

It should be noted, there is no explicit Biblical command instructing believers to pray for the dead. Similarly, there is no Biblical command forbidding the practice. Yet, in three accounts, the Bible favorably refers to this practice. The first of these is a statement by the Archangel Raphael that God heard the prayers of Tobit, which he offered when he buried the dead.[458]

The second of these instances concerned certain Israelites who had fallen in battle against a Syrian army, around the year 165 BC. Judas Maccabees, their leader, came to mourn their deaths and realized that they were wearing idolatrous tokens. Judas and his men prayed for

---

13:9, Psalm 12:6, 66:10). See also Wisdom 3:5-7, Isaiah 4:3-4, Job 23:10, 1 Peter 1:6-7.

[455] Sister Faustina, *Diary of Sister Maria Faustina Kowalska*, Marian Press, 2004, entry 20.

[456] Cf. Sanhedrin 104a; Telushkin, Rabbi Joseph, *Jewish Literacy*, William Morrow and Company, 2001, pages 696-697. Rabbi Akiva, a prominent Jewish leader from the first century AD, composed the *Kaddish* after having what he understood to be a prophetic vision of a person's soul undergoing the pains of the Final Judgment. The soul spoke to Rabbi Akiva and asked for prayers.

[457] Telushkin, Rabbi Joseph, *Jewish Literacy*, William Morrow and Co., 2001, pg 697.

[458] Cf. Tobit 12:12.

the dead soldiers asking God to forgive their sins. Moreover, Judas took up a collection and sent moneys to Jerusalem to provide for a sin offering. In so doing, the Bible tells us, Judas "acted very well and honorably, taking account of the resurrection."[459]

The third Biblical reference is from Paul's second letter to Timothy. Paul offers a prayer for a friend, Onesiphorus, who appears to have died: "May the Lord grant that he will find mercy from the Lord on that Day [of Judgment]."[460] Elsewhere in that letter, Paul offers condolences for Onesiphorus' family.[461]

The Bible also records prayers for the dead offered by Elijah, Elisha, Jesus, Peter, and Paul that resulted in a deceased person coming back to life.[462] Granted, these prayers had a purpose differing from those that seek mercy in the Final Judgment; yet, they do indicate that God hears the prayers we offer for persons who have died. This is relevant to the role of the Holy Spirit, because if such prayers are righteous before God, then the Holy Spirit, who is the Artisan of Prayer, is present and operative in those prayers. Attitudes of the flesh that resist such prayers or teach against them stifle the Spirit's work.

Dear Holy Spirit, Thank you for the revelation of various truths concerning final things. I wish to experience more than this life. I wish to experience life-eternal with you in heaven. Please continue your good work of sanctification within me so that I may enter heaven one day pure and holy. Thank you for the gift of Purgatory. I pray that your purifying efforts within me come to completion in this life making Purgatory unnecessary for me. But if I need it, I am glad it is there. For all the souls in Purgatory, and for my family and friends who have preceded me in death, I pray for mercy on the day of Judgment. In Jesus' name I pray, Amen.

---

[459] 2 Maccabees 12:43 (NRSV). Cf. 2 Maccabees 12:44-46.
[460] 2 Timothy 1:18 (NIV).
[461] Cf. 2 Timothy 1:16, 4:19.
[462] Cf. 1 Kings 17:17-24, 2 Kings 4:32-35, John 11:38-44, Acts 9:36-43, 20:7-12.

Holy Spirit's Sacramental Grace

Go into the whole world and proclaim the gospel to every creature. Whoever believes and is baptized will be saved.

Mark 16:15-16 (NAB)

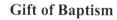

15   **Gift of Baptism**

The work of the Holy Spirit in our lives is always about grace. God's grace, in all its many forms, we ought to desire and appreciate. This is most certainly true of God's sacramental graces. As Pope Benedict XVI taught, "All the sacraments, each in its own way, communicate divine life to human beings, thanks to the Holy Spirit who works within them."[463] Through the sacraments, the Spirit frees souls from spiritual and moral bondage, provides inner healing, and builds souls up in holiness and strength.

The seven sacraments of the Catholic Church are Baptism, Holy Eucharist, Reconciliation, Confirmation, Anointing of the Sick, Holy Orders, and Holy Matrimony. With each sacrament, there is an "epiclesis" – a prayer that calls for the action of the Holy Spirit. Pope John Paul II taught, "The Holy Spirit is . . . the source and principle of the sacramental life through which the Church draws the strength of Christ, participates in his holiness, is nourished by his grace, and grows and advances on her journey towards eternity. The Holy Spirit . . . is the living source of all the sacraments."[464]

Each sacrament is a gift of God. These portals of grace are critical aids in our spiritual journeys. Celebrated worthily, each is an opportunity to experience the presence and action of the Holy Spirit. When we celebrate a sacrament unworthily (by going through the motions, or lacking faith, or lacking any real desire for holiness), the sacrament yields no benefit to us. Thus, it is important that a vibrant preaching of God's Word accompany each sacrament, which the Spirit uses to build up our faith, helping dispose our hearts to worthily receive the grace offered.[465]

The sacramental life begins with Baptism. The Bible's first mention of baptism is in reference to the ministry of John the Baptist. John was the last prophet of the Old Covenant. He was God's anointed herald who went before Jesus preparing his way. John's baptismal ministry involved immersion into water, as persons repented of their sins. Each recipient received God's forgiveness. The Bible tells us that those persons who received John's baptism and later encountered Jesus

---

[463] Pope Benedict XVI, homily, June 12, 2011. Cf. CCC sections 1116, 1129.

[464] Pope John Paul II, GA, January 30, 1991, section 1.

[465] Cf. CCC section 1133; Pope John Paul II, GA, April 21 1993, section 4. See also Galatians 6:7.

were able to grasp the truths Jesus proclaimed. Conversely, those who refused John's baptism and later encountered Jesus rejected Jesus.[466]

During his public ministry, Jesus also had a baptismal ministry. The Bible mentions it, but says little about it other than that it occurred and Jesus' disciples were the ones actually baptizing people.[467] How similar this baptism was to John's baptism or the Sacrament of Baptism in the era of the Church is not known to us.

Jesus instituted the Sacrament of Baptism, as a normal practice in the Church, shortly before his ascension into heaven. He commanded his Apostles saying, "[G]o and make disciples of all nations, baptizing them in the name of the Father and of the Son and of the Holy Spirit, and teach them to obey everything I have commanded you."[468]

Baptism is critically important to our Christian walk because it confers the gift of the Holy Spirit who comes to dwell within us, cleansing us of original sin and of all sin.[469] This first installment of God's love provides us "entry into the life of the Most Holy Trinity"[470] and membership into the Body of Christ.[471] As Jesus, by the power of the Holy Spirit, partook of our human nature at the Incarnation, by the power of the same Spirit at Baptism, we partake of Jesus' divine nature. This fulfills an ancient promise: "I will put my Spirit in you."[472]

The grace of Baptism allows a person to become "a new creature," "an adopted child of God," "a partaker of the divine nature," and "a temple of the Holy Spirit."[473] The Catholic Church teaches, "The Most Holy Trinity gives the baptized [person] sanctifying grace . . . enabling them to believe in God, to hope in him, and to love him . . . giving them the power to live and act under the prompting of the Holy Spirit through the gifts of the Holy Spirit; [and] allowing them to grow in goodness through moral virtues."[474]

---

[466] Cf. Luke 7:29-30.

[467] Cf. John 3:22, 4:1-2.

[468] Matthew 28:18-20 (NIV). Cf. CCC sections 1213-1284.

[469] Cf. Acts 2:38, 18:24-19:7, 22:16, Romans 6:3-4, Titus 3:5, Hebrews 10:22, 1 Peter 3:20-21; CCC sections 1262-1266.

[470] CCC section 1239. Cf. 2 Corinthians 1:22, 5:5, Romans 8:23.

[471] Cf. 1 Corinthians 12:13.

[472] Ezekiel 36:27 (NIV).

[473] Cf. 2 Corinthians 5:17, 2 Peter 1:4, Galatians 4:5-7, 1 Corinthians 6:15, Romans 8:17, 1 Corinthians 6:19.

[474] CCC section 1266.

Paul referred to this sacrament when he spoke of "one Lord, one faith, one baptism."[475] When, in the Nicene Creed, we profess our belief in "one baptism for the forgiveness of sins," we are referring to this sacrament.[476]

The Catholic Church teaches, "Baptism seals the Christian with the indelible spiritual mark (*character*) of his belonging to Christ. No sin can erase this mark, even if sin prevents Baptism from bearing the fruits of salvation."[477]

Triple immersion in the baptismal water is the most expressive way to administer Baptism. However, from ancient times, the Church has also administered Baptism by pouring the baptismal water three times over the candidate's head. As a candidate is immersed in water, or as water is poured over their head, the celebrant (usually a priest or deacon) invokes the name of the Holy Trinity: *I baptize you in the name of the Father, and of the Son, and of the Holy Spirit.*[478] Baptism is a sacrament we receive only once.[479] The epiclesis for this sacrament occurs when the priest prays over the baptismal water, asking God to send his Spirit upon the water.[480]

In the early Church, most Baptisms were of adults. However, over time, the practice of baptizing children and infants became the dominant practice. This seems underway in Biblical times, when Peter baptized Cornelius' whole household and Paul baptized Lydia's household and that of a jailer.[481] Today, some Christian denominations question the propriety of infant Baptisms. They suggest that a person must first reach the age of reason before receiving this sacrament, yet there is no scripture instituting an age requirement. Moreover, we know that at God's instruction,[482] entry into the Old Covenant was administered to infants by circumcision, and Baptism is entry into the New Covenant. We also know that John the Baptist was "filled with the Holy Spirit even from birth."[483]

---

475 Ephesians 4:5 (NJB).
476 Cf. CCC section 977.
477 CCC section 1272. Cf. Romans 8:29; Council of Trent (1547): DS 1609-1619.
478 Cf. Matthew 28:19; CCC sections 1239, 1278, 1284.
479 Cf. Ephesians 4:5; CCC sections 1246, 1272, 1280.
480 Cf. CCC section 1238.
481 Cf. Acts 10:47-48, 16:14-15, 30-33.
482 Cf. Genesis 17:10-14.
483 Luke 1:15 (NIV).

The Catholic Church teaches that "Born with a fallen nature and tainted by original sin, children also have need of the new birth in Baptism[484] . . . The Church and the parents would deny a child the priceless grace of becoming a child of God were they not to confer Baptism shortly after birth.[485] . . . Since the earliest of times, Baptism has been administered to children, for it is a grace and a gift of God that does not presuppose any human merit."[486]

Dear Jesus, Thank you for the seven sacraments of your Church, which you instituted for our good. Thank you especially for the gift of Baptism and the indwelling of the Holy Spirit in my life, by which I became a member of your mystical Body. Thank you for the graces and charisms given to me at that time. I beg you, I beg the Spirit, to strengthen and enliven those graces in my life, most especially the gifts of faith, hope, and love. Thank you. Amen.

---

[484] Cf. Council of Trent (1546): DS 1514; Colossians 1:12-14.
[485] Cf. CIC, can. 867; CCEO, cann. 681; 686, 1.
[486] CCC sections 1250, 1282. Cf. St. Augustine, Letter to Boniface, Bishop (98:2).

Gift of Holy Eucharist

16

Of the Church's seven sacraments, many consider Holy Eucharist to be the most visibly Christ-centered. Yet, as with all the sacraments, it involves the action of the Holy Spirit, for it is the Holy Spirit who, at Mass, transforms the bread and wine into Jesus' body and blood.[487] The epiclesis for this sacrament comes during the Eucharistic prayer.[488] As the priest prays to the Father in Eucharistic Prayer II: "Make holy . . . these gifts, we pray, by sending down your Spirit upon them . . . so that they may become for us the Body and Blood of our Lord Jesus Christ."[489]

Holy Eucharist gets its name from saints Luke and Paul who use the Greek word "*eucharistein*"[490] (which means "thanksgiving") to refer to this meal. We give thanks to God for the gift of his Son, the gift of new life in his Son, and the gift of his Son's body and blood that feed our souls. Jesus instituted the Sacrament of Holy Eucharist at the Last Supper. As we hear in Matthew's gospel, "While they were eating, Jesus took bread, gave thanks and broke it, and gave it to his disciples saying, 'Take and eat; this is my body.' Then he took the cup, gave thanks and offered it to them, saying, 'Drink from it, all of you. This is my blood of the covenant, which is poured out for many for the forgiveness of sins.'"[491] In Luke's Gospel, Jesus gives the command: "[D]o this in remembrance of me."[492]

When Catholic priests offer the Eucharistic prayers at the altar of God, such prayers are a memorial of Jesus' one, eternal sacrifice at Calvary.[493] They do not re-sacrifice Jesus. Instead, the Holy Spirit makes present to us, in the form of bread and wine, Jesus' sacrifice on the Cross – *his body and his blood.* By faithfully participating in this sacrifice, we, in the words of St. Paul, "proclaim the Lord's death until he comes."[494]

---

[487] Cf. CCC sections 737, 1353, 1375.

[488] Cf. CCC sections 1105, 1353.

[489] The Roman Missal (2010), Eucharistic Prayer II.

[490] Cf. Luke 22:19, 1 Corinthians 11:24. See also Matthew 26:26, Mark 14:22 – '*eulogein*' and CCC sections 1328, 1359-1362.

[491] Mathew 26:26-28 (NIV). Cf. Mark 14:22-25, Luke 22:14-20, 1 Corinthians 11:24-25; CCC sections 1322-1419.

[492] Luke 22:19 (NJB). Cf. 1 Corinthians 11:24-25.

[493] Cf. CCC sections 1362-1372, 1545.

[494] 1 Corinthians 11:26 (NRSV). Cf. Pope John Paul II, EE, section 11.

When Jesus first taught about Holy Eucharist, he described himself as "the Bread of Life," "the Bread from heaven," and "the living bread."[495] He told his disciples, "I am the living bread that came down from heaven; whoever eats this bread will live forever; and the bread that I will give is my flesh for the life of the world."[496]

When Jesus prophesied about "the bread that I will give" he was referring to Holy Eucharist. Our challenge is to realize that this gift is himself – his body, blood, soul, and divinity. By the power of the Holy Spirit, the bread and wine offered at Mass cease to be. We receive Jesus under the appearance of bread and wine. What, or rather who, we receive is the Father's only Son, the Lamb of God who takes away the sins of the world. This is not a minor point of Christian theology, for the reality of which we speak is Jesus, in the flesh, coming to us as food for our souls.

When the Catholic Church teaches that Holy Eucharist is "the source and summit"[497] of the Christian life, it is because Jesus' most intimate presence to believers in the present age is Holy Eucharist. Jesus comes to heal us, to strengthen us, and to commune with us. As he said, "This is my body, which is for you"[498] and, in another place, "[M]y flesh is real food and my blood real drink."[499]

At the Incarnation, Jesus defied human logic and by the power of the Holy Spirit became a human being, an embryo in the womb of Mary. He also defies human logic when by the power of the same Holy Spirit he becomes "real food" for our faith journey.

The work of the Holy Spirit in the Eucharistic meal is not merely to make Christ present to us, but also to make us worthy receptacles of Jesus. The Spirit comes to sanctify us and to increase his presence in our lives. For as we consume Jesus worthily, the Holy Spirit in us increases. As Saint Ephraim taught: "He called the bread his living body and he filled it with himself and his Spirit. . . . He who eats it with faith, eats Fire and Spirit. . . . Take and eat this, all of you, and eat with it the Holy Spirit."[500]

---

[495] Cf. John 6:32-35, 41, 48, 51, 58.
[496] John 6:51 (NAB). Cf. Exodus 14:4, Psalm 78:24 (25), Wisdom 16:20.
[497] CCC section 1324. Cf. Second Vatican Council, LG, section 11.
[498] 1 Corinthians 11:24 (NJB).
[499] John 6:55 (NJB).
[500] St. Ephraim, as quoted by Pope John Paul II, EE, section 17.

Receiving Jesus Worthily. In his first letter to the Corinthians, the Apostle Paul emphasized the importance of receiving Holy Eucharistic worthily. He warns us, "Whoever . . . eats the bread or drinks the cup of the Lord in an unworthy manner will be answerable for the body and blood of the Lord. Examine yourselves, and only then eat of the bread and drink of the cup. For all who eat and drink without discerning the body, eat and drink judgment against themselves. For this reason many of you are weak and ill, and some have died."[501] This warning concerning illness and death only makes sense when we realize Holy Eucharist is not a mere symbol, it is Jesus.

We receive Jesus worthily only with the help of the Holy Spirit. This requires, first, that we receive Jesus with faith, recognizing that Jesus is truly present in the sacrament. Without faith, we may consume Jesus, but we will not receive him. Second, we should receive him with clean hearts. Thus, Paul instructs us to examine our consciences before receiving Jesus – better that we judge ourselves first and seek forgiveness, than to casually receive the Lord as though our hearts were clean, when in fact they may not be clean.[502] On this point, we should regularly seek the Spirit's healing in the Sacrament of Reconciliation; and we should not receive Holy Eucharist if we have serious sins for which we have not received absolution.[503] Third, we should receive Jesus with thanksgiving focused on the wonderful Gift we are receiving. Fourth, we should "discern the body" – not just the Lord's physical body we are about to receive, but also his mystical body, the community. We should not come to receive the Lord while holding grudges against others.[504] *Jesus gives us his body, to build up his body.* We must do our part.

When we receive Jesus worthily, we not only receive him, but he also receives us.[505] He receives each of us personally and he receives us as a community. If we enter fully into the mystery of this sacrament, the Holy Spirit unites us in friendship with Jesus and, if we cooperate, the Holy Spirit unites us in friendship with all fellow believers – not just those present, not just fellow Catholics, but all fellow Christians. When we receive Jesus worthily, the Holy Spirit is secretly at work healing the wounds of our separation.

---

[501] 1 Corinthians 11:27-30 (NRSV).
[502] Cf. 1 Corinthians 11:28.
[503] Cf. CCC section 1415; 1 Corinthians 5:6-8.
[504] Cf. Matthew 5:23-24.
[505] Cf. Pope John Paul II, EE, section 22.

In the United States and elsewhere, a common practice has formed over the last several decades whereby persons who are not able to receive Holy Communion come forward at Mass, as Holy Communion is distributed, to receive a blessing.[506] They may be unable to receive Holy Eucharist due to a lack of faith in Jesus as God, or a lack of faith in Jesus' real presence in the sacrament, or because they are not Catholic, or due to serious unconfessed sin, or because they have not received their first Holy Communion. Such persons signal the priest or extraordinary minister that they desire a blessing by crossing their arms over their chests. It should be noted that some dispute the propriety of this practice. Neither the Vatican nor the U.S. Conference of Catholic Bishops has ruled on this practice.[507]

As it concerns communion services in Protestant communities, it is right for them to describe the bread and wine that they distribute as only a symbol. By breaking communion with the Catholic Church and the Sacrament of Holy Orders, their ministers do not have the charism through which the Holy Spirit makes Jesus present in his body and blood.[508] "Nevertheless," taught Pope John Paul II, "when [they] commemorate the Lord's death and resurrection in the Holy Supper, they profess that it signifies life in communion with Christ and they await his coming in glory. . . . [Catholics may join worship services in Protestant communities but] while respecting the religious convictions of these separated brethren, [Catholics] must refrain from receiving the communion distributed in their celebrations, so as not to condone an ambiguity about the nature of the Eucharist and, consequently, to fail in their duty to bear clear witness to the truth."[509]

When we choose to enter the mystery of the Mass, clothed in faith, we can experience the Eucharistic gift as a wonderful foretaste of

---

[506] Generally, only priests use the formal words of blessing: "I bless you in the name of the Father, Son, and Holy Spirit." Extraordinary ministers pray that God would bless the person, for example: "May God bless you this day. Amen."

[507] It is reported in many editorials that a Fr. Anthony Ward, SM, of the Vatican's Congregation for Divine Worship and the Discipline of the Sacraments issued a private letter (Protocol 930/08/L, dated November 2008) on the matter. The letter acknowledged that the Congregation was considering the practice, though it had not ruled on it. The letter otherwise shared certain guidelines for distribution of Holy Eucharist whereby Fr. Ward discouraged the practice of blessings.

[508] Certain Christian churches, such as the Orthodox and Coptic churches, have maintained apostolic succession. Their priests have the charism or faculty to offer the Eucharistic prayers for their communities. Each of these communities has its own rules for receiving Holy Eucharist, which should be respected.

[509] Pope John Paul II, EE, section 30. Cf. CCC section 1400.

the "supper of the Lamb" mentioned in the Book of Revelation.[510] Yet when we consume this gift and do not believe in the Beauty present, when we merely go through the motions of receiving the sacrament with little or no faith in Jesus or his Eucharistic presence, we generally feel nothing.

As each of us comes to understand the true wonder of the Eucharistic Meal, we quickly realize the appropriateness of kneeling during the Eucharistic prayer – Jesus, our Lord and Savior, through whom the universe was made, is entering our presence, ushered in by the Holy Spirit. It is also appropriate to kneel when Jesus is formally presented to the community: "Behold the Lamb of God, behold him who takes away the sins of the world."[511] All true reverence of Jesus in these moments is our cooperation with the Holy Spirit who inspires such reverence.

Receiving Holy Communion at Mass and in the silence thereafter is a uniquely sacred moment. It is a time to experience the presence of Jesus in our lives, in the power of his Spirit. It is not a time to rush out of Church so as to get an early start to the rest of our day. Instead, it is a time to dwell in the presence of our Savior who we have just received in a very special way. It is a time for quiet adoration and communion with our Lord. The Catholic Church teaches that in the liturgy of the Mass, the high point of which is the Eucharistic Meal, we find "the most intimate cooperation of the Holy Spirit and the Church."[512]

Holy Spirit, Thank you for the gift of Jesus two thousand years ago in Mary's womb. Thank you, as well, for the gift of Jesus at every Mass. Please awaken me ever more deeply to the truths of Jesus' real presence in Holy Eucharist. Convict my heart of the need to seek absolution for my serious sins before receiving Jesus. Help me to be a worthy Temple for Jesus every time I receive him. Help me to receive him each time with faith, reverent devotion, and abundant thanks. In the name of Jesus, I pray. Amen.

---

[510] Cf. Revelation 19:9. See also 1 Corinthians 11:20.
[511] The Roman Missal (2010).
[512] CCC section 1108.

17   Gift of Reconciliation

On the first Easter, after Jesus had risen from the dead, he came to his closest disciples and breathed on them saying, "Receive the Holy Spirit. If you forgive anyone's sins, they are forgiven; if you retain anyone's sins, they are retained."[513] Through this act, Jesus conferred upon the Apostles a charism to participate in his ongoing ministry of forgiveness. Through the centuries, this ministry evolved into the Sacrament of Reconciliation. The charism to participate in this ministry is passed on by bishops to priests, through the laying on of hands at ordination.

The power and authority to forgive sins in the Sacrament of Reconciliation is a ministry of the Holy Spirit working through a bishop or priest.[514] It is comparable to the power and authority James talks about concerning what will become known as the Sacrament of the Anointing of the Sick. James instructs elders of the Church to pray for sick persons and anoint them with oil. He tells us that if the ailing person "has sinned, he will be forgiven."[515] By God's design, in both of these sacraments, Jesus extends divine forgiveness, by the power of the Holy Spirit, through a human instrument.

Yet many protest saying, "I don't need a priest to repent of my sins" and "God does not need a priest to extend his forgiveness." There is truth in both of these statements. Nevertheless, God, in his infinite wisdom, for reasons that defy normal human logic, has given certain human intermediaries – *priests* – the power and authority to dispense certain of his graces. Similarly, God does not need human intermediaries to heal those who are physically or mentally ill, and yet by his wisdom, God gives some a charism for miraculous healings.

As it concerns the power and authority to forgive sins that Jesus gave to his Apostles, most certainly Jesus intended for them to use it. Not only did Jesus mean for them and their fellow bishops and priests through the centuries to use this gift, he also meant for believers to make use of it as well. When we avoid this sacrament, we avoid Jesus who instituted the sacrament and we avoid the Spirit of Jesus who works miracles of forgiveness and inner healing through it.

---

[513] John 20:22-23 (NJB). Cf. CCC sections 1422-1498.
[514] Cf. St. Augustine, sermon 71, section 28; St. Ambrose, *On the Holy Spirit*, Book III, section 137.
[515] James 5:15 (NIV). Cf. CCC section 1520.

There is an interesting parallel here between the ordained priesthood of the Old and New Covenants. In both cases, by God's design, priests are empowered to declare people clean. In ancient Israel, the Levitical priests would examine those healed of leprosy and declare them clean. Today, through the Sacrament of Reconciliation, priests declare repentant sinners forgiven – that is to say, clean of the spiritual leprosy of sin. In both cases, people are restored to their community. This sacrament is directed toward ongoing healing, conversion, and sanctification. On the part of the believer seeking forgiveness, this sacrament involves not merely the confession of sins, but also the renouncing of sins, contrition for the harm our sins cause, and a commitment, no matter how imperfect, to go and sin no more.

Pope John Paul II taught, "[T]he conversion of the human heart . . . is an indispensible condition for the forgiveness of sins . . . Without a true conversion, which implies inner contrition, and without a sincere and firm purpose of amendment, sin remains unforgiven."[516] The Holy Spirit aids us in this process by "convincing" us of our sins. "[H]e makes man realize his own evil and at the same time directs him toward what is good."[517] Our challenge is to cooperate. When seeking the grace offered through the Sacrament of Reconciliation, it is right for us to examine our consciences, to identify and reflect upon our sins, and to regret those sins and repent. We should do so realizing that the Lord does not spurn a contrite heart.[518]

Perhaps the most wonderful gift we can give to God is the gift of our brokenness, our sinfulness, and our woundedness, acknowledging we need God's forgiveness and love. These things are the only things in our lives that truly belong to us and, as odd as it may seem, the gift of these to God is a precious gift. For when we give these to God, we are saying we do not want them. We can then seek a clean heart from the only one who can give it – the Lord. With David we should pray, "Create in me a pure heart, O God, and renew a steadfast spirit within me. Do not cast me from your presence, or take your Holy Spirit from me. Restore to me the joy of your salvation."[519]

Beyond the confession of sins, the Sacrament of Reconciliation includes a confession of faith – that Jesus is Lord. That he is the Son of

---

[516] Pope John Paul II, DeV, section 42.
[517] Pope John Paul II, DeV, section 42.
[518] Cf. Psalm 51:17 (verse 19 in some translations).
[519] Psalm 51:10-12 (NIV) (verses 12-14 in some translations).

the living God. This we do when we sincerely pray our Act of Contrition. If we so repent of our sins, then "he who is faithful and just will forgive us our sins and cleanse us from all unrighteousness."[520] The grace the Holy Spirit conveys by this sacrament is not merely forgiveness. Often there is peace, a healed heart, a lifting away of burdens, an awakening of purpose, or a freeing from demonic oppression. Catholics should regularly seek healing through the Sacrament of Reconciliation. They should seek it whenever they have committed grave sin and otherwise monthly.

While this sacrament communicates forgiveness for our sins, it does not remove all the effects of our sins. We must still deal with the consequences of our actions. Nor does this sacrament remove the temptation of our flesh, but it does weaken those temptations, and it empowers us with greater strength to resist sin and defeat it.

In the past several decades, fewer and fewer Catholics have availed themselves of the grace God offers through the Sacrament of Reconciliation. We have avoided it, and thereby we have avoided God. Some of us may stay away due to our ignorance of the grace offered. But perhaps most of us stay away due to fear or pride.

- We fear taking ownership of our sins.
- We fear being embarrassed as we verbalize our sins.
- We fear giving up sinful ways that we have learned to enjoy.
- We fear that God will call us to greater holiness.
- We fear other people's reaction to us if we get serious about pursuing holiness – they might judge us, ridicule us, or withdraw their friendship.

We must not be afraid. Too much is at stake. When we stay away from the Sacrament of Reconciliation due to our cowardliness, we prolong the harm of sin not only in our own lives, but also in the lives of all with whom we interact. We need to turn to God, and with the Spirit's grace be reconciled to him, and to choose the pathways of holiness to which he calls us.

Seriously, has anyone ever felt dread after genuinely repenting of their sins and receiving forgiveness in this sacrament? Sure, in the confessional, as we confess our sins, it may be difficult. But when we

---

[520] 1 John 1:9 (NRSV). Cf. Proverbs 28:13.

sincerely do so, we leave the sacrament feeling peace and joy. Burdens are lifted away. We are washed clean on the inside.

Now some of us may go to Confession and not have a positive experience. That might be the case if we are unwilling to repent, or if we want to rationalize our sins, or we blame others for our sins, or we otherwise resist the process. And others of us may get a stodgy priest. But the vast majority of us walk away refreshed and better equipped to continue our journey of faith.

Truly, each visit to the Sacrament of Reconciliation is an opportunity to encounter God, to encounter Jesus who waits for us in this sacrament, and the Holy Spirit who works through this sacrament. It is a chance for the Holy Spirit to free us from the bonds of sin and to pour healing ointments into our hearts, minds, and interior wounds. Each time we sincerely repent of our sins and turn to Jesus in this sacrament, we are changed, sometimes radically so.

Concerning Jesus' presence in the Sacrament of Reconciliation, Pope Francis teaches, "[T]he Lord always gets there before us, he gets there first, he is waiting for us! To find someone waiting for you is truly a great grace. You go to him as a sinner, but he is waiting to forgive you. . . . The Lord is waiting for us . . . to offer us his love. And this fills your heart with such wonder that you can hardly believe it, and this is how your faith grows – through an encounter with a Person, through an encounter with the Lord."[521]

Come Holy Spirit. Thank you for your work of renewal in the Sacrament of Reconciliation. Please open my eyes to the truths of this sacrament, of the Gospel, and of the wonders of forgiveness.

Please help me to encounter Jesus ever more intimately in this sacrament. Help me to realize he is there even before I arrive. Jesus is there wanting to forgive me, waiting for me to seek forgiveness. He is there because he loves me. You are there because you love me.

In my weakness, have pity on me. Despite the pain it may cause me, please show me my sins. Please fill the caverns of my heart and mind with your light, and drive out the darkness. Please help me repent from all sin in my life. Please guide me. Please heal me. Please restore me to the Body of Christ. In Jesus' name I pray, Amen.

---

[521] Pope Francis, Address in St. Peter's Square, May 18, 2013.

18   Gift of Confirmation

As with Baptism, the Sacrament of Confirmation involves the gift of the Holy Spirit. In Confirmation, Jesus pours the Spirit of God afresh into our hearts strengthening our Baptismal grace, allowing us to be united more fully with his Body (the Church), enabling us for greater holiness, and empowering us for service in God's kingdom.[522] In the Bible, we find this sacrament conferred through the laying on of hands, by Peter and John to believers in Samaria.[523] We also read of Paul conferring this sacrament on certain disciples from Ephesus.[524]

Isaiah prophesied the spiritual gifts we associate with Confirmation, gifts that were distinguishing marks of Israel's Messiah: the gifts of wisdom, understanding, knowledge, right judgment, courage, piety, and fear of the Lord.[525] Jesus is the Messiah, and as the Holy Spirit incorporates us mystically into Jesus' body at Baptism, we receive these gifts. If we are open to the Spirit's action at Confirmation, the Holy Spirit strengthens these gifts within us, helping us to grow in holiness. Confirmation can also be a time for receiving or releasing the power of other spiritual gifts in our lives, as the Spirit wills. The opening up of this, the charismatic dimension of our personal lives, helps us to participate in specific areas of service to which the Holy Spirit calls us. Each Christian through Baptism and Confirmation is "assigned to an apostolate by the Lord himself."[526]

---

[522] Cf. CCC sections 1285-1321; Pope John Paul II, GA, October 14, 1998, section 3.

[523] Cf. Acts 8:14-17. When the disciples in Samaria became believers, Philip baptized them and they received the indwelling of the Spirit. When the Bible later states that the Spirit "had not yet fallen upon any of them" (Acts 8:16), it means they did not as yet have the anointing of power that we associate with the Apostles' experience at Pentecost. This did happen when Peter and John visited them and laid hands on them (the Sacrament of Confirmation).

[524] Cf. Acts 19:1-7. In the case of disciples from Ephesus who had received only the baptism of John, when Paul met them, he administered two sacraments: Baptism and Confirmation. They received not only the indwelling of the Spirit, but also the release of the Spirit's charismatic power. In Eastern Rite (Orthodox) Churches, Confirmation is administered with Baptism. Baptism, First Holy Communion, and Confirmation are administered together, even to infants.

[525] Cf. Isaiah 11:2.

[526] Second Vatican Council, AA, section 3. Cf. Romans 8:28, 1 Corinthians 7:17, Ephesians 2:10, Titus 2:14.

Those who approach Confirmation worthily receive authority and power "to give an adult witness in Christ and to take up . . . [their Christian] responsibilities more consciously and deliberately."[527]

Both Baptism and Confirmation are an opportunity to be immersed in the Spirit. The first, associated with water, brings an interior cleansing and the indwelling of the Spirit. It is an anointing oriented to relationship with God – to faith, holiness, and salvation. The second, associated with fire, brings power. It is an anointing oriented to service in God's kingdom. If we approach the Sacrament of Confirmation worthily, the Spirit who has been with us from Baptism is revealed to us in new ways for new purposes.

Jesus offers Confirmation as a "Pentecostal" moment, a moment when the Holy Spirit provides us strength and power to be his witnesses to a disbelieving world. It involves "a special outpouring of the Holy Spirit as once granted to the apostles on the day of Pentecost."[528] Through Confirmation, the Holy Spirit directs us from within to our role in the community of believers, equipping us with power to serve in that role.

As the Apostles administered Confirmation in the early Church, today bishops (or their designees) administer Confirmation. They do so through the laying on of hands, anointing a recipient's head with sacred oil, as they pronounce the words "Be sealed with the Gift of the Holy Spirit."[529] While we speak of the bishop as the one who administers this sacrament, truly it is Jesus who sends his Spirit, working through the bishop. The "seal" mentioned in the bishop's blessing is an indelible mark of ownership on our soul, placed there by the Holy Spirit.[530] This seal marks us as persons belonging to God.

The epiclesis for Confirmation occurs in stages: first when the bishop as part of the Chrism Mass of Holy Week consecrates the sacred oils, then in the celebration of Confirmation when the bishop extends his hands over those receiving the sacrament asking for an

---

[527] Pope John Paul II, GA, September 21, 1994, section 4. Cf. Acts 1:8; CCC section 1303.

[528] CCC section 1302.

[529] CCC section 1320. For a singular bishop, it would be the laying on of the hand (one hand, not both). Cf. CCC sections 1300, 1320.

[530] Cf. 2 Corinthians 1:21-22, Ephesians 1:3, 4:30; CCC sections 1295-1296.

outpouring of the Holy Spirit, and then in the actual administration of the sacred oil.[531]

Preparing to Receive Confirmation Worthily. The Catholic Church teaches, "A candidate for Confirmation . . . must profess the faith, be in the state of grace, have the intention of receiving the sacrament, and be prepared to assume the role of disciple and witness to Christ."[532]

"One of the highest responsibilities of the people of God is to prepare the baptized for confirmation. Pastors have the special responsibility to see that all the baptized reach the completion of Christian initiation and therefore that they are carefully prepared for confirmation."[533] "*Preparation* for Confirmation should aim at leading the Christian toward a more intimate union with Christ and a more lively familiarity with the Holy Spirit – his actions, his gifts, and his biddings – in order to be more capable of assuming the apostolic responsibilities of Christian life."[534]

Powerful preaching, study of God's Word, and much prayer should accompany a person's preparation for Confirmation. The purpose of the preaching and study is to build up faith in Jesus, encourage holiness, and foster hopeful expectation that the Spirit will radically touch a person's life in accord with the Father's will. "More intense prayer should prepare one to receive the strength and graces of the Holy Spirit with docility and readiness to act."[535]

A Scandal in Our Day. We speak of Confirmation with the words "power," "fire," "holiness," "service," and "readiness to act." However, if we look around us, it often seems that there is very little evidence of these spiritual attributes in the lives of confirmed Christians. We might ask: Where is the holiness? Where is the fire? Have they experienced Pentecost? Have I experienced Pentecost?

Today, many who receive Confirmation are distracted teenagers merely going through the motions of the sacrament with inadequate preparation, a profound lack of faith, little or no commitment to Jesus as Lord of their lives, and little or no desire to serve God's kingdom.

---

[531] Cf. CCC sections 1297-1300.
[532] CCC section 1319.
[533] Introduction to the Rite of Confirmation, August 22, 1971, section 3.
[534] CCC section 1309.
[535] CCC section 1310. Cf. Acts 1:14.

As a result, they are not open to the dynamic action of the Holy Spirit. The grace conferred can lie dormant in their hearts overgrown with worldly distractions, darkness, and sin. For many, their adult witness to Jesus becomes one of lukewarmness, hypocrisy, and rebellion.

Many receiving the sacrament of Confirmation fail one of the sacrament's most basic requirements – to be in a state of grace. Fulfillment of this requirement is gravely hampered not merely by the preponderance of sexual sin, materialism, and the abuse of alcohol and drugs epidemic among teens, but even more so by their lack of faith in God. They do not love God with their whole heart, mind, and soul. Perhaps it is also fair to say, some don't even have a desire to love God. They love the cultural icons, lifestyles, worldly ambitions, sins, and other forms of emptiness that fill their lives. With respect to this sacrament, many teens treat it as graduation out of the Church.

Paul's chastisement of Christians living in Galatia who rejected the Spirit's grace is relevant to many today: "Are you so stupid? After beginning with the Spirit, are you now ending with the flesh?"[536] Some people today who have fallen away from the faith may be fortunate and return to it later in life, at which time the Spirit unexpectedly awakens in them truths, purposes, and charisms that they have spent their life ignoring. But we ought not live life foolishly supposing a later return to God. We ought not live life missing thousands of opportunities to be God's blessing to others. The time for conversion is now.

Heavenly Father, Thank you for the seal of the Holy Spirit in the Sacrament of Confirmation. Thank you for the Spirit's grace meant for the strengthening of my spirit and soul. Please forgive me for all the ways I have failed to live up to the graces and responsibilities of this sacrament. I want to be a holy and bold witness for Jesus – your Son and my Savior. Please anoint me afresh with your Holy Spirit and awaken in me the graces of my Baptism and Confirmation.

Come Holy Spirit. Please stir within me. Please fill my heart with your wisdom and love. Please strengthen my faith in Jesus. Please awaken in me a new joy to seek, know, and serve Jesus. Please inflame my heart with an ardent love for Jesus. I want to be "on fire" for him. I want to serve him faithfully. Please help me. Amen.

---

[536] Galatians 3:3 (NAB). Cf. Hebrews 6:4-5.

19 Gift of Anointing of the Sick

The sacramental graces of the Spirit are also at work in the Anointing of the Sick, which is administered to persons who are seriously ill or dying.[537] A serious illness may be physical, mental, emotional, or spiritual. In the case of persons who are dying, this sacrament is sometimes called Extreme Unction. As with the Apostle's ministries of healing, this sacrament involves an anointing with sacred oil.[538] The epiclesis proper to this sacrament occurs when the priest, in administering the sacrament, lays hands on the sick and prays over them.[539]

The grace associated with the Anointing of the Sick includes interior "strengthening, peace, and courage to overcome the difficulties that go with the condition of serious illness or the frailty of old age. This grace is a gift of the Holy Spirit, who renews trust and faith in God and strengthens against the temptations of the evil one[540] . . . This assistance from the Lord by the power of his Spirit is meant to lead the sick person to healing of the soul, but also of the body if such is God's will. Furthermore, 'if he has committed sins, he will be forgiven.'"[541]

Though it may not be immediately obvious, the grace to persevere faithfully through an illness cleaving to Jesus is more beneficial to our spiritual life than the miraculous healing we might otherwise prefer. It is worth recalling Paul's disclosure of an affliction in his life.[542] Three times, he pleaded with God, "heal me;" to which God replied, "My grace is sufficient for you, for power is made perfect in weakness."[543] God still miraculously heals bodies of disease and other afflictions, through this sacrament and apart from it, and we may rightly ask for such healing, yet the healing of our interior life is much more important. Either way, the healing is a work of the Holy Spirit.

Lord God, Thank you for the gift of the Anointing of the Sick. For all who seek its grace, may their hearts be open to your action. May you have mercy on them and bring forth miracles of healing. Amen.

---

[537] Cf. CCC sections 1499-1532.
[538] Cf. Mark 6:13, James 5:14.
[539] Cf. CCC section 1519.
[540] Cf. Hebrews 2:15.
[541] CCC section 1520. The interior quote is from James 5:15. Cf. Council of Trent (1551): DS 1717
[542] Cf. 2 Corinthians 12:7, Galatians 4:13-14.
[543] 2 Corinthians 12:9 (NRSV).

20 Gift of Holy Orders

Holy Orders is the sacrament given to bishops, priests, and deacons as they assume their particular roles in the Church.[544] At priestly and deaconate ordinations and the installation of new bishops, the Holy Spirit anoints recipients through the laying on of hands by a bishop and the prayers of consecration. At this time the Holy Spirit imparts to them a special character associated with their new role, and equips them with special graces to serve as "ministers in the New Covenant."[545] For priests, this includes sacred powers to forgive sins in the name of God and to celebrate Mass.[546] The prayers of consecration are the epiclesis for this sacrament.

The sharing of the Spirit in these instances recalls the sharing of the Spirit in the days of both Moses and Elijah, when special spiritual powers for leadership were transferred from one person to others.[547] In New Testament times, this sharing of the Spirit began when Jesus anointed his Apostles with the Spirit on the first Easter.[548] Paul refers to this sharing in his letter to Timothy, reminding Timothy of his own ordination.[549] Luke, in the Book of Acts, mentions this sharing of the Spirit as the Apostles ordained the Church's first deacons.[550]

Roles. Bishops and priests represent two degrees of participation in the Church's ministerial priesthood. They are consecrated and set apart to proclaim the Gospel, lead liturgical worship, administer the sacraments, and pastor communities. As with their counterparts in the Old Covenant, bishops and priests in the New Covenant are "chosen from among mortals" by God, and they are "put in charge of things pertaining to God on [the people's] behalf, to offer gifts and sacrifices for sins."[551] Bishops, as successors to the Apostles, lead faith communities that typically include a collection of many parishes. Priests are co-workers with the Bishops.

---

[544] Cf. CCC sections 1536-1600.

[545] Cf. 2 Corinthians 3:6.

[546] Cf. John 20:22-23, 2 Timothy 1:6; CCC section 1556; Pope Leo XIII, DI.

[547] Cf. Numbers 11:16-30, 27:18-20, 2 Kings 2:9-18.

[548] Cf. John 20:22-23.

[549] Cf. 1 Timothy 4:14, 2 Timothy 1:6.

[550] Cf. Acts 6:1-7.

[551] Hebrews 5:1 (NRSV). Cf. Acts 20:28, Ephesians 4:11, Romans 12:3-8, 1 Corinthians 12:27-29; CCC sections 1539, 1578.

Deacons are also ordained ministers. They too are clergy. Their role, though, is different from that of priests. They do not have the faculties to celebrate Mass or to forgive sins. Their role is one of service to the community. Commonly, they assist in proclamation of the Gospel at Mass, religious education, baptisms, marriages, funerals, social services, counseling, and such other activities as the bishop or the pastor in the parish to which they are assigned directs them.

Celibacy and the Priesthood. Normally, priests in the Catholic Church take vows of celibacy and thus do not marry. They are, as Jesus taught, men who renounce marriage for themselves and, by God's grace, choose to be eunuchs for the kingdom of God.[552] Paul suggested that God gives some a charism of celibacy through which the Spirit imparts graces to avoid sexual temptation, allowing them to serve the Lord without that distraction.[553] Exceptions to the Church's discipline of priestly celibacy relate to certain Middle Eastern rites within the Catholic Church and with respect to married clergy of other Christian denominations who convert to Catholicism and become Catholic priests. Deacons may be married.

Religious Life. In addition to the priesthood and deaconate, some are called to religious life which can include those in religious orders, be they priests, monks, nuns, brothers, or consecrated laity. These are persons who, in community, dedicate themselves to a life of service to the Church. This could be a life of prayer or teaching or social outreach. Those in religious life who are not priests or deacons do not receive the Sacrament of Holy Orders. However, they do receive special graces of the Spirit associated with their roles.

The Calling. The Holy Spirit calls and prepares persons for the roles of bishop, priest, deacon, or religious.[554] Concerning the role of ministerial priests, the Bible tells us "[N]o one takes this honor upon himself but only when called by God, just as Aaron was."[555] Persons discern their possible calling through prayer, study of God's Word, religious and community service, moral obedience, and spiritual direction. In their respective roles, they serve worthily only by the grace of the Holy Spirit.

---

[552] Cf. Matthew 19:12. Cf. CCC section 1579.
[553] Cf. 1 Corinthians 7:7.
[554] Cf. Acts 20:28 regarding bishops.
[555] Hebrews 5:4 (NAB). Cf. CCC section 1578.

Dear Jesus, Thank you for the gift of your Church and the offices in the Church that you established. Thank you for all bishops, priests, deacons, and other religious who serve the Church in various roles. Please purge from their ranks those who, for whatever reason, do not belong. Please bless, strengthen, and protect those who do belong. By the power of your Spirit, please build them up in faith, holiness, and love. Build them up with divine wisdom and understanding. Please baptize them afresh with your Spirit.

Come Holy Spirit, come and renew the Church throughout the world and renew those who have been called to leadership in the Church. Please bring forth in them ever more strongly the spiritual gifts that you have given them. Individually and as groups, may they be "on fire" for Jesus. Fill them, please, with an insatiable desire to know and study the Word of God, to live it, and to boldly proclaim it. Bring forth in many of them, profound gifts of preaching and evangelization. May a New Evangelization fill the Church, bringing forth a Great Awakening of faith among the People of God. I specifically pray for blessings upon _____.

I pray for more holy and faith-filled priests in the Church. For those you have called in the past, but they did not hear you, please keep speaking to them and impress upon them your will. Please bless all seminaries and seminarians. Please reform all seminaries to be bastions of holiness, orthodoxy, and vibrant faith in Jesus. Purge from the Church's seminaries all false ideas, false teachers, demonic oppression, lukewarmness, and confusion. Shut down those that, in your wisdom, need to be shut down.

Lord please bless all formation programs for deacons and religious. I pray for renewal in these programs in accordance with your perfect will. Please send us more holy and faith-filled deacons and religious to serve in various capacities as you see best.

Lord, if you are calling me to a new role in the Church – perhaps as a priest, deacon, or religious – please help me to hear that calling and to respond with faith and love. I ask for a fresh movement of your Spirit in my life, helping me to serve in whatever capacity you would have me serve your Church. In the name of Jesus I pray, Amen.

21   Gift of Holy Matrimony

Of the seven sacraments, the active work of the Holy Spirit may be least obvious in Holy Matrimony.[556] Yet, if we understand the Holy Spirit truly as the Spirit of Love, then we should see that it is only by the Spirit's grace that holy marriages exist. As the Holy Spirit is the bond of reciprocating love uniting the Father and the Son, similarly he is the bond of reciprocating love uniting husband and wife in all holy marriages. Many lesser loves and false loves fill the natural realm and, perhaps, most marriages. God's love is different. It is perfect, pure, and holy. It is oriented to our eternal salvation.

Marriage: It's Purpose. To rightly appreciate the union we call marriage, we must first recognize that it exists not as a creation of human design for our sake, but as a creation of God's design for our sake. It exists for husbands and wives, for children, and for families, who together form a domestic church. It is ordered to the good of the family and the good of society. An authentically Christian family is a communion of persons united together foremost by the common bond of faith in Christ and by a mutual love and respect for one another.

While couples rightly desire happiness in marriage, the purpose of marriage is holiness. Marriage, rightly embraced, is a workshop in holiness. It exists as an institution to help spouses draw closer to God and become the persons God intends each to be. Holy spouses help one another grow in faith, hope, and love. Together they help one another and their children get to heaven – that is one of the purposes of marriage.[557] Thus, not only do holy marriages originate in God, but God is their proper end.

Rightly embraced, marriage helps both spouses learn to give generously and show mercy. In marriages open to the Spirit's graces, both spouses are transformed into holier, more loving, more self-less, more faith-filled persons. Mutual forgiveness, love, respect, and patience make for the strongest and holiest of marriages, all a gift from God to those open to receive.

Pope Benedict XVI taught, "Marriage is truly an instrument of salvation, not only for married people but for the whole of society.

---

[556] Cf. CCC sections 1601-1666.
[557] Cf. CCC section 1534.

Like any truly worthwhile goal, it places demands upon us, it challenges us, it calls us to be prepared to sacrifice our own interests for the good of the other. It requires us to exercise tolerance and to offer forgiveness. It invites us to nurture and protect the gift of new life. Those of us fortunate enough to be born into a stable family discover there the first and most fundamental school for virtuous living and the qualities of good citizenship."[558]

As an institution, marriage is for the present age. In eternity, St. Paul tells us, marriage is something that passes away.[559] Jesus taught, "[A]t the resurrection men and women do not marry."[560]

Grace in Marriage. The Catholic Church teaches, "In the epiclesis of [Holy Matrimony] the spouses receive the Holy Spirit as the communion of love of Christ and the Church.[561] The Holy Spirit is the seal of their covenant, the ever-available source of their love and the strength to renew their fidelity."[562] The epiclesis for this sacrament occurs in the nuptial blessing at the wedding ceremony, after the Our Father prayer. Thereafter, the spouses become the ministers of this sacrament: husband to wife and wife to husband.[563] Throughout their marriage, as they love in accordance with the Spirit's inspirations, they impart divine graces to the other.

The Holy Spirit sanctifies marriages from within, from within the challenges of daily life, even amid disagreements, mistakes, hurts, and trials. Jesus, through the Holy Spirit, provides the strength by which both spouses are able to be subject to one another – the grace by which husbands love and serve their wives as Christ loves and serves his Church, and the grace by which wives, in turn, love and serve their husbands.[564] St. Paul taught that the Holy Spirit provides a special charism, a unique portal of grace into one's heart, specifically associated with marriage.[565] Perhaps, for far too many marriages, this charism lies dormant and unused.

---

[558] Pope Benedict XVI, GA, May 5, 2010.
[559] Cf. 1 Corinthians 7:31; CCC section 1619.
[560] Matthew 22:30 (NJB). Cf. Mark 12:25.
[561] Cf. Ephesians 5:32.
[562] CCC section 1624.
[563] Cf. CCC section 1623.
[564] Cf. Ephesians 5:21-33; CCC section 1642.
[565] Cf. 1 Corinthians 7:7.

Human Sexuality and Marriage. After the preparations, prayers, and promises associated with the marriage ceremony, a couple consummates their marriage in the sexual act. In its own way, the sexual act is to be a prayer as not only two bodies unite, but two spirits as well – as the two become one flesh.[566] When the Holy Spirit is welcomed in this setting, sexual union enhances the Christian faith of both husband and wife. In such cases, the two become not merely one flesh, but one flesh in Christ. When the Spirit's love rather than humanity's lusts govern the marital bed, then the love of sexual union is of heaven. It is a love that promotes healing, peace, joy, and unity. Such unity is a work of the Holy Spirit who knits together the hearts of husbands and wives.

Healing in Marriage. As two people enter marriage, whether they realize it or not, they are incomplete persons, with interior wounds, character flaws, patterns of sin, and areas of underdeveloped virtue. Part of the grace of marriage is the opportunity for each spouse to bring God's healing touch to the wounds of the other, and to bring a watchful eye and support to the other's fight against sin and for virtue. Praying together, in the Spirit, drawing closer to one another in God's presence, letting God's Spirit bathe them both in love are the more intimate aspects of holy marriages, intimacy not only with one another, but also with God.

As the Holy Spirit can bring life to a new marriage, he also can bring new life to struggling marriages. Fr. Raniero Cantalamessa suggests "The Holy Spirit wants to repeat in every couple the miracle of the wedding at Cana: the Spirit wants to transform the water into wine; the water of routine, of lowered expectations, of coldness, into the heady wine of newness and of joy. Important to know, the Spirit *is* the wine."[567] Ways to invite the Holy Spirit into a marriage is for both spouses to purposely pursue the disciplines of a holy life together, pray together, go on retreats together, attend a Life in the Spirit seminar together. The Holy Spirit is still in the miracle business, and he can heal any marriage and any person.

Marriage as Sacrament. The challenge in marriage, as in all the sacraments, is to participate in the sacrament worthily. Grace flows as

---

[566] Cf. Matthew 19:4-6, Genesis 2:24. Note, Jesus' use of the word "flesh" refers to their physical bodies and not metaphorically to their sins, as St. Paul uses the term.
[567] Cantalamessa, Fr. Raniero, *Come, Creator Spirit*, Liturgical Press, 2003, pages 92-93. Cf. Pope John Paul II, GA, March 9, 1994, section 3.

we embrace, with faith and reverence, the presence of God in the sacrament. As sacrament, Holy Matrimony is a transforming experience through which the Spirit helps both husband and wife find their deepest and truest self. It is something to be celebrated, enjoyed, and lived for God's glory. Though we emphasize here the holiness of marriage, it must be said that where there is true holiness there is true happiness, deeper joy, and lasting peace as well, all fruit of the Spirit.

Heavenly Father, Thank you for the gift of holy matrimony. Please pour out your Spirit afresh on all marriages [and my own marriage]. Please wash away the world's filth, lies, and hurts. Please bring forth new life, wonder, renewed friendship, and love. Please deliver husbands and wives from the evils attacking their persons and marriages. Please heal them. Please revive them. Please make each one of them holy. Amen.

Dear Mary, you who interceded for the couple at Cana when Jesus performed his first miracle, please intercede before the throne of Jesus on behalf of _____. Please pray that the love of the Spirit be poured afresh into their lives and marriage[s] to cleanse, heal, and strengthen them. St. Joseph, please pray for them. St. Raphael, patron saint of Christian marriages, please pray for them. Amen.

Holy Spirit's Charismatic Grace

There are different kinds of gifts, but the same Spirit. There are different kinds of service, but the same Lord. There are different kinds of working, but the same God works all of them in all men. Now to each one the manifestation of the Spirit is given for the common good.

1 Corinthians 12:4-7 (NIV)

| 22 | **Spiritual Gifts (Charisms)** |

The ministry of the Holy Spirit is all about grace, all about God's love, his power, his truth poured out upon the elements of creation. Much of that grace touches our humanity through spiritual gifts or charisms.[568] These gifts are portals into a believer's heart through which the Spirit's supernatural power flows. Each gift is an anointing from God, a means by which the Spirit builds us up from within in faith and equips us for service in God's kingdom.[569]

Each spiritual gift is a sacred power. Each is an invitation for believers – individually and in community – to participate ever more fully in the life and works of the Holy Spirit. Charisms make the pursuit of holiness and service in God's kingdom exciting because we experience the power of God flowing through us. "In a special way," said Pope John Paul II, "the Triune God shows his sovereign power in the gifts."[570] The Second Vatican Council declared that the "Holy Spirit constantly brings faith to completion by His gifts."[571] Fr. Francis Martin notes that the Holy Spirit does so "by making the revelation of Jesus Christ personal and life changing."[572]

All of the spiritual gifts are, by definition, supernatural; they come into our lives as gifts of the Holy Spirit. There may be natural talents or learned skills with the same name, but they are not charisms. Natural talents come to us through our physical birth; charisms come to us as part of our spiritual rebirth. While we can use our natural talents for good or bad purposes, the Spirit works through a charism only for good.[573] As Pope John Paul II observed, "[A] charism is not genuine unless it leads to proclaiming that Jesus Christ is Lord."[574]

Charisms are, as Pope Benedict XVI taught, "not something we can merit or achieve, but only receive as pure gift."[575] Yet even as we

---

[568] The English word charism comes from the Greek word "*charisma*" (or plural, "*charismata*") which means "free gift."

[569] Cf. Ephesians 4:11-13; Pope John Paul II, GA, March 9, 1994; Cantalamessa, Fr. Raniero, *Come, Creator Spirit*, Liturgical Press, 2003, page 174.

[570] Pope John Paul II, GA, March 9, 1994, section 3.

[571] Second Vatican Council, DV, section 5.

[572] Martin, Fr. Francis, *Baptism in the Holy Spirit*, Franciscan Univ., 1986, page 54.

[573] Cf. Huntington, Eryn and Weddell, Sherry Anne, *Discerning Charisms*, The Siena Institute Press, 2002, page 9.

[574] Pope John Paul II, GA, August 5, 1998, section 2. Cf. 1 Corinthians 12:1-3.

[575] Pope Benedict XVI, homily at the 2008 World Youth Day, July, 20, 2008.

receive and use the Spirit's gifts, they do not belong to us. They belong to the Holy Spirit. Joseph with respect to the gift of interpreting dreams, Solomon with respect to the gift of wisdom, and Paul with respect to the gift of preaching rightly acknowledged that the power belongs to God.[576]

There are countless spiritual gifts, of which the Bible mentions over fifty.[577] These gifts include those that we commonly associate with the Sacrament of Baptism: faith, hope, and love; and those strengthened in the Sacrament of Confirmation: wisdom, understanding, knowledge, counsel, courage, piety, and fear of the Lord. These gifts help us grow in holiness.

We traditionally refer to faith, hope, and love, as "theological virtues." They are "theological" because they have a direct bearing on our relationship with God. However, before these are virtues, which involves the cooperation of our wills, they are first gifts of God. They are gifts infused in our hearts empowering us to live as children of God.[578] For purposes of our study, we treat these gifts as charismatic because they animate and inform all the other spiritual gifts that we commonly consider charismatic. They are the foundation for Christian morality and Christian service.

The Holy Spirit equips us with certain charisms so that we might serve God's kingdom in a particular way, filling certain roles or purposes in the Church community. As Paul tells us, "There are different kinds of spiritual gifts but the same Spirit; there are different forms of service but the same Lord; there are different workings but the same God who produces all of them in everyone."[579] Some of these gifts seem more modest in nature, and others more extraordinary, but all of them are important. The Spirit's service-oriented gifts include teaching, healing, pastoring, leadership, prophecy, tongues, hospitality, helpfulness, mercy, and casting out demonic spirits.

The Holy Spirit does not give spiritual gifts only to a saintly few. Instead, he distributes them, as he wills,[580] to "the faithful of every rank."[581] "To each individual, the manifestation of the Spirit is given

---

[576] Cf. Genesis 41:16, Wisdom 8:21, 1 Timothy 4:13-14.
[577] See Appendix 2.
[578] Cf. CCC sections 1266, 1812, 1813.
[579] 1 Corinthians 12:4-6 (NAB). Cf. Romans 12:3-6.
[580] Cf. 1 Corinthians 12:11, Hebrews 2:4.
[581] Second Vatican Council, LG, section 12.

for some benefit."[582] All believers, even those with mental, emotional, or physical limitations, have spiritual gifts and all are to participate in the community of believers using their gifts. The Holy Spirit dispenses his gifts with the needs of individuals and communities in mind. In most faith communities, there is the fullness of gifts, all complementing one another. Yet far too often, these gifts lie dormant.

We might think of the Holy Spirit as a great reservoir of water, with ourselves as dams holding back the water, and the charisms given to us are floodgates. Only as we open the floodgates, does the Spirit's living water – *his power* – flow, first as a trickle, then a stream, and finally as a rush of divine energy. God provides the floodgates and the living water. We open those floodgates with faith and obedience to the Spirit's inspirations. Ignorance, sin, fear, and worldly distractions shut these floodgates and suppress the flow of the Spirit's power.

The Church's Charismatic Dimension. The Second Vatican Council reminds us, "It is not only through the sacraments and the [hierarchal] ministries of the Church that the Holy Spirit sanctifies and leads the People of God . . . [but also by] 'allotting his gifts to everyone according to his will.'"[583] Pope John Paul II taught that these two channels of grace, the institutional and charismatic dimensions of the Church, are "co-essential . . . to the Church's constitution. They contribute, although differently, to the life, renewal, and sanctification of God's People."[584] He described the Church's "charismatic dimension as one of her constitutive [essential] elements."[585] He referred to the modern era as a time of "providential rediscovery of the Church's charismatic dimension."[586]

Rediscovery of the Church's charismatic dimension is important because a proper emphasis on the Spirit's gifts can radically change people, communities, the Church, and indeed the world. We cannot attain the fullness of God's will for our lives without them. Moreover, there is blessing to be experienced in community through the gifts of others that we will miss out on if we, as community, do not allow the

---

[582] 1 Corinthians 12:7 (NAB). Cf. Ephesians 4:7-8, 1 Peter 4:10.

[583] Second Vatican Council, LG, section 12. The interior quote is from 1 Corinthians 12:11. Cf. CCC section 768.

[584] Pope John Paul II, address to ecclesial movements, May 30, 1998, section 4. Cf. Pope John Paul II, GA, June 24, 1992, section 9.

[585] Pope John Paul II, address to ecclesial movements, May 30, 1998, section 4.

[586] Pope John Paul II, address to ecclesial movements, May 30, 1998, section 4.

Spirit to bring forth his gifts. Thus, St. Paul said of the spiritual gifts, "I do not want you to be uninformed."[587]

Receiving and Experiencing the Release of Charisms. Spiritual gifts can come into our lives much like seeds planted in the ground. Both the budding forth and the release of a gift can happen immediately with robust vigor, or it may happen gradually – each a function of God's grace and our cooperation with his grace. Sometimes a recipient may experience a profound awareness that something has happened. As Pope John Paul II taught, some gifts "burst in like an impetuous wind, which seizes people and carries them to new ways of missionary commitment to the radical service of the Gospel . . . and instilling . . . an ardent desire for holiness."[588] Other times, gifts may quietly and beautifully grow within us, without our being aware of it.

The Sacrament of Baptism is the normal means by which persons receive charisms. These are strengthened in Confirmation and as we actively pursue our faith in Jesus. As St. Cyril taught adult converts prior to the Sacrament of Baptism, "My final words, beloved ones, . . . are words of exhortation, urging all of you to prepare your souls for the reception of the heavenly charisms."[589]

The experience of many Biblical figures suggests that the Holy Spirit can and does impart charisms apart from Baptism,[590] including the gift of faith present in the life of an adult believer prior to Baptism.[591] Jesus' parable of the talents suggests that by being good stewards of existing gifts, God may reward us with more gifts.[592] In addition, Paul's exhorts believers to eagerly desire spiritual gifts, suggesting that the Spirit may give some gifts because we seek them not for our own glory but for the building up of others.[593] Charisms unique to the ministerial priesthood (authority to forgive sins in the name of God and to make the body and blood of Jesus physically present at Holy Mass) are conferred at ordination.

---

[587] 1 Corinthians 12:1 (NRSV).
[588] Pope John Paul II, address to ecclesial movements, May 30, 1998, section 5.
[589] St Cyril of Jerusalem, *Catechetical Lecture* #18, section 32.
[590] For example: Moses, the prophets, the judges, David, etc in the Old Testament and Cornelius and his household in the New Testament (Acts 10:1-8, 44-48).
[591] Cf. CCC sections 1248-1249.
[592] Cf. Matthew 25:14-30, Luke 19:12-27.
[593] Cf. 1 Corinthians 14:1.

It is common for the power of various gifts to be released in times of worship, faithful celebration of a sacrament, in prayer groups through the laying on of hands, while listening intently to God's Word, or while serving God in some task and the gift is needed. As discussed in chapter 7, the initial experience of charisms bursting forth with energy and excitement often comes when we are baptized in the Holy Spirit, as was the case with the Apostles at Pentecost.

The Second Vatican Council declared that charisms should "be received with thanksgiving and consolation, for they are perfectly suited to and useful for the needs of the Church."[594] Pope John Paul II taught that they should be "received in gratitude both on the part of the one who receives them, and also on the part of the entire Church."[595]

While the Apostle Paul encourages believers to desire all the spiritual gifts,[596] too often we do not desire them and the ones we have are, as Pope Paul VI suggested, "buried and suffocated."[597] They are buried beneath ignorance, pride, fear, and our lack of faith. They are buried beneath the confusion, busyness, and distractions of everyday life, and there they can lie dormant for years or a whole lifetime. Some, guided by a false sense of modesty, bury the Spirit's gifts thinking that they do not need them to be good Christians, never realizing that part of being a good Christian is our openness to the Spirit's gifts.

Many Christians fear the Spirit's charismatic grace. We wonder, what might God call me to do with his gifts? Might he call me to move to some far away country to work as a missionary? Some of us fear embarrassment: What will others think of me if I step out in faith and use the gifts God has given me? Will others think of me as a Jesus-freak or a holy roller? What if I fail? Will people be disappointed in me? Whatever our fears, we must respond with faith, knowing that God is present in the moment helping us.

Discernment of Our Gifts. As believers, we need to discern the spiritual gifts entrusted to us and strive to use those gifts in a responsible manner. Discernment takes time, particularly as it concerns the more extraordinary gifts. The same Spirit who endows us with spiritual gifts aids our discernment. He is the anointing of which John

---

[594] Second Vatican Council, LG, section 12. Cf. CCC sections 799-800.
[595] Pope John Paul II, CL, section 24. Cf. Pope John Paul II's GA, March 9, 1994.
[596] Cf. 1 Corinthians 14:1.
[597] Pope Paul VI, EN, section 70.

speaks: "[T]he anointing you received from him remains in you, and you do not need anyone to teach you . . . his anointing teaches you."[598]

Prayer, study of God's Word and Church teachings, active ministry, the help of qualified spiritual directors, and the help of persons who maturely use a particular gift are the common means by which the Spirit helps us discern. In the process of discernment, Paul tells us, "[T]est everything and hold on to what is good."[599]

Many charisms are given as a means by which the Holy Spirit intends to work through us in various forms of service.[600] Thus, a better understanding of our charisms helps us to better understand and live God's calling for our lives, for we cannot meet the demands of our vocation on natural strength alone. A better understanding of our gifts can also give rise to periodic changes in our areas of service as we search for our proper place in the community of believers. Leaders, for their part, should be sensitive to this, cooperating with the Spirit, striving to place the right people in the right roles.

God fills our lives with many blessings, including natural talents, learned skills, material privileges, unique experiences, access to resources, key relationships, opportunities, and spiritual gifts. We should use all blessings in a way pleasing to God, remembering that to whom much is given, much is required.[601] Each form of blessing can be put to work for God's kingdom, but it is important to distinguish spiritual gifts from strengths and talents that are of the natural realm.

For example, consider the talents of artists. Consider poets such as Maya Angelou or Robert Frost, musicians such as Yo-Yo Ma or Eric Clapton, singers such as Ella Fitzgerald or Placido Domingo, public speakers such as Winston Churchill or John F. Kennedy, or painters such as Vincent Van Gogh or Claude Monet. All of these individuals are or were exceptionally talented. Yet, even as some of them may have used their unique skills at times for a sacred purpose, in perhaps most cases or even in all cases, they were exercising a natural talent and not a spiritual gift.

---

[598] 1 John 2:27 (NIV). Cf. 1 Corinthians 2:12.
[599] 1 Thessalonians 5:21 (NJB).
[600] Cf. Second Vatican Council, LG, section 4; Pope John Paul II, GA, February 6, 1991.
[601] Cf. Luke 12:28.

Generally speaking, when we experience the natural talents of artists, we are attracted to them, their artistic genius, or the beauty or power of their work or their message. With a charism, whether we realize it or not, we are attracted to God who is at work in and through the charism. Think of the writers of the Bible. In the case of the psalmist, the prophet Isaiah, or the writer of Job, for example, we might say that they were wonderfully talented at the craft of writing. However, most of the Biblical writers were not as naturally gifted. Yet they all had a charism for spiritual writing. *Their words had power because the Holy Spirit anointed their words for his purposes, despite what at times may have been the presence of a natural limitation.* Think of Peter, an uneducated fisherman, who by the power of the Holy Spirit became an accomplished preacher and evangelist. His words may not have been artistic by secular standards, but the Holy Spirit anointed his speech with unseen graces. Whether the spiritual gift is hospitality, healing, administration, or mercy, with a charism it is the power of the Holy Spirit at work.

Each of the Holy Spirit's service-oriented gifts enable us to be ministers of God's grace in some unique way. By faith, we exercise the power of these gifts, but it is in love that this power is perfected. As we mature in our Christian walk, as we grow in holiness and love, we become more effective minister's of the grace entrusted to us.

As we discern our spiritual gifts, we must be careful that such analysis does not inadvertently become an occasion for vanity, pride, envy, or competition. Properly naming our gifts is not as important as humbly using them in service to God. In the discernment process, we must also be careful not to let our ambitions or our natural talents confuse us. Because we want a particular role in the community does not mean God desires that we serve there. Nor does it mean he will or has given us charisms for that role. Because we have a natural talent that we put to impressive use in secular settings, does not mean we have a charism with the same name, to be used in God's kingdom.

Charisms are of God and will manifest themselves for God's purposes. They are a function of God's desires, not ours. What we are discussing has ramifications not only for front-line ministerial teams, but also with various councils and boards at the parish, diocesan, hospital, university, and other levels of the Church. So often, these councils or boards are made up of persons who have distinguished themselves in the secular world with their natural talents or learned skills. They might be noted for their business acumen and human wisdom. But how do these compare with the Spirit's charisms of administration and divine wisdom? How much better when Church councils are composed of persons who have been baptized in the Holy Spirit and are walking maturely in spiritual gifts relevant to the roles in which they serve. Think of the individuals Jesus chose to be the premier leaders of his Church; none of them were distinguished by worldly standards. However, after Pentecost, they were all filled with the Spirit of God and serving with charisms given by the Holy Spirit. Perhaps that should be the standard for all boards, councils, and committees within the Church, at all levels.

Regulating the Use of Spiritual Gifts. Pope John Paul II declared that all charisms belong to "the ordinary life of the Church."[602] Toward that end, bishops and local pastors are responsible for overseeing a community's teachings on spiritual gifts and determining the authenticity of the more extraordinary ones and regulating them.[603] While the Catholic Church has not provided a list of the more extraordinary gifts, perhaps these include charisms associated with priestly offering of the Eucharistic prayers, priestly forgiveness of sins in the Sacrament of Reconciliation, discernment of Church doctrine, proclamation of the Word, prophecy, tongues, casting out demonic spirits, and miraculous healings. All of these gifts belong to the ordinary life of the Church; and most or maybe all of these gifts also belong to the ordinary life of every parish community. Proper pastoral oversight will vary depending on a host of circumstances, the purpose of which is to aid, not stifle, the Spirit's activity.

Spiritual Gifts and One's Status before God. Receiving spiritual gifts in no way exalts a person in God's eyes.[604] Jesus makes this quite clear in a stern warning he gave concerning the Final Judgment. He stated that there will be individuals who receive and exercise extraordinary charisms and perform great works of service for the Church who, on the Day of Judgment, will hear the words, "I never knew you; go away from me, you evildoers."[605] Jesus' warning prompts us to embrace our spiritual gifts with God's will and his glory in mind and not our own.

---

[602] Pope John Paul II, GA, March 24, 1993, section 6.
[603] Cf. 1 Thessalonians 5:12, 19-21; LG, section 12; CCC section 801.
[604] Cf. Romans 12:3-8, 1 Corinthians 4:7.
[605] Matthew 7:23 (NRSV).

Counterfeit Gifts. With each gift of the Spirit, there are counterfeit gifts of the world and of Satan, which can mislead people. Every counterfeit gift does harm. False faith does harm, as does false hope, false love, false wisdom, false prophecy, and false teachings. Yet the reality of counterfeits in every realm of spiritual giftedness must not dissuade us from faithfully seeking that which is authentic and appreciating it in ourselves and in others.

With Gifts Comes Responsibility. As given, gifts of the Spirit are possibilities, special privileges, supernatural talents.[606] The Catholic Church teaches that each service-oriented gift is a privilege that enables us "to collaborate [with God] in the salvation of others."[607] Each is "a duty," as Pope John Paul II put it, "stemming from the very fact of the gift received, which creates a responsibility and demands a commitment."[608] When we ignore God's gifts, we are shirking a responsibility, which is one meaning of Jesus' parable of the talents. In that parable, the master looks upon the servant who buried his talents and rebukes him saying, "You wicked and lazy servant!"[609] The master then takes away the talents previously given to that servant and gives them to others. Jesus' rebuke concerns spiritual gifts and has implications not only for individuals, but for communities too.

We should learn also from the experience of Samson, in the Old Testament. In his childhood, "the spirit of the Lord began to stir in him."[610] In time, that stirring manifested itself in mighty deeds of strength. So long as Samson was faithful to God, this gift was with him. When he behaved foolishly and took the gift for granted, God took the gift away. After Samson endured great suffering due to his foolishness and repented, God restored his gift. But Samson could have avoided much suffering had he not taken the gift for granted.

Truly, when due to sin, or ignorance, or lack of interest, or fear, we ignore God's purposes with respect to charisms, we are in rebellion against God. Just as we must respect and make use of the Spirit's sacramental graces, so also we must respect and make use of the Spirit's charismatic graces. If we ignore these, we do so not only to our own detriment, but also to the detriment of the community we are a

---

[606] Cf. Sheed, Frank J., *The Holy Spirit in Action*, Servant Books, 1981, page 83.
[607] CCC section 2003.
[608] Pope John Paul II, GA, March 9, 1994, section 7. Cf. CCC section 799.
[609] Matthew 25:26 (NJB). Cf. Luke 19:22.
[610] Judges 13:25 (NRSV).

part of and those we might help. Truly, the charismatic experience is not an end unto itself, but rather a means to quicken our faith in Christ and equip us for service in God's kingdom.

Gifts to God. The Holy Spirit does not give us his gifts that we would ignore them. Thus, referring to one of Timothy's spiritual gifts, Paul instructed him, "Do not neglect your gift."[611] "[F]an into a flame the gift of God that you possess."[612] When we use the Spirit's gifts worthily, the result is a virtue, our gift back to God. Virtues are our response to the Spirit's gifts, often through the formation of good habits. Virtues are always a verb, always associated with doing, always an act of our will inspired and supported by God's grace.

Being Wise Stewards of Our Gifts. The Spirit's gifts are all good; they are all perfect and from above.[613] However, we who receive the gifts are not perfect. With any new spiritual gift, it begins developing within a person who is usually not yet mature in his faith walk and certainly not mature in his use of a gift that he is only beginning to realize he has. As Jesus in his humanity "grew in wisdom,"[614] we too must grow in our gifts. We do this only with the help of the Spirit.

Peter tells us to use our gifts "to serve others, faithfully administering God's grace in its various forms."[615] When he says "faithfully," he means when it is easy and when it is challenging, when we are acknowledged for our efforts and when we are not. In our service, we must remember that we are working for God. We are privileged to be administering his grace.

Spiritual Gifts and Community. By his work through various charisms, the Holy Spirit connects the People of God in community, equipping us to work together in teams. Yet for his greater purposes to be fulfilled, believers must accept, appreciate, and use their gifts in concert with others, guided by the Holy Spirit. Pope John Paul II taught that God gives us differing gifts with the broader needs of the community in mind:"[K]eep in mind that spiritual gifts are to be accepted not only for one's personal holiness, but above all for the good of the Church. . . . Because of these charisms, the community's life is full of spiritual wealth and every kind of service. And diversity

---

[611] 1 Timothy 4:14 (NIV).
[612] 2 Timothy 1:6 (NJB).
[613] Cf. James 1:17.
[614] Luke 2:52 (NIV).
[615] 1 Peter 4:10 (NIV).

is necessary for a greater spiritual wealth: everyone makes a personal contribution which the others do not. The community lives on the contribution of all."[616] There is a richness that communities sorely lack, if the gifts of the many lie dormant and unused.

It is customary for persons with similar gifts and a common calling to gather in communities, such as a religious order or a parish ministry. In the Apostolic Church, for example, the community that travelled with St. Paul shared, perhaps, similar gifts of evangelization and administration – as they went about establishing many new churches. In Church history, many religious communities formed around a dominant charism shared with their founder. For example, the communities that formed around saints Francis of Assisi, Dominic de Guzman, Ignatius of Loyola, and Alphonsus Liguori were great preachers, great evangelists. The communities that formed around saints Francis Cabrini and Katherine Drexel were teachers. Those that formed around saints Benedict and Bernard were prayer warriors. Those that formed around saints Mother Teresa and Vincent de Paul had a heart for the poor; and those that formed around Josephine Potel, Camillus de Lellis, and John of God took care of the sick.

In a mature community, even one organized around a particular form of service, there will be the fullness of spiritual gifts. The challenge for a community organized around a dominant gift is to appreciate all the gifts given to the community and not just the dominant gift. Truly, absent an awakening and responsible use of the Spirit's many charisms in the community, communities cannot attain the fullness of God's perfect will for them.

Jesus, Thank you for the charismatic dimension of your Church and my life. I ask forgiveness for my ignorance or lack of appreciation of this in times past. I seek forgiveness for the extent to which I have buried or ignored the charisms you have given to me. Lord, please awaken within me a new appreciation of this aspect of Christian life. Please baptize me afresh in your Holy Spirit, and may the charisms and other graces of my Baptism and Confirmation be enlivened. May the charisms you have given me blossom to full beauty and bear much pleasing fruit for your kingdom. In your holy name I pray, Amen.

---

[616] Pope John Paul II, GA, June 24, 1992, section 3.

23   Gift of Faith

Pope John Paul II clearly taught, "[The gift of faith] is the fundamental gift given by the Holy Spirit for the supernatural life."[617] The gift of faith makes relationship with God possible. It is the capacity to know and trust God. If we persistently engage this gift, it will direct us from within toward our eternal destiny in God.

The Book of Hebrews describes the spiritual gift of faith as "the realization of what is hoped for and evidence of things not seen."[618] When the writer refers to something that is "hoped for," he is referring to the deeper meaning of life, which we find only in relationship with God. Our experience of God is the "evidence of things not seen." It is a way of knowing that transcends the physical world. In the natural realm, *seeing is believing*; but in the supernatural realm, *believing is seeing*. This believing does not originate from our imagination or intellect, but from our experiences of God as he reveals himself to us.

Pope Francis described the gift of faith this way. "Faith is born of an encounter with the living God who calls us and reveals his love, a love which precedes us and upon which we can lean for security and for building our lives. . . . Faith, received from God as a supernatural gift, becomes a light for our way, guiding our journey through time."[619]

Our experience of faith begins as we first encounter the Spirit. Even infant children, who do not yet have a developed intellect, can receive the Spirit and experience the gift of faith, if only in seedling form. This commonly happens through the Sacrament of Baptism.[620]

Virtue of Faith. The virtue of faith is our acceptance and worthy use of Spirit's gift of faith. It is an authentically human act, whereby we respond to God's revelation of himself and we choose to seek God, trust his ways, and obey his commands for love of him. *Faith is the living of life differently because we are in relationship with God.*

The virtue of faith is not an intellectual belief that God exists or agreement with any belief system about God. Belief that God exists is

---

[617] Pope John Paul II, GA, May 8, 1991, section 1. Cf. Mark 16:16, John 3:16, 36, 6:40, 47; CCC sections 153, 161, 1253.
[618] Hebrew 11:1 (NAB).
[619] Pope Francis, LF, section 4.
[620] Cf. Pope John Paul II, CT, section 19.

not even a virtue. The devil, for example, and all his demons believe in God's existence.[621] They know about God's power and many of the truths we find in the Bible. However, they do not have faith in God. They do not know and trust God. Sadly, that may also describe many people today who call themselves Christian.

The virtue of faith is not an activity of the mind, but of the heart, for as the Bible tells us, "one believes with the heart."[622] Our minds have a role to play, but faith is foremost a matter of the heart. Pope John Paul II taught that the virtue of faith, "in its deepest essence, is the openness of the human heart . . . to God's self-communication in the Holy Spirit."[623] This self-communication of the Spirit leads us from within to our salvation in Christ. We grow in faith as we come to know Jesus, ever more intimately, as Lord and Savior, and as Teacher and Friend. This knowing begins in earnest as we make an explicit personal commitment to Jesus and begin embracing the disciplines of a holy life.[624] We grow in faith the more we learn to depend on God for everything, daily submitting our intellect, will, and emotions to the overriding authority of his Spirit.

The virtue of faith matures as we freely commit our entire selves to God in loving obedience.[625] This happens only as we allow our relationship with God to become the most important relationship in our lives. How important is faith? The Bible tells us, "without faith it is impossible to please God"[626] and "the righteous live by their faith."[627] The Catholic Church teaches that faith is "already the beginning of eternal life."[628]

In his letter to the Galatians, Paul tells us, that Jesus died on the cross "so that we might receive the promise of the Spirit through faith."[629] Two important ways we receive the Spirit "through faith" are prayer and Bible study. Faith is all about relationship, which is to say,

---

[621] Cf. James 2:19.

[622] Romans 10:10 (NAB).

[623] Pope John Paul II, DeV, section 51.

[624] Cf. Pope John Paul II, CT, section 19.

[625] Cf. CCC section 1814.

[626] Hebrews 11:6 (NIV).

[627] Habakkuk 2:4 (NRSV). Cf. Romans 1:17, Hebrews 10:38.

[628] CCC section 163.

[629] Galatians 3:14 (NAB).

it is all about prayer: *no prayer, no faith; little prayer, little faith.*[630] In prayer, we truly learn how awesome God is and who we really are as creatures in his kingdom. It is through prayer that he commonly heals, renews, and directs the lives of the faithful. Paul also tells us that study of the Gospel message is critical to growing in faith, for "faith comes from . . . hearing the word of Christ."[631]

When we embrace the gift of faith and live it, we step into the gift of right standing before God. Says Paul, "The righteousness from God comes through faith in Jesus Christ to all who believe."[632] The expression "righteousness from God" means "right standing." It comes from God as a gift. We accept that gift into our lives "through faith in Jesus Christ." Such faith includes obedience, for in the same letter Paul discusses "the obedience of faith,"[633] an "obedience, which leads to righteousness."[634]

For Christians and Jews, Abraham, the great patriarch of ancient Israel, is our *father in faith.* He was unique for his close relationship with God. Because of this close relationship, he was wonderfully obedient to God's many commands, including some that were exceptionally difficult to understand and follow. At times, those commands tested his faith, exposing it for what it was at a given point in time. By obedience and perseverance, his faith grew in strength.

For us, to live *the obedience of faith,* we need the interior help of the Holy Spirit, and we ourselves must be committed to the task. God will test our faith, regularly, through the trials of life. In the testing, if we persevere, clinging to God, our faith grows stronger even as we stumble and periodically fall. Through it all, we must reject all fear, which is an enemy to faith.[635] For good reason, over three hundred times in the Bible, we hear the command, "Be not afraid."

Faith and Works. Faith, our trust in God, and works, our loving obedience to God's commands, go hand and hand. As St. James taught, "[J]ust as a body without a spirit is dead, so also faith without works is

---

[630] Cf. Scanlan, Fr. Michael, *Appointment with God*, Apostolate of Family Consecration, 1987, page 10.

[631] Romans 10:17 (NJB).

[632] Romans 3:22 (NIV). Cf. Romans 4:13, 10:4, Hebrews 11:7.

[633] Cf. Romans 1:5, 2:13, 16:27; Second Vatican Council, DV, section 5; CCC sections 1814-1816.

[634] Romans 6:17 (NIV).

[635] Cf. Pope Francis, comments in St Peter's Square, May 18, 2013.

dead."[636] And elsewhere, "faith without deeds is useless."[637] Paul tells us that all humanity was "created in Christ for good works, which God prepared beforehand to be our way of life."[638] He encourages us to live lives "rich in good works."[639]

Faith and good works go together. However, sometimes what looks like faith, for example intellectual beliefs, religious pride, or legalistic behavior, is not faith at all. In addition, works intent on manipulating God's judgment are not works of faith. Works of faith are done for love of God.

In our faith journeys, we often must go through the motions of obedience or religious practice when we do not feel the faith, or understand a command, but we do it anyway out of love or respect for God, or out of our desire to love and respect God. This is faith, perhaps early in its development. Often, an apprentice to any activity will engage in behaviors that initially do not make sense, or do not seem natural, but in time, they do. Some use the expression "fake it until you make it" or "acting as if" to refer to a person's sincere efforts to obey, when their intellect or emotions are not yet in agreement. In our faith journeys, this is all good, a work of the Holy Spirit.

It is through *the humility of faith* that the power of the Holy Spirit is most active in our lives, often as the enabling means for other spiritual gifts (such as prophecy, healing, mercy, courage, wisdom, or teaching). This is what Jesus is referring to when he says, "Whoever believes in me, as scripture says: 'Rivers of living water will flow from within him.'"[640]

Common Good. Our faith in God is in one sense a personal matter with God and, at the same time, it is a public matter. God is the God not only of you and me, but also of all creation. The Christian faith is meant to be lived in community. It is meant to be shared. We have no greater possession, no greater treasure to share with others than our faith in Jesus. And in such sharing, we grow in faith.

Pope Francis wrote about the connection between faith and the common good of society and noted, "The individual's act of faith finds

---

[636] James 2:26 (NAB).
[637] James 2:20 (NJB). Cf. Matthew 22:11-14.
[638] Ephesians 2:10 (NRSV).
[639] 1 Timothy 6:18 (NAB). Cf. Galatians 5:6, Titus 2:14.
[640] John 7:38 (NAB).

its place within a community, within the common "we" of the people who, in faith, are like a single person. . . . Faith is truly a good for everyone; it is a common good. Its light does not simply brighten the interior of the Church, nor does it serve solely to build an eternal city in the hereafter; it helps us build our societies [today] in such a way that they can journey towards a future of hope."[641]

Are We Living Our Faith? Pope Paul VI taught, "[E]ither we live our faith [in Jesus] with devotion, depth, energy, and joy or that faith will die out."[642] We all should challenge ourselves, in a practical everyday sense: who or what do we have faith in, really? Is God the supreme object of our faith or other things or persons? Consider how you spend your time and your money. What fills your private thoughts, your daydreams, and your words of praise? Is God pre-eminent? Are you a different person because of your close relationship with Jesus?

Beyond the ordinary gift of faith or a saving faith, there is a gift of faith listed by St. Paul as a service gift.[643] It is great confidence in the power of God that inspires a person toward miracles and mighty deeds.[644] This is the faith the size of a mustard seed that is able to move mountains.[645]

Jesus, Faith in you is everything. It is the gateway to truth, to eternal life, and to heavenly purpose. Jesus you are Lord! You are the Son of the living God! The Father, you, and the Holy Spirit are God. I believe in you Jesus, please help my unbelief. I pray for a deeper awareness of you and your commands. I want my life unambiguously centered on you. I ask that the Holy Spirit strengthen my capacity to know, trust, and obey you.

Come Holy Spirit, come. Please inflame my heart with an abiding love for Jesus and faith in him. Help me to know Jesus more fully and to trust him with my life. Teach me to follow him wholeheartedly. In Jesus' name I pray, Amen.

---

[641] Pope Francis, LF, sections 7, 51.
[642] Pope Paul VI, public address, May 19, 1975.
[643] Cf. 1 Corinthians 12:9; Pope John Paul II, GA, May 8, 1991, section 2.
[644] Cf. 1 Corinthians 12:10.
[645] Cf. Matthew 17:20.

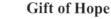

24 Gift of Hope

Hope is another important gift of the Holy Spirit. In our everyday use of the word, hope is the desire or expectation of some perceived good. People commonly hope for money, fame, jobs, physical beauty, winning contests, getting out of trouble, etc. Some of what we might call our "everyday hopes" can have a proper place in our lives. On the other hand, some hopes can do damage by distracting us from our relationship with God.

The spiritual gift of hope is an expectant joy that awaits the fulfillment of God's promises, most especially the promise of eternal salvation.[646] It is not wishful thinking, rather it is confident assurance born of our relationship with God, whom we have come to know and love. Our hope, truly, is in Jesus, in whom we find the "Yes to all God's promises."[647] Like all spiritual gifts, divine hope comes only from the Holy Spirit.

Peter speaks of the Christian life as "a new birth into a living hope."[648] This living hope is our relationship with Jesus through the ministry of the Holy Spirit. This living hope unclogs and expands the pipelines of our hearts allowing the Spirit's grace to flow more freely through us. This living hope brings new desires: desires for holiness, truth, goodness, and purity. It gives us new insights and new attitudes. Because of it, we learn to live differently, with new priorities and a new joy. In times of trial, this living hope comforts us.

Divine hope brings transformation and as it does, the Apostle John teaches, it purifies us, by raising our minds to God.[649] Thus, Paul tells us to be "joyful in hope, persevere in hardship, keep praying regularly."[650] "For in hope we are saved."[651] Isaiah prophesied, "[T]hose who hope in Yahweh will regain their strength, they will sprout wings like eagles, though they run they will not grow weary, though they walk they will never tire."[652]

---

[646] Cf. CCC section 1817; Colossians 1:23, Titus 3:7.
[647] 2 Corinthians 1:20 (NJB).
[648] 1 Peter 1:3 (NRSV).
[649] Cf. 1 John 3:3.
[650] Romans 12:12 (NJB).
[651] Romans 8:24 (NRSV).
[652] Isaiah 40:31 (NJB).

Like a piece of armor, "the hope of salvation"[653] is a helmet that protects our minds from evil, sometimes by illuminating the false hopes that may also be present in our lives. The Holy Spirit helps us discipline our lesser hopes and purge destructive hopes. For most of us, this happens gradually over time, but often there are distinct moments when we experience a dramatic change, when we find freedom from false hopes or false understandings and we learn to hope in Jesus.

Virtue of Hope. When we embrace God's gift of hope and worthily apply it in our lives, the result is the virtue of hope. It is unshakeable confidence in the promises of God. This virtue growing within us is our gift back to God. It is our choice to desire and seek fulfillment in God, even in life's darkest moments. It is the choice to delight in the Lord, rather than the enticements of the world. Peter speaks to this virtue when he says, "[P]ut all your hope in the grace brought to you by the revelation of Jesus Christ."[654]

The virtue of hope is a discipline that keeps our minds and hearts focused on God, his promises, and his truths. It is not about periodically wanting God to move in our lives, it is confidence that indeed he is moving in our lives, even when we cannot sense it. From the Bible, we see this virtue wonderfully manifest in the lives of Abraham and Sarah who "hoping against hope"[655] trusted God's seemingly preposterous promises. Hope guided them to their destiny.

The virtue of hope protects us from discouragement; it sustains us during times of trial; it focuses the gaze of our hearts on the heavenly reward that awaits those who keep their faith in Jesus. Strengthened by this hope, we learn to find freedom from selfishness and to appreciate and experience more deeply God's love.[656] Even in the most dire of circumstances, such as the plight of wartime prisoners in an enemy's concentration camp, divine hope buoys believers who rest in the promises of Christ. Hope reassures us of God's love for us and his divine presence, even as evil seems to have its way.

As regards preaching, very often divine hope blossoms in people when a priest or minister vibrantly preaches about sin, the Final Judgment, heaven, and hell. At first, we may not feel hope because

---

[653] 1 Thessalonians 5:8 (NJB). Cf. Ephesians 6:17.
[654] 1 Peter 1:13 (NJB).
[655] Romans 4:18 (NRSV).
[656] Cf. CCC section 1818.

such preaching draws attention to the reality of sin in our lives and its consequences. Yet as we learn of God's mercy, his forgiveness, his healing touch to those who repent, the message of sin can awaken hope and greatly facilitate the processes of conversion.

Human Optimism and Divine Hope. Optimism is a natural form of hope that is born of a positive attitude. It is a disciplined belief that everything will end well. For all its potentially favorable attributes, optimism is not divine hope. Human optimism can participate in the virtue of hope, if it helps direct our will, our intellect, and our emotions toward God. However, sometimes, if we are not careful, such optimism can work contrary to God's commands. It can be a "god" of the self-will in our lives.

An example of worldly hope disguising itself as divine hope is the so-called "prosperity gospel," which incorporates God's name in pursuit of personal wants. This heresy mistakenly believes that God has bound himself by his own Biblical promises to give us worldly prosperity, often in the form of financial blessings. It tries to manipulate God to serve our desires. Though the message of the prosperity gospels tickles the ears of many, it nevertheless has its origin in a worldly spirit, not the Holy Spirit.

Hope in Community. Divine hope sustains not only persons, but also communities. Indeed, God intends us to share our hope with others. That is why Peter instructs us to always be ready to give an account "for the hope that is in you."[657] For her part, the Church sows the seeds of this hope when she boldly proclaims the good news of Jesus – first through preaching, but also through ministries of healing, charity, and fellowship that give divine hope a human touch.

The experience of divine hope is not merely for church communities, but also for families, friendships, workplaces, towns, and even nations. Nations often place their hope in leaders, armies, political systems, economic structures, social policies, technological advancements, and strategic alliances. The Bible's great civil leaders taught that nations should place their hope in God.[658]

---

[657] 1 Peter 3:15 (NAB).

[658] Cf. Deuteronomy 1:29-32 (Moses), Numbers 14:6-9, (Joshua), 1 Samuel 17:47 (David), 2 Chronicles 20:5-22 (Jehosaphat), 1 Maccabees 3:19 (Judas Maccabees). See also Psalms 25:3, 33:17-22, 42:5, 130:7, Zechariah 4:6.

Enemies of Hope. In our lives, the main enemies of hope are presumption, indifference, and despair. Presumption: We can falsely suppose our own salvation. Indifference: We can choose to ignore the importance of God, placing our hope in worldly things. Despair: We can think it impossible that God would extend his kindness to me.

We counteract these snares by seeking first the kingdom of God through a deepening relationship with Jesus. Paul also emphasizes the importance of praying for hope. He prayed for fellow Christians – "[May] the God of hope fill you with joy and peace . . . so that in the power of the Holy Spirit you may be rich in hope."[659] Prayers of praise and thanksgiving foster hope, by helping us focus our minds on God, and off ourselves and off life's worries, distractions, and worldly wants. Bible study helps us grow in hope by reminding us of God's promises, encouraging us to trust those promises, and reminding us of God's many wonderful deeds. Paul tells us that the Bible was written so that "we might have hope."[660]

Trials can also be a time to grow in hope. Often it takes a seemingly hopeless situation to bring us to our knees, before we allow divine hope to flourish within us. When life is going smoothly, we can forget about God and rely on ourselves, others, or things apart from God. Often, it takes a trial to remind us of God in whom we should place our hopes.

Paul tells us, we should "boast in our hope of sharing the glory of God. And not only that, but we [should] also boast in our sufferings, knowing that suffering produces endurance, and endurances produces character, and character produces hope, and hope does not disappoint us, because God's love has been poured into our hearts through the Holy Spirit."[661]

The Father pours the Spirit into our hearts so that "we might become heirs according to the hope of eternal life."[662] As the Spirit speaks to all of us, "I know well the plans I have in mind for you, says the Lord, plans for your welfare, not for woe! plans to give you a

---

[659] Romans 15:13 (NJB).
[660] Romans 15:4 (NIV).
[661] Romans 5:2-5 (NRSV).
[662] Titus 3:7 (NRSV).

future full of hope."[663] So then, "Let us keep firm in the hope we profess, because the one who made the promise is trustworthy."[664]

> *Sweet Holy Spirit, You are the Spirit of Hope. In my weakness, in my struggles, please come and help me. Please free me from all sadness and despair, and fill me instead with angelic hope. Please lift the gaze of my heart to heaven. Please focus my heart and mind on Jesus and his promises. May your graces of hope buoy me in turbulent times. May your graces help keep the peace and joy of my heart stable. Please make me aware of and purge from my life all false and misplaced hopes. I do not want to hope in the world or in worldly things. I want that hope that comes only from you. Amen.*

---

[663] Jeremiah 29:11 (NAB).
[664] Hebrews 10:23 (NJB).

25 Gift of Love

The Bible tells us that "the love of God has been poured into our hearts by the Holy Spirit"[665] and that this love is God himself, for "God is love."[666] Of course, God's love is not the world's love; it is not about human desires, likes, or feelings, or a system of philosophical values. Rather, God's love is the Holy Spirit, the bond of perfection, infinitely holy and pure.

In Greek, the language of the New Testament, there are four different words for our one English word "love." They are "*storge*," "*eros*," "*philia*," and "*agape*."[667] In the Biblical framework for love, the first three of these are natural forms of love. The last of these is supernatural; it is a work of the Holy Spirit in us and through us.

Type of Love	English Translation	Example
Storge	Affection	Mentor for a protégé
Eros	Romance	As between spouses
Philia	Friendship	Good friends
Agape	Selfless giving	Charity to others

Each of the natural loves, in its proper context, is a blessing to life, yet each can be distorted causing damage to our spiritual and emotional health. Only as the natural loves are lived properly are they a blessing. Sin, in all its many forms, is the perversion, distortion, or rejection of love.

Agape (pronounced "ah-gah-pay") is God's love for us. This is the love Jesus lived and taught. This love comes from God; it is a gift infused into our hearts by the Holy Spirit, a gift to be lived. Agape is selfless giving that can transform each of the natural loves, taking them to greater levels. Through agape, the Holy Spirit perfects our faith in and our relationship with God. For centuries, Christians translated agape into English as "charity." Agape is a spiritual gift that enables us to "love God above all things for his own sake, and our neighbor as ourselves."[668] The Biblical texts that follow concern agape love.

---

[665] Romans 5:5 (NJB).

[666] Cf. 1 John 4:8, 16.

[667] Cf. C. S. Lewis, *The Four Loves*.

[668] CCC section 1822.

Christianity associates agape with the Father's gift of the Son. The Apostle John tells us, "God's love was revealed among us in this way: God sent his only Son into the world . . . to be the atoning sacrifice for our sins."[669] Truly, throughout time, God has expressed his love in countless ways; but its supreme expression is Jesus. It is Jesus laying down his life for us.

The Holy Spirit leads every believer who lets him to the crucified Jesus and through Jesus to the Father. This is why Paul boasted of preaching a crucified Christ.[670] This is why Catholics pray the sorrowful mysteries of the rosary and the Stations of the Cross. Because, along with the Incarnation, the Cross is the greatest act of love, ever. Amid the horrid reality that is the Cross, there is immense, unfathomable beauty because of the One who died there. We go to the Cross to learn how much our God loves us. We stand at the foot of the Cross to honor Jesus' supreme act of love and to open our own hearts to his gift of the Holy Spirit.

At the Last Supper, Jesus prayed to the Father on his disciples' behalf "that the love which you [Father] loved me may be in them."[671] The love by which the Father loved Jesus is the Holy Spirit. Jesus desires that the Father fill all humanity with that very same love, that very same Person. This isn't mere poetic language. It is literal truth.

God loves us, each and every human being, by name. He loved us before he created us. Before time began, he chose us to be his own. He chose each person who has ever lived and who ever will live to be a beloved child in his kingdom. Our life is a gift of God's love, and in that same love, our lives are sustained. Even as we sin, even as we suffer under the weight of our sin, even if we ignore and reject God, he sustains our lives in his love. His creativity, his forgiveness, his healing power, his wisdom, his commands, his correction, his patience, and even his wrath are all expressions of his love.

Pope John Paul II poignantly taught, "Man cannot live without love. He remains a being that is incomprehensible [to] himself, his life is senseless, if love is not revealed to him, if he does not encounter love, if he does not experience it and make it his own, if he does not

---

[669] 1 John 4:9-10 (NRSV). Cf. John 3:16.
[670] Cf. 1 Corinthians 1:23, 2:2.
[671] John 17:26 (NJB).

participate intimately in it. This . . . is why Christ the Redeemer 'fully reveals man to himself.'"[672]

The gift of love is the capacity to love with God's own love, and to live life in the Spirit of Love. It is the "principal gift of the Holy Spirit."[673] Through faith, our relationship with God is established, but it is by love that our relationship with God is perfected. Thus, Paul could say, "[I]f I am without love, I am nothing."[674]

Virtue of Love. Our gift of love to God is the virtue of love. This is an act of our will choosing to love God and others in the power of God's own love. This cooperation with God manifests itself in various ways, but most obviously in obedience to God's commands. Jesus told his Apostles, "If you love me, you will keep my commands."[675]

When asked what were the greatest commands of Jewish Law, Jesus replied, "*Love the Lord your God with all your heart and with all your soul and with all your mind.* This is the first and greatest commandment. And the second is like it: *Love your neighbor as yourself.*"[676] How do we do this? First, we must learn to love God above all things and to let that love give order and orientation to our lives. To love him, though, we must first know him and trust him. We cannot truly love anyone whom we do not first know.

God is the Eternal Cause of all beauty, all truth, all goodness, and all love. To God the Father, our Creator; to God the Son, our Savior; to God the Holy Spirit, our Helper, we owe our deepest love and devotion. To love God, we must be persons of prayer and obedience. Prayer. Worship. Time together. Obedience. This is how we come to know and love God.

Jesus is our model for love – not only our love for God, but also our love for others. He told his closest disciples, "I give you a new commandment, that you love one another just as I have loved you."[677] Yet, how did Jesus love? He, who was greater than the entire universe,

---

[672] Pope John Paul II, RH, section 10.
[673] CCC section 1971.
[674] 1 Corinthians 13:2 (NJB).
[675] John 14:15 (NRSV). Cf. 1 John 5:3, Deuteronomy 5:10, 7:9, Nehemiah 1:5, Daniel 9:4.
[676] Matthew 22:37-39 (NIV). Cf. Mark 12:28-34, Luke 10:25-28, Deuteronomy 6:5, 10:12, Leviticus 19:18.
[677] John 13:34 (NRSV).

became one with us. He, who is worthy of being supremely exalted, chose to serve others. He touched people, and the power of the Spirit flowed out from him to bless others. Though he was innocent, he accepted humiliation and died for our sins.

Truly, a proper love of others flows from our love of God. The Apostle John tells us quite bluntly, "If anyone says, 'I love God,' but hates his brother, he is a liar; for whoever does not love a brother whom he has seen cannot love God whom he has not seen."[678] Our love of God is most tested in our daily interactions with our fellow human beings. What spirit is at work in us in our various interactions? Is it the Holy Spirit? Our challenge is to engage everyone from a place of lowliness and Godly joy, free from envy, pride, anger, lust, competitiveness, etc.

In his beautiful prose, often read at weddings, Paul describes the virtue of love, both what it is and what it is not. Says Paul, "Love is patient; love is kind; love is not envious or boastful or arrogant or rude. It does not insist on its own way; it is not irritable or resentful, it does not rejoice in wrongdoing, but rejoices in the truth. It bears all things, hopes all things, endures all things."[679] What is interesting about this passage on love is that Paul does not equate love with a feeling. He describes what it is and is not by listing behaviors, because love finds its proper expression not in our emotions, but in our actions.

We are to love others, but whom, specifically? Our families and friends? Yes, but such love will not distinguish anyone as a Christian, for even pagans know how to love family and friends.[680] God challenges us to love our neighbors who we know and don't know, who we like and don't like. He challenges us to love everyone, even our enemies. We are to love them despite how they have offended us. We are to bless our enemies, show them mercy, and pray for them.[681] We are to love all, including the unlovable, and we can only do this with the Spirit's supernatural help. To love as God loves, we need his grace at work in us.

If, with the natural loves, we might say that we love another person *because* _____; with agape, we might say we love another

---

[678] 1 John 4:20 (NAB).

[679] 1 Corinthians 13:4-7 (NRSV). Cf. Romans 12:9, 16-17, 1 John 3:18.

[680] Cf. Matthew 6:46-47, Luke 6:32-36.

[681] Cf. Matthew 5:44, Luke 6:26-27, Romans 12:14-16, 1 Peter 2:23.

person *despite* _____.[682] With agape, we love not for what we receive in return, but because love is our nature.

When Paul tells us that love "endures all things," he is saying that it is "long suffering." Whether we are suffering on our own or with others, divine love is patient, holding up under pressure supported by grace. Love trusts on God. Love waits on God with faith. Love worships and thanks the Lord even when times seem at their worst.

Echoing Israel's prophets, Jesus taught that our love must include acts of kindness to persons who are hungry, poor, sick, aging, and in prison. Love demands that we serve them. As Jesus lowered himself to serve humanity, his followers must lower themselves and serve humanity as well. This was the point of Jesus' parable of the Good Samaritan. Jesus would make this point even stronger when – in the story of Lazarus and the rich man and in the parable of the sheep and the goats – he linked the gift of eternal salvation with the love each person shows to the weak.[683] When we show kindness to those in need, we show it to Jesus; and when we deny kindness to those in need (through selfishness, fear, resentment, greediness, racism, indifference, gossip, or neglect) we deny kindness to Jesus.

At the Last Supper, Jesus further emphasized the importance of service when he got on his knees and washed his disciples' dirty feet. Then he said to them, "Do you realize what I have done for you? You call me 'teacher' and 'master,' and rightly so, for indeed I am. If I, therefore, the master and teacher, have washed your feet, you ought to wash one another's feet. I have given you a model to follow . . . If you understand this, blessed are you if you do it."[684]

Christian love requires forgiveness. Judaism, of the Law and the prophets, spoke passionately of forgiveness. God's own example was one of repeated forgiveness toward Israel despite her many transgressions. Peter asked Jesus how often we should forgive those who offend us. Seven times, perhaps? Was this the limit for Christians? No, said Jesus, not seven times "but seventy-seven times."[685] Practically speaking, he is saying that there is no limit. How do we do this? Only with the Spirit's help. It is all about the Spirit's

---

[682] Roberts, Oral, *The Baptism with the Holy Spirit*, Oral Roberts, 1964, page 68.
[683] Cf. Luke 16:19-31, Matthew 25:31-46. See also James 2:14-17.
[684] John 13:12-17 (NAB).
[685] Matthew 18:22 (NJB).

grace enabling us to choose mercy and not condemnation; it is a choice to carry no bitterness, no matter how bad an offense or how great our pain, and even if others are not sorry or they continue their bad behavior. It does not mean we are a doormat, or that we forget, or that we enable future bad behavior. Sometimes love requires dramatic actions to punish bad behavior or to separate ourselves from certain toxic people. Love is not a feeling but rather a choice, a choice to hold no grudge, to resist all tendencies to evil in us, and choose mercy. Love, in the form of forgiveness, is also one of the most powerful tools with which to fight evil in our own lives. When we choose to forgive, the Spirit's grace flows through us with much greater intensity.[686]

Paul described agape as the preeminent spiritual gift from God and the preeminent gift to God. He extols the wonders of faith, hope, and love, but "the greatest of these is love."[687] He tells us, "[T]he only thing that counts is faith working through love."[688] In addition: "Owe nothing to anyone, except to love one another."[689] It is "the most excellent way."[690]

Holy Spirit, from the Sacred Heart of Jesus please come. You, who are Love, please come. Please renew me in spirit, soul, and body with your light and your love. Holy Spirit, breathe in me. Inflame my heart with a love of God: Father, Son, and Holy Spirit. Turn the gaze of my heart to heaven. Come sweet Spirit and teach me your ways. Teach me to love with the love of heaven. Teach me to love not only God, but with that same love, please teach me to love the people in my life, even those who seem most unlovable. Help me to forgive those who have hurt me. Please free me from all unforgiveness, all bitterness, and all grudges. I renounce such evil and choose to forgive. I choose to love. Help me to serve others with your love, particularly those in need. Please help me to love with a love that endures difficult trials with a joyful and peaceful heart. In Jesus' name, I pray. Amen

---

[686] Cf. Mark 11:23-25.
[687] 1 Corinthians 13:13 (NRSV).
[688] Galatians 5:6 (NRSV).
[689] Romans 13:8 (NAB). Cf. Romans 12:16.
[690] 1 Corinthians 12:31 (NIV). Cf. 1 Corinthians 14:1.

Gift of Prophecy

26

One of the more interesting gifts of the Holy Spirit is the gift of prophecy. Saint Paul told Christians in Corinth to "strive eagerly for the spiritual gifts, above all that you may prophesy . . . [and again] strive eagerly to prophesy."[691] "I would like all of you to speak in tongues, but even more to prophesy."[692]

For Paul, prophecy is a highly esteemed gift bestowed not on a privileged few, but potentially upon many. It is the supernatural ability to communicate a message or revelation on the Holy Spirit's behalf.[693] "The Spirit of the Lord spoke through me; his word was on my tongue."[694] In most cases, the message is for another individual, a small group, a ministry team, or a local community. A prophetic message may be a single word, a scripture verse, a paragraph, an image, or a vision. It may be divine insight into the meaning or application of God's Word to a particular situation. Occasionally, a prophecy may be about future events. Usually, it is about the present.

Some with a prophetic gift may merely feel an inspiration to speak, knowing only the first few words and the message forms as they speak or begin to write.[695] Others may first receive a revelation from the Spirit – something they hear, or a vision they see, or a piece of knowledge they suddenly know[696] – that the Spirit inspires them to share. What by the Spirit's grace a person sees, hears, or suddenly knows is the gift of "revelation"[697] or "word of knowledge."[698] What he or she communicates on the Spirit's behalf is the prophecy. Not all revelations lead to prophecy.

Usually when we talk about seeing, hearing, or knowing, we are referring to the use of our physical senses – our eyes and ears. We can also see, hear, and know things by the internal working of our mind – our intellect, will, emotions, memories, and imagination. Divine

---

[691] 1 Corinthians 14:1, 39 (NAB).

[692] 1 Corinthians 14:5 (NJB).

[693] Cf. 1 Corinthians 12:10, 2 Peter 1:21, Nehemiah 9:30, Zechariah 7:12.

[694] 2 Samuel 23:2 (NIV).

[695] Cf. Matthew 10:19-20, Mark 13:11, Luke 12:11-13, Jeremiah 20:9.

[696] Cf. Numbers 24:4, 15-16.

[697] Cf. 1 Corinthians 14:6, 30, 2 Corinthians 12:1,7, Ephesians 1:17.

[698] Cf. 1 Corinthians 12:8.

revelation is different. It comes to us by way of the Holy Spirit dwelling in our spirits.

It is possible for someone to have a prophetic gift and not hear or see anything. They may speak an anointed message and be totally unaware that the Holy Spirit is using them. Yet those to whom the Lord is speaking receive the message. This may be the case with people who more consciously possess other gifts, such as counseling, hospitality, intercessory prayer, or the priestly charism in the Sacrament of Reconciliation. Other times, a person may be speaking their own thoughts and suddenly he or she senses another voice at work in them. Fr. Raniero Cantalamessa describes it is "as if a wave on a different frequency inserts itself into [a person's] voice. The person becomes suddenly aware of an inner stirring, of a power and a conviction"[699] that is of God. In such instances, it is usually not necessary to indicate what you are feeling, but merely cooperate in the moment and let the Holy Spirit use that utterance to touch the mind and heart of the intended audience.

Evangelists, preachers, and teachers are also communicators, who proclaim the Gospel to others and thereby share in the prophetic ministry of the Church. Yet such efforts generally do not include the gift of prophecy. These persons proclaim the general message of the Church given by God, however, their communications involve study and preparation. Such work is very different from the gift of prophecy.

In Old Testament times, the prophetic gift seemed to manifest in the lives of only a few persons, some of whom are remembered in history, such as Elijah, Elisha, Isaiah, Ezekiel and Jeremiah. This gift seemed to flourish with a much higher frequency in Apostolic times, not only in the lives of major figures such as Peter, Paul, and John, but also ordinary believers such as Ananias (who baptized Paul), Agabus, Silas, Judas (a companion of Silas), Philip an early deacon, and Phillip's four daughters. The prophetic gift flourished so much so that Paul provided instruction for its use in local prayer meetings.[700]

From Biblical accounts and early Church history, it appears that the prophetic gift flourished within many Christian communities for

---

[699] Cantalamessa, Fr. Raniero, *Sober Intoxication of the Spirit: Part Two* (Servant Books, 2012, page 92.
[700] Cf. 1 Corinthians 14:26-33.

the first two centuries of· the Church.[701] According to St. John Chrysostom, a Doctor of the Church, "Every church had many who prophesied."[702] However, it rapidly declined in the late second and third centuries after the Montanism and the Manichaeism heresies. Both heresies involved false prophets who claimed to be the Holy Spirit and who claimed to have revelations whose importance surpassed that of Jesus and the Apostles.[703] As these heresies were condemned, the gift of prophecy received less attention – not by any expressed edict of the Church, but perhaps by an abundance of caution.

In the fourth century, as adult converts prepared for the Sacrament of Baptism, St. Cyril, also a Doctor of the Church, prayed, "God grant that you may be worthy of the charism of prophecy."[704] Yet through the centuries, apart from the experiences of certain saints and mystics, the manifestation of this gift seems to have been a rarity.

Public Versus Private Revelation. We should note that there are two types of revelation: public and private. Public revelation is the Bible's definitive revelation of Jesus, his mission, the Father's plan for salvation, and his Law. Through Sacred Scripture, God speaks to everyone, in every generation. The Catholic Church teaches that no new public revelation is to be expected before Jesus' Second Coming.[705] In addition, the Christian faith "cannot accept 'revelations' that claim to surpass or correct the Revelation of which Christ is the fulfillment, as is the case in 'certain non-Christian religions and also in certain recent sects which base themselves on such 'revelations.'"[706]

Apart from the New Testament books, all that is truly the gift of prophecy in the Christian era is private revelation. Through private revelation, God speaks through persons at a given moment in time, helping others to grow in faith and to live the one true public revelation of Jesus.[707] All authentic Marian apparitions and the mystical

---

[701] Cf. *Didache* (Teaching of the Apostles), chapter 13; St. Cyril of Jerusalem, *Catechetical Lecture #17*.

[702] St John Chrysostom, *On 1 Corinthians*, Homily 32:2, (PG 61:265).

[703] Cf. St. Cyril of Jerusalem, *Catechetical Lecture #16,* sections 8-10.

[704] St. Cyril of Jerusalem, *Catechetical Lecture #17*, section 37.

[705] Cf. Second Vatican Council, DV, section 4; CCC sections 66-67; 1 Timothy 6:14, Titus 2:13.

[706] CCC section 67. Religious groups who claim special revelations that surpass or correct the Gospels include Islam, Latter Day Saints (Mormons), Jehovah's Witnesses, Seventh Day Adventists, Unification Church (Moonies), and Christian Scientology.

[707] Cf. CCC section 67; Pope Benedict XVI, VD, section 14.

experiences of such saints as Francis of Assisi, Thomas Aquinas, Catherine of Sienna, John of the Cross, Margaret Mary Alacoque, Faustina Kowalska, and Padre Pio are private revelations. The Church, through a bishop or pope, has recognized only a few such private revelations. This is not to suggest that the Church rejects most private revelations. Rather, most private revelations are meant for individual persons or small groups, and not the broader Church. Thus, they are not all investigated, nor could they all be.

What the Gift of Prophecy is Not. The gift of prophecy is not a means for persons to seize control of the future. Prophecy is not about fortune telling, astrology, palm reading, tarot card reading, or any other practices forbidden by God.[708] These other practices are of the devil.

Putting the Prophetic Gift to Work. As with all spiritual gifts, the one who has a prophetic gift needs to learn how to responsibly use the gift. For all to whom the Spirit bestows the prophetic gift, it will take time to grow accustomed to it, and to use it in a mature manner. Toward that end, it helps to have the aid of faith-filled mentors already walking in this gift. It is not uncommon for those with a prophetic gift to at first be timid about speaking prophetic utterances. Even so, if the Holy Spirit is urging them to speak, then they have a duty to speak.[709] Having said that, the means of communication may be tempered by the situation, as in the case of Nathan's rebuke of King David.[710]

St. Paul counsels that in prayer meetings, everyone who feels a prophetic urge is not to speak at the same time. Prophetic urges are not uncontrollable ecstasies. Says Paul, "The spirits of prophets are subject to the control of prophets. For God is not a God of disorder but of peace."[711] Persons are to prophesy in an orderly manner.

Jesus said, when he discussed the gift of prophecy in his own ministry, "I did not speak on my own, but the Father who sent me commanded me what to say and speak."[712] Jesus' reference to what to "say and speak" can, in English, sound redundant. But in the original Greek, what to say (from the Greek "*lego*") refers to the substance of

---

[708] Cf. Exodus 22:18, Leviticus 19:31, 20:6, Deuteronomy 18:9-13, Jeremiah 29:8; CCC sections 2115-2117; Pope Benedict XVI, *Jesus of Nazareth*, Part I, Doubleday, 2007, pages 2-4.

[709] Cf. Exodus 3:15-18, Ezekiel 3:18-21, 33:1-9, Jeremiah 1:7, 23:28.

[710] Cf. 2 Samuel 12:1-15.

[711] 1 Corinthians 14:32-33 (NIV).

[712] John 12:49 (NAB).

the message, the words to use. What to speak (from the Greek "*laleo*") includes the sense of how to convey or say the message.[713] In this regard, how we convey a message, even a rebuke, must be tempered by love. "Though I have the power of prophecy . . . if I am without love, I am nothing."[714] For those with a prophetic gift, it is right, particularly in sensitive situations, to ask the Holy Spirit how he wants the prophetic word communicated. "*Holy Spirit, please guide me not only in what to say, but also in how to say it.*"

For persons with a prophetic gift, who want to grow in this gift, Fr. Cantalamessa counsels that they must focus on three things – prayer, humility, and love. *Prayer* is obvious. It is the principal way we grow in our overall relationship with God and learn to hear his voice. *Humility*, as mentioned in a previous chapter, is our openness to the action of the Spirit, our lowliness, our desire for God to be praised and not ourselves. *Love* is the preeminent virtue. If we are to communicate anything on God's behalf, we must do so with his own essence, with love. If we are lacking in any of these areas, Fr. Cantalamessa tells us, we should turn to God and ask for what we lack – for a heart of prayer, a heart of humility, and a heart of love.[715]

Some prophetic communications may involve physical actions. This was the case with Jeremiah who purchased a clay jug and broke it in front of the leaders of Jerusalem to illustrate the punishment God was going to inflict on the city; with Isaiah whom the Lord told to walk naked and barefoot through Jerusalem as a sign of the punishment to be inflicted against Egypt; and with Agabus who took Paul's belt and tied himself up with it to show what was going to happen to Paul.[716]

For those with a prophetic gift, their responsibility is to deliver the message. Typically, it is not their role to interpret what they think the message might mean. It will be for others to discern that.[717] If they do participate in discerning the message, it is vital that they distinguish the message as received from their thoughts about its possible meaning, lest they muddle the Spirit's message with their own ideas.

---

[713] Cf. Damian Stayne, Lecture on the Charism of Prophecy, Augusta GA, July 2012.
[714] 1 Corinthians 13:2 (NJB).
[715] Cf. Cantalamessa, Fr. Raniero, *Sober Intoxication of the Spirit: Part Two* (Servant Books, 2012, pages 104-106.
[716] Cf. Jeremiah 19:1, 10, Isaiah 20:2-4, Acts 21:11.
[717] Cf. 1 Corinthians 14:29.

When a member of a community asserts that they have or may have a prophetic gift, what is the proper response? First, the leaders of the community (pastor or prayer group leader) need to discern whether the person actually has a prophetic gift and, if so, how to faithfully accept this work of the Holy Spirit into the community. In this regard, Paul tells us to "test everything; hold fast to what is good."[718]

As it concerns a person who purportedly has a prophetic gift, relevant concerns are the person's spiritual maturity, mental and emotional health, history of agreement or disagreement with Church teachings, history of walking in the prophetic gift, and whether they are in bondage to any serious sin.

Persons with the gift of prophecy can and do make mistakes. They can speak what seems to be of God, but in a particular instance speak from their own mind. Alternatively, they can receive a message, but communicate their interpretation of the message when they should communicate the message as received. Or they can communicate the words accurately, but do so in the wrong frame of mind, accompanied by attitudes, gestures, or excitement that confuse the message.

As for the meaning of an authentic prophecy, often it is unclear in the moment and can be understood only in the course of time. When discerning the meaning of a prophetic message, the person or community to whom the message is directed should first take it to God in prayer. The Holy Spirit who gives the message is ultimately the one who must reveal its meaning. Discernment, then, is not merely an exercise in human reasoning.

A famous story illustrates the importance of careful discernment. The story involves St. Francis of Assisi praying in the ruins of an old chapel. He heard the Lord speak to him, "Rebuild my house, which lies before you in ruins." At first, Francis thought the Lord's instruction concerned the building he was praying in. So, for the next several weeks, he and a crew of other men set out to repair the chapel. The Lord would later make it clear, he was not referring to the chapel, but to the Church universal. The rebuilding effort was to be through preaching, prayer, poverty, and love. The Spirit filled Francis with the grace to boldly proclaim the Gospel of Jesus as an itinerate preacher.

---

[718] 1 Thessalonians 5:21 (NRSV). Cf. 1 John 4:1-6.

Four criteria normally accompany a true prophecy.[719] First, the purported prophecy does not conflict with Sacred Scripture or Church teachings. The Spirit, who is the author of prophecy, Sacred Scripture, and Church doctrines, does not contradict himself. Second, the fruit of the Spirit, such as truth, love, and peace are present. Discerning this criterion can be a challenge particularly when the purported prophecy is a rebuke, a call to reform, or a message otherwise resisted by the intended audience. The lack of peace among those who resist the message is not a violation of this criterion. Third, the person who purportedly has the gift of prophecy willingly submits to pastors of the Church. This can be a serious challenge for persons with a prophetic gift: they must exercise patience, even as they may at first, or even for a while, be rejected and ignored. Fourth, the purported prophecy, if faithfully embraced, serves to build up the faith of a person or community.

Often a prophecy does not stand alone. God may confirm a message through other events, a miraculous sign, a Biblical passage brought to one's mind, the counsel of a wise person, or by allowing others to receive the same message. Persons discerning a purported prophecy should be alert to possible confirmations. Those who discern on behalf of a community should be carefully selected; they should be prayerful persons, with the gift of divine wisdom, and with a strong understanding of the Bible and Church teachings.

Hold Fast to What is Good. If someone discerns that a prophecy is of God, they should hold on to it and, from time to time, ponder its meaning. When they have discerned a proper meaning, they should let it comfort, instruct, admonish, or encourage them, as the case may be.

False Prophecies. Within Christian circles, false prophecies are messages allegedly from God given by (1) fakes who knowingly attempt to manipulate or please others for some purpose or gain, (2) persons who hear the voice of a demon, (3) persons who are mentally ill, and (4) persons who are misled by their own imagination. Christians should ignore their messages. When a Christian with a legitimate gift of prophecy appears to make a mistaken utterance, some refer to the mistaken utterance as a "non-prophecy."

---

[719] Cf. Pope John Paul II, GA, June 24, 1992, sections 5-9; Pope Benedict XVI, VD, section 14.

Outside of Christian circles, the world abounds with would-be prophets who urgently pedal their revelations, predictions, and advice. This includes those of the occult: fortune tellers, astrologers, spirit mediums, and their like. We must avoid such persons, for any other-than-natural power they may have comes from the devil. Other false prophets include those of a worldly nature, so-called visionaries in politics, sociology, academia, science, technology, economics, business, and entertainment whose urgent messages distract people from the truth of Jesus Christ.

Being Open to the Gift of Prophecy. While there may be false forms of prophecy, there is nevertheless an authentic gift of the Spirit that we are to know about and, as Paul instructs, we are to eagerly desire it and welcome its use in community.[720] He tells us, "Do not despise prophetic utterances."[721] Everyone who prophesies "speaks to men for their strengthening, encouragement and comfort."[722] Those who walk responsibly in this gift "build up the community."[723]

Paul encourages "all" believers to be open to the manifestation of the prophetic gift in their lives. "Now I should like all of you to speak in tongues, but even more to prophesy. . . . For you can all prophesy one by one, so that all may learn and all be encouraged."[724] Said Moses, in his day, "Would that all the Lord's people were prophets."[725]

And what is the effect of prophetic utterances on a nonbeliever or a skeptic who walks in on a prayer meeting and encounters the Spirit of God working powerfully through prophetic utterances? Paul tells us. "[T]he secrets of his heart [would be] revealed; and so he would fall down on his face and worship God, declaring that *God is indeed among you.*"[726] The secrets Paul refers to here are not the sordid details of one's sins made public, rather it is a particular insight on some matter that reaches deep within him and awakens faith.

Prophetic Office. Apart from the gift of prophecy, a charism that the Holy Spirit may give to many, is the office of prophet, a role assigned to very few. In Old Testament times, Moses, Elijah, Elisha,

---

[720] Cf. 1 Corinthians 14:1-5, 26-33, 39.
[721] 1 Thessalonians 5:20 (NAB).
[722] 1 Corinthians 14:3 (NIV).
[723] 1 Corinthians 14:4 (NJB).
[724] 1 Corinthians 14:5, 31 (NAB).
[725] Numbers 11:29 (NRSV).
[726] 1 Corinthians 14:25 (NJB).

Isaiah, and Jeremiah held the prophetic office. In New Testament times, Paul describes this office as an essential function within the Church's hierarchy: "Some people God has designated in the church to be, first, apostles; second, prophets; third, teachers."[727]

In the modern era, several popes in various moments of their pontificate have functioned in a prophetic role, not merely teaching on a particular matter, but prophesying to the whole Church on behalf of the Spirit. This includes Popes John XXIII, Paul VI, John Paul II, Benedict XVI, and Francis. It is not their custom to declare their prophetic utterances as such, but when one reads their key writings, one may appreciate that certain of them offer more than sound teaching, but also a word from the Lord for our times. This includes Pope Paul VI's encyclical *Humanae Vitae*, in which he foretold the decline of western culture due to the rising tide of sexual immorality and moral lapses that stem from artificial birth control; or, Pope John Paul II's encyclical *Redemptoris Missio*, wherein he issued a call to the Church to embrace its primary mandate to evangelize the world; his encyclical *Centesimus Annus*, in which he chastised the world systems of both communism and capitalism; and his encyclical *Evangelium Vitae*, in which he stressed the imperative to protect unborn human life. This was also the case a little over a century ago when Pope Leo XIII had a prophetic vision in which he saw the unleashing of evil upon the world in what would be the 20th century. From that vision he felt inspired to compose the Prayer to St. Michael that was said regularly at the end of Masses around the world for the next sixty years. In the first year of his pontificate, Pope Francis perhaps more through actions than words, has been a prophet of God's love as he has engaged in outreach to those who are suffering.

Holy Spirit, St. Paul instructed us to strive eagerly for all the spiritual gifts, most especially to prophesy. Lord, help me to hear your voice and to speak your words, as you would have me. I want to be your spokesperson, and to do so with love. I ask that the gift of prophecy be manifested in my life, to your glory. I want to have your words of encouragement and insight to help build up the faith and holiness of others and of the Church. I bless your holy name. Please use me dear Lord to bless others. In Jesus' name I pray, Amen.

---

[727] 1 Corinthians 12:28 (NAB). Cf. Ephesians 4:11.

27　Gift of Tongues

The gift of tongues is one of the more mysterious works of the Holy Spirit in the life of a Christian. It is the supernatural ability to communicate with speech beyond one's natural ability. This includes the supernatural ability to:

- speak to God in an unfamiliar language, in prayer or song;
- speak to foreigners in their native language; and
- speak to others in a language you know, but with much greater clarity, boldness, and effect.

At one of his post-resurrection appearances, Jesus prophesied concerning the gift of tongues. He said that one of the signs that will accompany those who believe in him, is that "they will speak new languages."[728] Weeks later, in Jerusalem, fulfillment of this prophecy began with the Apostles who spoke in tongues at Pentecost.[729] The Bible also mentions manifestations of this gift in Caesarea (around the year 43 AD), Ephesus (around the around the year 53 AD), and Corinth (around the around the year 55 AD).[730] These references appear to be the passing mention of what may have been a very common experience in the Apostolic Church.

An Unrecognizable Prayer Language. In his first letter to the Corinthians, Paul discussed the gift of tongues manifesting as an unrecognizable language used for prayer. Though to most listeners such prayer sounds like gibberish, truly it is the Holy Spirit speaking (or praying) through us in the language and words the Spirit chooses. Said St. Paul, "Those who speak in a [prayer] tongue speak to God . . . not to other people."[731] "Nobody understands them, since they are speaking mysteries in the Spirit."[732] They may be speaking a human language, but it is always a language they have never before learned.

While we may normally think of prayer as originating from our own mind, a prayer tongue originates in our spirit, in a language given by the Holy Spirit. Even as the Holy Spirit provides the words for a

---

[728] Mark 16:17 (NAB).
[729] Cf. Acts 2:4, 1 Corinthians 14:21.
[730] Cf. Acts 10:46, Acts 19:6, 1 Corinthians 12:10, 14:4-25.
[731] 1 Corinthians 14:2 (NJB).
[732] 1 Corinthians 14:2 (NSVR).

prayer tongue, people who possess this gift have control over their use of it. They turn it on or off.

Paul taught that when a person prays in tongues, the Spirit strengthens that person's spiritual life.[733] Humble surrender to the quiet rhythms of this gift helps believers experience deeper intimacy with God. It also helps us learn to surrender more and more of our lives to the flow of the Spirit.

In our spiritual walk, it is okay if we do not pray in tongues, so long as it is because the Spirit has not given us this gift. However, if the Spirit has given us this gift, we should allow the Spirit to awaken this gift within us, and we should regularly put the gift to good use. Those of us who do so with faith and love will grow in holiness. From the New Testament accounts, it would seem that this was a gift given to many in that day, and perhaps many in every generation, as the Spirit wills.

Today, many who experience the release of this gift do so in prayer meetings through the laying on of hands, or in private prayer when it just comes over them, or when they are singing praises to God. It is a spiritual gift that commonly manifests in persons who have been "baptized in the Holy Spirit" as discussed in chapter 7. Yielding to this gift requires faith, a willingness to surrender our voices and sense of dignity to the Holy Spirit, letting the Spirit speak through us, even though we have no idea what he is saying. In most instances, it is believed that such prayers are prayers of praise and thanksgiving.

Prayer tongues is not a gift reserved for the most holy among us, but rather it is a gift given to persons of every rank, helping all with this gift to grow in holiness. In fact, its manifestation in the Bible often came upon persons new to the faith. Paul exclaimed, "I would like every one of you to speak in tongues . . . [and] I thank God that I speak in tongues."[734]

Jubilation. St. Augustine and other fathers of the Church used the term "jubilation" to describe something similar to St. Paul's description of prayer tongues. It was, as Augustine taught, a song from the heart that defied normal speech. He said, "Think of people who sing at harvest time, or in the vineyard, or at any work that goes with a

---

[733] Cf. 1 Corinthians 14:4.
[734] 1 Corinthians 14:5, 18 (NIV).

swing. They begin by caroling their joy in words, but after a while they seem to be so full of gladness that they find words no longer adequate to express it, so they abandon distinct syllables and words, and resort to a single cry of jubilant happiness. Jubilation is a shout of joy; it indicates that the heart is bringing forth what defies speech. To whom, then, is this jubilation more fittingly offered than to God who surpasses all utterance?"[735]

St. Teresa of Avila described her experiences of jubilation as follows. "Our Lord sometimes bestows upon the soul a jubilation and a strange kind of prayer, the nature of which it cannot ascertain. . . . If He grants you this favor, you may give Him hearty praise and know that such a thing really happens. . . . May it please His Majesty often to bestow this prayer upon us since it brings such security and such benefit. For, as it is an entirely supernatural thing, we cannot acquire it."[736]

Allowing Prayer Tongues to be Manifested. Paul instructed the Christian community in Corinth – "[D]o not forbid speaking in tongues."[737] He did so because he understood the blessing embedded in this gift. Yet, because of the immature reaction to this gift by some in Corinth (by both recipients and non-recipients of the gift), Paul rebuked the community against pride and strife. Their local controversies, however, did not result because of the gift, but rather because of human brokenness. If the gift was the problem, then the Holy Spirit would be to blame. Paul exhorts those with the gift to always use it in love; for without love, a person praying in tongues is just "a noisy gong or a clanging cymbal."[738]

While Paul encourages us to be open to the gift of prayer tongues, he also cautions us concerning its proper use in group settings. Leaders should not deliver a sermon while speaking in tongues because the assembly would not be edified, unless someone could interpret the message.[739] Generally, in a large gathering, it is not appropriate to pray aloud in tongues because such prayers could bother others, or cause

---

[735] Saint Augustine, *Exposition 2 on Psalm 32 [33]*, section 8, *The Works of Saint Augustine: A Translation for the 21st Century*, John E. Rotelle, O.S.A., ed., New York City Press, 1993, Part III, Volume 15, page 401.

[736] St. Teresa of Avila, *Interior Castles*, Chapter VI; Peers, E. Allison (translator), Doubleday, 1998, pages 167-169.

[737] 1 Corinthians 14:39 (NIV).

[738] 1 Corinthians 13:1 (NRSV).

[739] Cf. 1 Corinthians 14:6, 18-19.

confusion, or distract from a teaching. Yet in smaller settings, such as a prayer group, Paul encourages us to pray aloud in tongues, so long as we do so in an orderly manner.[740]

Cardinal Joseph Suenens, one of the four Moderators of the Second Vatican Council, offered this advice to those who are experiencing the initial release of this gift. If a person accepts it with humility, even with "the risk of appearing foolish or childish – he soon discovers the joy of praying in a way that transcends words and human reasoning, bringing great peace and an openness to spiritual communication with others. . . . When, in a prayer meeting, it takes the form of an improvised chant in tongues, it can assume, in musical terms, a rare beauty as well as a religious depth by which no one who listens without prejudice can fail to be impressed."[741]

Gift of Interpreting Tongues. St. Paul also mentions the gift of interpreting tongues. This gift is the supernatural ability to understand a message proclaimed through either prayer tongues or a human language that is not known by the interpreter. It is not the ability to translate individual words, but instead to understand the message. When the gift of interpreting tongues is manifested, generally it is as an ability to interpret a prayer tongue. It works much like the gift of prophecy, a means by which the Holy Spirit communicates a message.

Fear of Prayer Tongues. The gift of prayer tongues is manifest among many Christians today of most denominations. Believers unfamiliar with the gift are often apprehensive when they first hear it or hear of it. They fear that something inappropriate might be happening. *"This is not the Christianity (or the Catholicism) I grew up with or that I want to be a part of."* Yet, if it is an authentic movement of the Holy Spirit, a genuine part of the Christian experience handed down from the Apostles, it behooves all believers to overcome their fears and insecurities and welcome it. To resist the gift, in ourselves or in others, is to resist the One who gives the gift and operates through it. Such apprehensions are an obstacle to the Spirit's manifestation of this gift in our respective lives and our communities.

Truly, for those to whom the Lord has given the gift of prayer tongues, it takes faith to cooperate with its release and to learn how to maturely use it. Yet the benefit is great – deeper intimacy with God

---

[740] Cf. 1 Corinthians 14:22-40.
[741] Suenens, Leon Joseph, *A New Pentecost?*, Seabury Press, 1975, page 102.

and greater movement of the Spirit within us. Paul tells us to strive for all the spiritual gifts.[742] This includes the gift of tongues. If we are afraid or inhibited, we need to realize that such negative emotions are not from God, for all God's gifts are good. As the Lord manifests this gift within us, we should be thankful and use it regularly.

A Human Language Foreign to the Speaker. The gift of tongues manifested as a human language foreign to the speaker generally occurs among missionaries, helping them to evangelize peoples in foreign lands. This form of tongues appears to have been manifest to the Apostles at Pentecost, as bystanders from many foreign lands understood the Apostles each in their own native language.[743] Through Church history, missionary evangelists such as saints Francis of Assisi, Dominic Guzman, Anthony of Padua, and Francis Xavier enjoyed this gift, as do some missionaries today. As a missionary enters a foreign community, the Spirit intervenes, enabling them to speak the local language, which they have never learned.

A Human Language Familiar to the Speaker. The gift of tongues can manifest itself in a language familiar to the speaker, when his or her speech contains new attributes able to reach a particular audience. This manifestation helps a speaker more clearly proclaim the Gospel. The Bible speaks of the Holy Spirit filling the Apostles and enabling them on various occasions to speak God's Word in a familiar tongue, but with a new boldness and effect.[744] This manifestation might help a teacher reach an audience who by age, ethnicity, or life experience is very different from him or her. Pope John Paul II taught that persons with teaching or evangelizing roles should pray to the Holy Spirit for this manifestation of tongues – "the gift of speaking in a language understood by all the faithful."[745]

Tongues as a Service Gift. The gift of tongues is included by St. Paul among a list of spiritual gifts that are commonly referred to as service gifts.[746] They are gifts that help build up the community of believers as a whole, and not merely the individual with the gift. Concerning the gift of tongues, its use as a service gift is most obvious

---

[742] Cf. 1 Corinthians 14:1.
[743] Cf. Acts 2:1-11.
[744] Cf. Acts 4:8, 31, 1 Peter 1:12, 1 Corinthians 2:4-5, 13.
[745] Cf. Pope John Paul II, *Rise, Let Us Be On Our Way*, Warner Books, 2004, pg. 107.
[746] Cf. 1 Corinthians 12:10, 28-30, 14:26-28, Romans 8:27.

when the gift manifests itself for purposes of spreading the gospel, or, in the case of prayer tongues, when it is interpreted.

Yet the gift of prayer tongues, when it is not interpreted, is also a service gift. Our prayers of praise and thanksgiving through an inspired prayer language first and foremost serve God. Such prayers can also bring blessing upon others when we use the gift while interceding for them – for healing, or deliverance, or blessing. When we intercede for others using a prayer tongue, allowing the Spirit of God to speak through us, the words we speak will be the right words for the situation, even if we have no idea what those words mean. As St. Paul tells us, in such moments, "the Spirit" who speaks through us "intercedes for the saints in accordance with God's will."[747]

When those to whom the Lord has given the gift of prayer tongues use it worthily for intercessory purposes, they are ministers of the Spirit's power. They are instruments of his grace, positively impacting the lives of others. This gift, then, is a privilege. Moreover, it is a responsibility, one to be exercised regularly. As with all service-oriented gifts, so too with prayer tongues, to be an effective minister of the Holy Spirit's grace, we must actively pursue holiness and intimacy with God. In this way, we are clean instruments through which the Spirit can work unobstructed.

As for the intercessory use of prayer tongues, it is helpful to realize that those with this gift may use it in more instances than one might initially think. Some may find that they can use this gift in many group settings, even secular settings, by praying in tongues quietly. Some may find that they can pray in tongues with their mouth shut, not making a sound, but still allowing the Spirit to intercede through them in the moment.

Most of us may, upon first experiencing the gift of tongues in us, enjoy a certain excitement as the Spirit manifests his power in our lives in new ways. Our challenge is to never grow complacent about the value of such prayers for our own edification and for others. It is not about what we feel when praying such prayers, instead it is about the power of the Spirit flowing through us in such moments for the Spirit's purposes. As with all prayer, so also with praying in tongues, it greatly delights the devil when we grow bored and stop praying, falsely thinking our prayers are of little importance.

---

[747] Romans 8:27 (NIV).

Gift of Tongues As a Sign for Unbelievers. St. Paul taught that the gift of tongues is a sign, "not for those who believe but for unbelievers."[748] This is no doubt true, in a very positive sense, as it concerns the manifestation of tongues by missionaries in a foreign land helping them to proclaim the Gospel in a local language. It is a sign to the local people that God is working miracles through the missionaries. However, the context of Paul's statement concerns an unrecognizable prayer tongue and the sign implied is negative. Paul cites a prophecy uttered by Isaiah regarding strange new tongues that will proclaim the goodness of God and be rejected by many of God's own people.[749] They will exclaim, "you are out of your mind."[750] In such cases, prayer tongues is a sign that exposes the lack of faith among believers. It exposes our lack of faith as it concerns the fullness of God's economy of grace.

While Paul teaches that the gift of tongues is a sign for unbelievers, we must also recognize that for believers who experience the release of this gift in their own prayer life, it is also a sign. It is a sign of God's presence. It is a sign of God's power. It is a sign of God's love. This sign helps build faith and encourages us to a deeper, more intimate prayer life.

Holy Spirit, St. Paul said that he would like it if everyone spoke in tongues and he thanked God that he did. If the gift of tongues is a charism that you want manifested in my life, may your will be done. I choose to be open to this gift however you manifest it in the Church or in me. Please deliver me from all fear, doubt, and confusion in regards to this spiritual gift. I love you Lord, and I choose to accept any new language you have given me or want to give to me. May any such gift blossom and grow in me in ways pleasing to you. I praise your holy name. And I thank you, in advance, for however you choose to answer this prayer. In the name of Jesus I pray, Amen.

---

[748] 1 Corinthians 14:22 (NAB).
[749] Cf. 1 Corinthians 14:21, Isaiah 28:11-12.
[750] 1 Corinthians 14:23 (NAB).

28   Gifts of Healing

In his first letter to the Corinthians, Paul provides a list of charisms the Spirit distributes to believers for the common good of the community. He refers to most of them as a singular "gift," such as the gift of wisdom or the gift of prophecy. When it comes to healing, he refers to "gifts" of healing.[751] These gifts are a special ability "to obtain graces of healing for others."[752] Such healing can be physical, psychological, emotional, or spiritual.

Those who participate in the Spirit's work of healing include priests who extend spiritual healing in the Sacrament of Reconciliation. Others bring sudden wellness to those suffering from physical illness or injury. Some participate in the Spirit's ministry of inner healing by listening, providing counsel, and prayer. Some participate on healing teams who pray over sick persons for a variety of afflictions. Others participate in deliverance ministries and expel demons.

Jesus' Ministry of Healing. An amazing aspect of Jesus' public ministry was the occurrence of so many miraculous healings. While the Gospels record several instances of Jesus healing a single person, repeatedly they tell of Jesus healing "many" or "all" who were sick. The Bible describes how "Jesus went around to all the towns and villages, teaching in their synagogues, proclaiming the gospel of the kingdom, and curing every disease and illness."[753] All who came out to see him tried to touch him, "for power came out from him and healed all of them."[754] "[A]ll who touched him were healed."[755] And "he drove out many demons."[756]

During Jesus' public ministry, he healed, perhaps, thousands of people from various infirmities. He did so because he felt compassion for the afflicted.[757] When disciples of John the Baptist came to Jesus asking if he was Israel's Messiah, Jesus replied by drawing their

---

[751] Cf. 1 Corinthians 12:9; CCC 1508.

[752] CDF, *Instruction on Prayers for Healing*, September 14, 2000, section 3.

[753] Matthews 9:35 (NAB). Cf. Matthew 4:23, 8:16, 12:15, 14:35-36, 15:30-31, Mark 1:34, 3:10, 6:56, Luke 4:40, 5:17, 6:17-19, 7:21, 9:11, Acts 10:38.

[754] Luke 6:19 (NRSV).

[755] Matthew 14:36 (NIV).

[756] Mark 1:34 (NAB). Cf. Matthew 4:24, 8:16, 28-34, 9:32-33, 12:22, 15:21-28, 17:14-18, Mark 1:23-26, 32-34, 5:1-20, 7:24-30, 9:17-29, Luke 4:33-35, 41, 6:18, 8:26-37, 9:38-43.

[757] Cf. Mathew 9:35-36, 14:14, 20:34, Mark 1:41, 6:34, 8:2; CCC sections 1503-1505.

attention to his healing ministry. Said Jesus, "Go and tell John what you have seen and heard: the blind regain their sight, the lame walk, lepers are cleansed, the deaf hear, the dead are raised, the poor have the good news proclaimed to them."[758] Of the six signs mentioned, five deal with physical healings and the sixth concerns spiritual healing.

In Jesus' humanity, the power to heal people of illnesses and to cast out demons came from the Holy Spirit.[759] As the Catholic Church teaches, "The Spirit filled Christ and the power of the Spirit went out from him in his acts of healing and of saving."[760]

To properly understand Jesus' healings, we must understand that all sickness, all disease, all psychological disorders, all birth defects, all addictions are forms of evil.[761] They are among the works of the devil that Jesus came to destroy.[762] They are all the result of living in a world wounded by sin. On occasion, there may be obvious links between a particular affliction and the sins of society, the sins of those around us, or our own sins, but usually there is not.[763] Healing is the eradication of an evil and its ill effects. Jesus came to heal the whole of each person – spirit, soul, and body. Forgiveness of sins was an essential part of his healing ministry.

Healing Ministries of the Church. Just as Jesus' public ministry brought healing to many who were suffering, so also the ministries of his disciples. During his public ministry, Jesus sent his Apostles out with instructions not only to proclaim the Gospel, but also to "Heal the sick, raise the dead, cleanse those who have leprosy, drive out demons."[764] To accomplish that aim, Jesus gave them "authority over unclean spirits, to cast them out, and to cure every disease and every sickness."[765] That authority, that power was the Holy Spirit.

Jesus also sent out some seventy-two other disciples on their own missions to proclaim the Good News. The Bible tells us that during their missions, "They drove out many demons, and they anointed with

---

[758] Luke 7:22 (NAB). Cf. Isaiah 35:4-6, 53:4, 61:1-2; Matthew 8:17.

[759] Cf. Luke 5:17, Acts 10:38 (healing); Matthew 12:28, Luke 11:20 (deliverance).

[760] CCC section 695.

[761] Cf. CCC section 1502; CDF, *Instruction on Prayers for Healing*, September 14, 2000, section 1.

[762] Cf. 1 John 3:8, Acts 10:38; MacNutt, Francis, *Healing*, Ave Maria, 2003, page 50.

[763] Cf. Exodus 15:26, Leviticus 26:14-17, Deuteronomy 28:15, 20-22, Romans 5:12; CCC section 1502.

[764] Matthew 10:8 (NIV). Cf. Mark 6:12-13, Luke 9:1-2; CCC sections 1506 - 1509.

[765] Matthew 10:1 (NRSV). Cf. Matthew 10:8, Luke 9:1-2, 10:8-9.

oil many who were sick and cured them."[766] They "went from village to village proclaiming the good news and curing diseases everywhere."[767] And when the seventy-two came back from their mission of evangelization, they rejoiced saying, "Lord, in your name even the demons submit to us!"[768]

After Pentecost, re-invigorated by the Holy Spirit, the Apostles preached of the Risen Jesus and continued their ministries of healing. So well known were their healings that great numbers of sick were laid down in the streets, so that Peter's shadow might fall on them as he walked by. People gathered from the towns around Jerusalem, bringing to the Apostles "their sick and those tormented by evil spirits, and all of them were healed."[769] People were healed in "the name of Jesus . . . through faith in him."[770] Such miracles included persons who had recently died coming back to life.[771] Phillip, an early deacon, had a ministry of preaching, exorcisms, and healing.[772] Paul's healing ministry included the use of religious relics, "face cloths or aprons that touched his skin were applied to the sick, [and] their diseases left them and the evil spirits came out of them."[773] James encouraged those who were sick to present themselves to the elders of their local church for prayers and anointing with oils.[774]

Healing ministries of the miraculous sort have continued down through the centuries, though with much less frequency compared to the Apostolic Church. Such ministries include those associated with Marian apparitions, such as in Lourdes, France. In addition, many have experienced the Spirit's healing touch through prayers to saints, contact with religious relics, and through the sacraments. When embraced with faith, all the sacraments can bring healing.

An interesting series of events concerning healing occurred in the life of St. Augustine. In the period leading up to his baptism, at age thirty-two, he had a miraculous healing. He had fallen ill from a

---

[766] Mark 6:13 (NAB).

[767] Luke 9:6 (NAB).

[768] Luke 10:17 (NRSV).

[769] Acts 5:16 (NIV). Cf. Acts 28:9.

[770] Acts 3:16 (NJB). Cf. Acts 3:6, 4:10, 30, Luke 10:17, John 15:16.

[771] Cf. Acts 9:36-43, 20:7-12.

[772] Cf. Acts 6:5, 8:6-8, 13.

[773] Acts 19:12 (NAB). Regarding the power of religious relics to bring God's healing graces to others, see also Numbers 21:8-9 and 2 Kings 13:20.

[774] Cf. James 5:13-15.

serious tooth ache and could not speak. When friends prayed over him, he was immediately healed.[775] Despite this, years later, he came to the conclusion that miraculous healings were a frequent phenomena only for the Apostolic Era.[776] Later, as Bishop of Hippo, he retracted this view,[777] after taking note of so many miraculous healings in his local community. He noted with keen interest the many healings that occurred alongside the administration of a sacrament, specifically Baptism and Holy Eucharist, those associated with religious relics, and those relating to his own prayers. He observed that after two years, there had been nearly seventy attested miracles in their community.[778]

Today, the more miraculous healing ministries seem to flourish in developing countries, particularly where missionaries are hard at work proclaiming the Gospel, and among the poor in traditionally Christian nations. Why in these places are sudden healings more prevalent? Perhaps, the less affluent persons in these communities, clergy and non-clergy, are much more open in faith to God's miraculous ways.

Prayers for Healing. Jesus prophesied that one of the distinguishing marks of the Church would be miraculous healings. "These are the signs that will be associated with believers: in my name they will cast out devils . . . [and] they will lay hands on the sick, who will recover."[779] "Amen, amen, I say to you, whoever believes in me will do the works that I do, and will do greater ones than these."[780]

Truly, anyone can pray for healing, for themselves or others. In fact, the Bible commands us, "[P]ray for each other so that you may be healed. The prayer of a righteous man is powerful and effective."[781] God also calls some to special ministries of healing and the Holy Spirit equips some with special charisms for this purpose.

Prayers for healing can take many forms. They can call upon Jesus, the Father, or the Holy Spirit. They can be long or short. They can involve the laying on of hands, use of blessed oils, words of command, and acts of faith. One of the shorter healing prayers in the Bible was Moses' prayer for his sister Miriam who had leprosy: "O

---

[775] Cf. Saint Augustine, *Confessions*, book IX, chapter 4.
[776] Cf. Saint Augustine, *On the True Religion*, chapter 25, section 47.
[777] Cf. Saint Augustine, *The Retractions*, chapter 12, section 7.
[778] Cf. Saint Augustine, *City of God*, book 22, section 8.
[779] Mark 16:17-18 (NJB).
[780] John 14:12 (NAB).
[781] James 5:16 (NIV).

God, please heal her."[782] And God did. The Holy Spirit, working through Peter, healed a crippled beggar. Peter's words of healing were "I have neither silver nor gold, but what I do have I give to you: in the name of Jesus Christ the Nazorean, rise and walk."[783]

Often, the grace of the Holy Spirit is conveyed through the laying on of hands. As in Apostolic times, the transfer of grace through the laying on of hands occurs firstly in the sacraments – namely, Baptism, Confirmation, Anointing of the Sick, and Holy Orders. Yet it can also relate to healing prayer that involves clergy and non-clergy. We know from Scripture that Jesus and his Apostles used the laying on of hands in their healing ministries.[784] A prayer minister, today, might place her hand on a person's head, or shoulder, or over the ailing part of his body, or hold hands with the sick person as she prays for healing.

When praying for the healing of others, ministers should seek the Lord's guidance in prayer. Often the Holy Spirit will reveal matters in the person's life that need to be addressed first. For example, the person may be harboring bitterness toward someone else that is an obstacle to healing; they may need to extend forgiveness to that person first or repent of some sin first, before they are able to receive healing from God. Or the Lord may reveal to the prayer minister a deeper need for healing in the person's life beyond his initial request. Maybe he is seeking healing in his marriage, when he first needs to experience emotional or psychological healing in his own life first before he can experience healing in his marriage. Prayer ministers need to be sensitive to the lead of the Spirit.

Inner Healing. Inner healing involves the healing of mental, emotional, and spiritual wounds. Often these wounds relate to traumatic events in our lives, perhaps as far back as childhood, wounds that can be very slow to heal. Moreover, the wounded person may be totally unaware of her wounds. Untreated, such inner sores can worsen, as persons do their best to cope with the challenges these hidden wounds create. Persons may cope with anger, alcohol, drugs, excessive work, pleasure seeking, hobbies, isolation, etc. Those with a gift of healing bring the light of the Holy Spirit to those wounds and memories through active listening, prayer, and consultation. The Holy

---

[782] Numbers 12:13 (NIV).
[783] Acts 3:6 (NAB).
[784] Cf. Mark 6:5, 8:23, 10:16, Acts 8:17-19, 13:3, 19:6; CCC section 699.

Spirit, the Oil of Gladness, works through these means. He cleanses our inner wounds, dressing them, and healing them.

Inner healing is most often a gradual process, rather than a sudden event, yet there are often distinct moments of breakthrough, distinct moments when persons tangibly feel the movement of God within them. Forgiveness is often a large part of this healing process, extending forgiveness to others and seeking forgiveness from God.

Deliverance Ministry. Deliverance ministries seek to free persons from demonic attacks. In the most severe of cases, it involves persons who are "possessed" by a demon or perhaps multiple demons. In such situations, which are exceptionally rare, a demonic presence is able to control the person's behavior for prolonged periods. In these cases, deliverance involves the expertise of an exorcist (a bishop or specifically designated priest) praying a specific rite of exorcism.

More commonly, deliverance ministries involve gifted and trained clergy and non-clergy who pray for persons "oppressed" by demons. In such cases, the demonic presence exerts influence on the person, but not control. Such prayers involve commands, "in the name of Jesus," for the demons to leave. The strength of deliverance ministries rests on the faith and spiritual authority of the prayer ministers and the cooperation of the person needing help. In all deliverance ministries, it is the Holy Spirit who expels the demons, working through the prayers, faith, and commands of the ministers. Often persons with interior wounds need deliverance prayer to first cast out a spiritual poison so that the inner wound can finally begin to heal.

Faith and Healing. In Jesus' day and today, the miracle of healing is manifest where there is faith. Several times in the Gospels, Jesus tells a victim that they experienced healing because of their faith.[785] On one occasion, Jesus celebrates the faith of others who brought their friend to be healed.[786] In other cases, the sick person was not present for the healing; someone else came to Jesus, in faith, on the sick person's behalf, and Jesus healed the sick person.[787] Conversely, on at least one occasion, Jesus "could not do any miracles . . . [because of the people's] lack of faith."[788]

---

[785] Cf. Matthew 9:2, 22, 29, Mark 5:34, Luke 7:50, 8:48, 50, 18:42. See also Acts 14:9.
[786] Cf. Mark 2:5.
[787] Cf. Matthew 8:10, 13, Mark 5:36, Luke 8:50.
[788] Mark 6:5-6 (NIV).

Not only is the faith of those who are sick important, but also the faith of God's ministers of healing.[789] The Gospels record an instance when Jesus' disciples were unable to cure a sick boy. When Jesus came upon the scene, he cured the boy and expressed disappointment with his disciples. The disciples asked why they were unsuccessful. Jesus answered, "Because you have so little faith."[790]

The faith required of us is faith in Jesus. He is the healer, his Spirit working through his servants. Worship of Jesus is perhaps the most helpful act of faith we can do to open our hearts to Jesus' healing power – prayers of praise and thanksgiving. A vibrant proclamation of God's Word also helps build up our faith. It should be noted, though, that unsuccessful attempts at healing are not necessarily attributable to lack of faith. The Lord has his purposes and timing.

What often distinguishes the prayers of those through whom miracles regularly occur is that they have faith *for miracles* and not merely faith *in the possibility of miracles*. Faith for miracles is deep trust in the Spirit; it is something we can ask for. As persons with a gift of healing draw closer to the Lord, a confidence emerges that comes not from themselves, but from the Holy Spirit.

God's Response to Prayers for Healing. God responds to some prayers for healing immediately. Other times, his healing is gradual or delayed. Sometimes his healing comes in a way not considered in the prayer. Sometimes the healing comes as we are extending love to God in worship. Sometimes it comes as we sit in the Lord's presence waiting with him. Sometimes the healing we request never comes.

Often God may demand something of us as part of a healing, to pick up our mats so to speak, as we hear in the Gospels. For some of us, that may mean that we must first repent of certain sins in our lives, that we must first let go of bitterness and unforgiveness, or embrace more sincerely Jesus' pathway of holiness. The initiative here is God's not ours; we can't earn healing by self-determined tasks.

When God does not respond as we ask, there can be a temptation to wallow in anger or despair. We can become self-absorbed in our pain. We must resist these feelings. As best we can, we must persevere, learning to lean on God in the midst of our suffering.

---

[789] Cf. Acts 3:16.
[790] Matthew 17:20 (NJB).

Times of illness can also be times, if we are open to it, for conversion to the Lord and deeper faith. It can be a time of purification and greatly increased holiness as we learn to ever more closely cling to Jesus and to unite our suffering with his. In Saint Paul's own life, God did not answer his prayers for his own healing. This did not mean that God had abandoned Paul.[791] There was purpose to it all. In weakness, Paul was made strong. The Lord told him, "My grace is sufficient for you, for power is made perfect in weakness."[792]

Medical Science and Medical Care. As we discuss miraculous healings, it is important not to diminish the value provided society by doctors, nurses, counselors, therapists, pharmacists, and researchers who use learned skills, medicines, and procedures to help bring healing to persons. The Bible tells us, "Hold the physician in honor, for he is essential to you, and God it was who established his profession."[793] The Bible also affirms the use of medicines, for the earth's medicinal herbs exist according to God's purpose.[794] Yet when we are sick, before we turn to medical science, we should first turn to God.[795]

Part of the Church's healing ministry includes medical attention and care for the sick and wounded. Through the years, the Catholic Church and other Christian communities have built many tens of thousands of hospitals, small and large, to serve local communities. Some religious orders have invested great amounts of time, service, and love building and maintaining hospitals to care for the sick – many among the poor who are so often underserved and most in need.

One of the more important healing ministries of the Church is to journey with people in tough times, including death, allowing ourselves to be an extension of Christ's love to them. We serve them and, in other ways, they may actually serve us.

Healing Society. Healing is not merely for individuals, it is also for relationships – for marriages, families, friends, co-workers, neighbors, local communities, and even whole societies, nations, and the Church. The healing of societies will generally come with a clear proclamation of truth and sincere efforts on the part of people to live

---

[791] Cf. 2 Corinthians 12:7-10, Galatians 4:13-14.
[792] 2 Corinthians 12:9 (NAB).
[793] Sirach 38:1 (NAB). Cf. Sirach 38:6-8, 12-14.
[794] Cf. Sirach 38:4-7.
[795] Cf. Sirach 38:9.

that truth in love. Often, this will be led by religious leaders whom the Spirit anoints for such purposes.

In Old Testament times, there were several instances when the remarkable movements of God's healing came by way of reforms the Spirit worked through civil leaders. This happened in the days of Moses, David, Hezekiah, and Jehoshaphat. These leaders embraced the Laws of God as their model for governance. As they did, grace flowed from heaven that brought healing to the people. God promised Israel, "If you pay attention to these laws and are careful to follow them, then the Lord your God . . . will love you and bless you, and increase your numbers. He will bless the fruit of your womb, the crops of your land . . . The Lord will keep you free from every disease."[796]

Jeremiah, living in a particularly decadent period of Jewish history, was one of Israel's harshest critics. He lived during a time when the people's love of God was weak, Sabbath commands ignored, the poor mistreated, greed ran rampant, sexual impurity abounded, and the people dabbled in various false religions. Yet, in the midst of it all, speaking to a people who were soon to be punished with the Babylonian Exile, Jeremiah prophesied hope. The Holy Spirit, speaking through him, promised a future time when "I will restore health to you, and your wounds I will heal."[797] However, that healing would only come as the people, collectively, repented of their sins and returned to God.[798] Then, and only then, they would learn the meaning of the words, "I am Yahweh your Healer."[799]

Dear Jesus, I know that you are still in the healing business. I pray for the faith to confidently call upon your healing grace. Please heal me of all infirmities of spirit, soul, and body. I also pray for healing in my family and in your Church. I pray for healing within and among Christian denominations, and within and among nations. I pray for a Godly peace to fill the hearts of all peoples. I pray for a new outpouring of the Holy Spirit as at Pentecost, bringing a vibrant and fresh proclamation of the Gospel to the world, with the conversion of hearts and the healing of lives. In your holy name, I pray. Amen.

---

[796] Deuteronomy 7:12-15 (NIV). Cf. Exodus 23:25-26, Deuteronomy 28:1-68, Leviticus 26:1-46, Isaiah 58:6-14.
[797] Jeremiah 30:17 (NRSV).
[798] Cf. 2 Chronicles 7:14.
[799] Exodus 15:26 (NJB).

Appendix 1 – Names for the Holy Spirit

Name	Bible Reference
Holy Spirit	Ps 51:11, Is 63:10, Ws 7:22, 9:17, Mt 1:18, 20, 3:11, 12:32, 28:19, Lk 1:15, 35, Jn 14:26, 20:22
Spirit of God	Gn 1:2, Ex 31:2, 35:31, Nm 24:2, Mt 3:16, 12:28, Ro 8:9, 14, Php 3:3
Spirit of the Lord	Jdg 3:10, 1Sm 16:13, 1Kgs 18:12, Is 11:2, 2 Cor 3:17
Spirit of the Living God	2 Cor 3:3
Spirit of the Sovereign God	Is 61:1
Spirit of Jesus	Acts 16:7
Spirit of Jesus Christ	Php 1:19
Spirit of Christ	Ro 8:9, 1Pe 1:11
Spirit of the Son	Gal 4:6
Spirit of Truth	Jn 14:17, 15:26, 16:13
Spirit of Faith	2 Cor 4:13
Spirit of Love	Gal 5:22
Spirit of Life	Ro 8:2
Spirit of Adoption	Ro 8:15, Gal 4:4-7
Spirit of Holiness	Ps 51:11, Ro 1:4
Spirit of Wisdom	Dt 34:9, Is 11:2, Wis 7:7
Spirit of Grace	Zec 12:10, Heb 10:29
Spirit of Petition	Zec 12:10
Spirit of Healing	1Cor 12:9
Spirit of Glory	1Pe 4:14
Spirit of the Promise	Gal 3:14, Eph. 1:13
Spirit of Judgment	Is 4:4
Spirit of Burning (Fire)	Is 4:4
Eternal Spirit	Heb 9:14
Good Spirit	Ne 9:20
Resolute Spirit	Ps 51:10
Generous Spirit	Ps 51:12
Holy Spirit of Discipline	Wis 1:5
Breath of God	Gn 1:2, Job 4:9
Breath of Life	Gn 2:7, Rev 11:11

Voice of (the living) God	Dt. 4:33, 5:25, 26, Is 66:6, Ps 29:7
Glory of the Lord (God)	Ex 40:34, 35, 1 Kgs 12:11, Tb 12:12, Rev 21:23
The Holy Appearance	2 Chr 20:21
Hand of the Lord	Ex 9:3, 13:3, 2Kgs 3:15, 1Chr 28:19, Tb13:2, Is 66:14, Lk 1:66
Finger of God	Ex 31:18, Dt 9:10, Lk 11:20
Gift of God	John 4:10
God's Glorious Arm	Is 63:12
Peace of Christ	Col 3:15
Advocate / Counselor / Helper	Jn 14:16, 26, 15:26, 16:7
Living Water	Jn 4:10, 7:38
Fountain of Living Water	Jer 2:13
River of Life	Rev. 22:1
Oil of Gladness (Joy)	Ps 45:7, Is 61:3, Heb 1:9
Anointing	1 Jn 2:27, Acts 10:38
Strength of the Lord	Mi 5:3
Power of God (the Lord)	1 Kgs 18:46, 2 Chr 30:12, Lk 5:17, 2 Cor 13:4
Power of the Most High	Lk 1:35
Power of the Lord	Lk 6:19
Power from on High	Lk 24:49
Power of the Resurrection	Php 3:10
Promise of the Father	Lk 24:49, Acts 1:4, 2:33
Bond of Peace	Eph 4:3
Bond of Perfection	Col 3:15
Lord	2 Cor 3:17
Lord of the Harvest	Mt 9:37
Light of Life	Jn 8:12
Giver of Life	2 Cor 3:6
Water of Life	Rev 22:17
Wisdom of God	Lk 11:49

Other Names Given by the Church and Christian Faithful

Amazing Grace
Bond of Love
Breath of the Father
Breath of the Risen Christ
Creator-Spirit
Father of the Poor
Light of Consciences
Fire of Love
Living Flame of Love
Font of Life
Lord & Giver of Life
Love of God
Sanctifier

Spirit of Freedom
Spirit of Hope
Spirit of Joy
Spirit of Light
Spirit of Peace
Spirit of Pentecost
Spirit of Prophecy
Spirit of Repentance
Spirit of Unity
Spirit-Paraclete
Soul of the Church
Sweet Anointing from Above

Appendix 2 – Spiritual Gifts (Charisms)

Gifts of the Holy Spirit	Biblical References

Principle Gifts Received at Baptism:

Faith	1 Cor 12:9, 13:13, Php 1:29
Hope	1 Cor 13:13, Php 1:19-20
Love	1 Cor 13:1-13, Ro 5:5, 1 Jn 7-21, 2 Tm 1:7
Wisdom	Is 11:2, Ex 31:3, 1 Cor 2:6-10, Eph 1:17, Acts 6:3, 10
Understanding	Is 11:2, Ex 31:3, 1 Cor 2:11, Acts 11:1-1, Eph 3:4-5
Counsel	Is 11:2, Acts 15:28, Wis 9:17
Knowledge / revelation	Is 11:2, Ex 31:3, Eph 1:17, 1 Pe 1:11-12, Lk 2:25-32
Courage / fortitude	Is 11:2, Wis 8:7
Fear of the Lord	Is 11:2, Acts 9:31, Sir 1:9-28, Prv 1:7, 19:9, 128:1
Piety	Is 11:2

Other Gifts

A heart of praise and worship .	Acts 10:46, Php 3:3
Ability to cast out demons	Mk 16:17, Mt 12:28, Lk 11:20
Ability to fight evil men	Acts 13:9-12
Access to the Father	Eph 2:18
Administration	1 Cor 12:28
Aids our efforts of obedience	1 Pe 1:2
Aids our prayer life	Ro 8:26-27
Art / Craftsmanship	Ex 31:1-5
Boldness to speak God's truth	Acts 4:8,13; 29-31
Call / anointing / vocation	1 Sm 16:13, Ez 2:2-8, Acts 6:1-6, 13:2-3
Calm in stormy times	Lk 8:22-25
Celibacy	1 Cor 7:7
Charm / graciousness	Sir 37:21
Comfort against fear	Hg 2:5
Consolation	Acts 9:31
Discernment of spirits	1 Cor 12:10
Encouragement / exhortation	Ro 12:8, Acts 11:23-24, 18:9-10
Faith	1 Cor 12:9

Fellowship with Holy Spirit	2 Cor 13:14, Php 2:1
Generosity / giving	Ro 12:8
Guards the deposit of faith	2 Tm 1:14; Acts 15:28
Guides us in the ways of truth	Jn 16:13
Guides us in the wilderness	Mk 1:2, Lk 4:1, Acts 13:4
Healing	1 Cor 12:9, 28
Helpfulness / assistance	1 Cor 12:28, 1Pe 4:11
Hunger for justice and peace	Is 42:1, 61:1-3
Inner strength, holiness	Eph 3:16, Php 1:19-20, Ps 51:10
Instruction	Jn 14:26, Acts 11:12, 13:2-4, 15:28, 16:6-10, Neh 9:20
Interpretation of dreams	Gen 40:8, 41:38
Joy – a rejoicing heart	Lk 10:21
Joy in the midst of distress	1 Th 1:6, Col:10-11
Justice	Wis 8:7
Justification before God	Ro 5:15-17
Knowledge of our sins	Jn 16:7-9
Leadership	Ro 12:8, Nu 11:16-17, 26-30, Jdg 6:14-16; 34
Mercy	Ro 12:8
Miracles	1 Cor 12:10
Miraculous transport	Acts 8:39-40, Ez 3:12-14, 11:24, 1 Kg 18:12
Moderation	Wis 8:7
Opens our hearts to truth	Is 6:5, Lk 2:27-35, Acts 16:14
Pastoring / counseling	Ro 12:7, Eph 4:11, Acts 20:25
Power	2 Tm 1:7
Preaching	Ro 12:8, Eph 4:11, 1Th 1:5, 1Pe 1:12
Prophecy	Ro 12:6, 1 Cor 12:10, 14:1-5, Acts 2:17-18, 10:9-20, 11:27-28, 15:32, 25:28, Lk 1:67, 1Pe 1:10-12, 2Pe 1:19-21, Nu 7:89, 12:6, 1Sm 10:10, Jl 2:28
Purity	Heb 9:14, Ps 51:2, Ez 36:24-27
Prudence	Wis 8:7
Repentant heart	Acts 11:18
Responsibility	Acts 20:28
Rest	Is 63:14
Righteous anger	1 Sm 11:6
Sacred scripture	Acts 1:16; 4:25, 2 Tm 3:16
Self control	2 Tm 1:7
Spiritual transformation	2 Cor 3:18

Strength and endurance	Jude 15:14, 2 Cor 20:13-30, Eph 3:16
Strength to be God's builder	Zc 4:6
Strength for physical combat	Jdg 14:6, 9, 15:14
Strength to resist temptation	Jas 4:7-8
Teaching	Ro 12:7, Eph 4:11, 1 Cor 2:13
Tongues (Speaking in)	1 Cor 12:10, 28, 14:1-19, Acts 2:4, 10:46
Tongues (Interpretation of)	1 Cor 12:10
Understanding of our gifts	1 Cor 2:12
Understanding of scripture	1 Cor 2:10-11
Unity to a group	2 Chr 30:12, Acts 4:32, Php 2:1-5
Utterance of Wisdom	1 Cor 12:8
Utterance of Knowledge	1 Cor 12:8
Warning	Acts 20:23, 21:4, 11, Neh 9:30
Words of correction	Acts 13:10-11
Words to speak when attacked	Mt 10:19-20, Acts 4:8

Other Gifts (noted from Christian experience)

Chastity in Marriage	Intercessory prayer
Chastity in Single Life	Martyrdom
Desire to know the Bible	Music / song
Desire for prayer	Scholarship / study
Desire for holiness	Voluntary poverty
Evangelistic fervor	Willingness / Courage to endure suffering
Hospitality	Writing

Appendix 3 - Fruit of the Spirit (Galatians 5:22-23)

Love

Joy

Peace

Patience

Kindness

Goodness

Faithfulness

Gentleness

Self-control

Appendix 4 - Resources

Scriptures in this book are taken from the four Biblical translations listed below.

NAB The New American Bible
New York, NY: Catholic Book Publishing Company, 1992

NIV The New International Version (Study Bible)
Grand Rapids, MI: Zondervan, 2002

NJB The New Jerusalem Bible (Saints Devotional Edition)
New York, NY: Doubleday, 2002.

NRSV New Revised Standard Version Bible (Catholic Youth Bible) Winona, MN: St. Mary's Press, 2000.

Other resources:

CCC Catechism of the Catholic Church, second edition, United States Conference of Catholic Bishops, 1994, 1997

DV Second Vatican Council, Constitution of the Church, *Dei Verbum* (Word of God)

LG Second Vatican Council, Constitution of the Church, *Lumen Gentium* (Light of the Nations)

AA Second Vatican Council, Decree on the Apostolate of the Laity, *Apostolicam Actuositatem* (Apostolic Activity)

AG Second Vatican Council, Decree on the Church's Missionary Activity, *Ad Gentes* (To the Nations)

LF Pope Francis's encyclical *Lumen Fidei* (The Light of Faith)

DCE Pope Benedict XVI's encyclical *Deus Caritas Est* (God is Love)

VD Pope Benedict XVI's Apostolic Exhortation, *Verbum Domini* (Word of the Lord)

RH Pope John Paul II's encyclical *Redemptor Hominis* (Redeemer of Man)

RM Pope John Paul II's encyclical *Redemptoris Missio* (Mission of the Redeemer)

DeV Pope John Paul II's encyclical *Dominum et Vivificantem* (Lord and Giver of Life)

EE	Pope John Paul II's encyclical *Ecclesia de Eucharistia* (Church of the Eucharist)
NMI	Pope John Paul II's Apostolic Letter *Novo Meillennio Ineunte*, (At the Start of the New Millennium)
CT	Pope John Paul II's Apostolic Exhortation *Catechesi Tradendae* (Catechesis in Our Time)
CL	Pope John Paul II's Apostolic Exhortation *Christifideles Laici* (Christ's Faithful People),
EN	Pope Paul VI's Apostolic Exhortation, *Evangelii Nuntiandi* (Evangelizing the World)
DI	Pope Leo XIII's encyclical on the Holy Spirit, *Divinum Illud Manus* (The Divine Hand)
GA	The statement of a pope at his weekly general audience.
AN	Angelus address by a pope.
RC	Regina Caeli address by a pope.
CDF	Congregation for the Doctrine of the Faith

Appendix 5 – Selected Bibliography

Church Fathers (Greek and Latin)

- St Hiliary's *The Trinity* and *Commentary on Psalms* (64 and 118)
- St. Athanasius' *Letters Concerning the Holy Spirit*
- St. Basil's *On the Holy Spirit*
- St. Cyril of Jerusalem's *Catechetical Lectures* (Lectures 16 and 17)
- St. Ambrose's *On the Holy Spirit*
- St. Gregory Nazianzen's *Orations* (Orations 31 and 41)
- St. John Chrysostom's *Homilies on the Acts of the Apostles*
- St. Augustine's *The Trinity* and his Pentecost sermons

14th - 19th Century Authors (Catholic and Orthodox)

- St. John of the Cross' *The Living Flame of Love*
- St. John of Avila's Pentecost Sermons *(The Holy Spirit Within,* Scepter Publishers, 2012)
- St. Seraphim's *On the Acquisition of the Holy Spirit*
- Bl. Elena Guerra's letters to Pope Leo XIII and *Rebirth in the Holy Spirit*
- Pope Leo XIII's encyclical *Divinum Illud Manus* (The Divine Hand)

20th - 21st Century Catholic Authors

- Pope John Paul II's encyclical *Dominum et Vivificantem* (1986), his 80 catechetical lectures on the Holy Spirit (1989-91), 28 catechetical lectures in the year of the Holy Spirit (1998), and his Pentecost sermons.
- Fr. Bill McCarthy's *The Holy Spirit in the Writings of Pope John Paul II* (St. Andrew's Productions, 2001)
- Fr. Edward O'Connor's *Pope Paul and the Spirit* (Ave Maria, 1978)
- Cardinal Leon-Joseph Suenens' *A New Pentecost?* (Seabury Press, 1974)
- Cardinal Suenens, et al, *Theological and Pastoral Orientations on the Catholic Charismatic Renewal* (1974) – a.k.a. The Malines Statement; republished under the title *Toward a New Pentecost for a New Evangelization* (Liturgical Press, 1993); *Ecumenism and Charismatic Renewal: Theological and Pastoral Orientations* (Servant Books, 1978)

- Fr. Raniero Cantalamessa's *Sober Intoxication of the Spirit* (Servant Books, 1989); *Sober Intoxication of the Spirit: Part Two* (Servant Books, 2012); *The Holy Spirit in the Life of Jesus* (Liturgical Press, 1994); *The Mystery of Pentecost* (Liturgical Press, 2001); *Come Creator Spirit* (Liturgical Press, 2003)

- Fr. Kilian McDonnell's (editor) *The Holy Spirit and Power: The Catholic Charismatic Renewal* (Doubleday, 1975)

- Ralph Martin's (editor) *The Spirit and the Church* (Paulist Press, 1976)

- Frank Sheed's *The Holy Spirit in Action* (Servant Books, 1981)

- Fr. Yves Congar's *I Believe in the Holy Spirit* (Seabury Press, 1983)

- *A Pastoral Statement on the Catholic Charismatic Renewal* (1984), U.S. Bishops' Liaison Committee with the Catholic Charismatic Renewal.

- Fr. Michael Scanlan's *Let the Fire Fall* (Franciscan Univ. Press, 1986)

- Fr. Francis Martin's *Baptism in the Holy Spirit* (Franciscan Univ., 1986)

- Fr. George Montague and Fr. Kilian McDonnell's *Fanning the Flame* (Liturgical Press, 1991)

- Patti Mansfield's *As by a New Pentecost: The Dramatic Beginning of the Catholic Charismatic Renewal* (Franciscan Univ. Press, 1992)

- Fr. Andrew Apostoli's *The Gift of God: The Holy Spirit* (Alba House, 1994); *The Comforter: The Spirit of Joy* (Alba House, 1995); *The Advocate: The Spirit of Truth* (Alba House, 1999).

- Alan Schreck's *Your Life in the Holy Spirit* (Word Among Us, 1995)

- *Grace for the New Springtime*, A Statement by the National Conference of Catholic Bishops on the Catholic Charismatic Renewal (1997)

- Eryn Huntington and Sherry Anne Weddell's *Discerning Charisms* (The Siena Institute Press, 2002).

- Fr. James Kinn's *The Spirit of Jesus in Scripture and Prayer*, (Rowan & Littlefield, 2004)

- Fr. Jacque Philippe's *In the School of the Holy* Spirit (Scepter, 2007)

- Fr. George Montague's *Holy Spirit, Make your Home in Me* (Word Among Us, 2008)

- International Catholic Charismatic Renewal Services Doctrinal Commission's *Baptism in the Holy Spirit* (ICCRS, 2012)

- Sister Ann Shield's *More of the Holy Spirit* (Word Among Us, 2013)

20th - 21st Century Protestant / Pentecostal Authors

- William Barclay's *The Promise of the Spirit* (Westminster, 1960)
- Karl Barth's *The Holy Ghost and the Christian Life* (Muller LTD, 1938)
- Dennis & Rita Bennett's *The Holy Spirit and You* (Bridge-Logos, 1971)
- Henry and Melvin Blackaby's *Experiencing the Spirit*, (Multnomah Books, 2009)
- Billy Graham's *The Holy Spirit* (Word Publishing, 1978)
- Kathryn Kuhlman's *The Greatest Power in the World* (Bridge-Logos, 1997)
- Catherine Marshall's *The Helper* (Chosen Books, 1978)
- Andrew Murray's *Experiencing the Holy Spirit* (Whitaker House, 1985)
- Watchman Nee's *The Holy Spirit and Reality* (Living Stream, 2001)
- David du Plessis' *A Man Called Mr. Pentecost* (Logos International, 1977); *Simple & Profound* (Paraclete Press, 1986)
- Oral Roberts' *The Baptism with the Holy Spirit* (Oral Roberts, 1964)
- R. C. Sproul's *The Mystery of the Holy Spirit* (Christian Focus Publications and Ligonier Ministries, 2009)
- Charles Stanley's *Living in the Power of the Holy Spirit* (Nelson, 2005)
- Charles Swindol's *Embraced by the Holy Spirit* (Zondervan, 2010)
- John Taylor's *The Go-Between God* (SCM, 1972)
- R.A. Torrey's *The Person and Work of the Holy Spirit* (Readaclassic.com, 2010)
- Smith Wigglesworth's *On the Holy Spirit* (Whitaker House, 1999)

Ecumenical

- Cardinal Leon-Joseph Suenens and Archbishop Michael Ramsey's *Come Holy Spirit* (Darton, Longman & Todd, 1977)
- Catholic/Pentecostal International Dialogue, *On Becoming a Christian: Insights from Scripture and the Patristic Writings* (Vatican website, 2009)

Appendix 6 – Acknowledgments

I am very thankful for the many encouragements and helps that I received while researching and writing *Gift of the Holy Spirit*. I want to specifically thank those who were kind enough to read drafts of the manuscript as it was being formed – Suzanne Barton, Chris Fenn, Chris Kellner, Al Forrester, Mark DuCharme, Ben Newland, Dr. John Hulsman, and Fr. Tim Hepburn. Their contributions to the book's content and style made it more substantive, more readable, and more relevant. Thank you.

I also want to acknowledge and thank those persons whose work greatly influenced the direction of this book. First, I want to acknowledge Pope John Paul II, who may have provided the most comprehensive exposition on the Holy Spirit of anyone in Church history. The bulk of his writings on the Holy Spirit are wonderfully presented in Fr. Bill McCarthy's *The Holy Spirit in the Writings of Pope John Paul II* (St. Andrew's Productions, 2001). Second, I found Fr. Michael Scanlan's writings quite inspiring, particularly his autobiography *Let the Fire Fall* where he beautifully shares his first-hand experiences of the Holy Spirit. Third, Fr. Raniero Cantalamessa's many books on the Holy Spirit are all outstanding. He faithfully and poetically shares many insights of the Spirit-led life. Fourth, I found David du Plessis' writings quite insightful. His life story and his ministry within early Pentecostalism and later to mainline Protestant churches, and then to the Catholic Church are extraordinary. Fifth, I am indebted to Blessed Elena Guerra and her work, though I was not able to locate the full text of any of her writings in English. Each of these five persons, in their own way, has been an apostle for the Holy Spirit. The universal Church and world are the better because of it.

Most importantly, I must acknowledge that in all the research, prayer, and writing associated with this book, I am indebted to the Holy Spirit who guided me. I am not a skilled writer. I am an accountant by training, much more adept with numbers than I am with words. For me, reading and writing are a chore, but by the Holy Spirit's grace I have been able to conceive and accomplish this work. To him be the glory, with the Father and Son, now and forever.

Appendix 7 – About the Author

Paul Ragan is a CPA by trade, a former audit partner with one of the big-four accounting firms. In 1997, he took a sabbatical from his accounting career to engage in various writing endeavors. In 1998, Paul attended a Life in the Spirit seminar at the Cathedral of Christ the King in Atlanta GA. At that seminar, he was baptized in the Holy Spirit. Afterward, he became actively involved in ministries at the Cathedral parish. Over the next fifteen years, he actively served in youth ministry, adult evangelization, Christ Renews His Parish, Knights of Columbus, Men's Club, parish pastoral council, and several prayer ministries. He also served on the Board of Directors of Catholic Social Services of Atlanta, as both Treasurer and Board Chair. Paul is passionate in his love for Jesus, the Father, and the Holy Spirit, and he is a frequent speaker and teacher on the Christian faith, Catholicism, and the Holy Spirit.

Made in the USA
Charleston, SC
16 March 2014